ENEMIES
OF ROME

BARBARIANS THROUGH ROMAN EYES

I. M. FERRIS

SUTTON PUBLISHING

This book was first published in 2000 by
Sutton Publishing Limited · Phoenix Mill
Thrupp · Stroud · Gloucestershire · GL5 2BU

This paperback edition first published in 2003

British Library Cataloguing in Publication Data
A catalogue record for this book is available from the British
Library.

ISBN 0 7509 3517 0

Typeset in 10.5/12pt Photina.
Typesetting and origination by
Sutton Publishing Limited.
Printed and bound in Great Britain by
J.H. Haynes & Co. Ltd, Sparkford.

CONTENTS

ACKNOWLEDGEMENTS

Almost inevitably, thanks and acknowledgement are due to a large number of individuals and organisations for different and various kinds of help and encouragement in writing this book.

Firstly I must thank the organisers of the Theoretical Roman Archaeology Conferences (TRAC) at Durham in 1994 and Sheffield in 1996, of the Theoretical Archaeology Group conference (TAG) at Bradford in 1995, and of the Roman Archaeology Conference (RAC) at Nottingham in 1997 for providing platforms on which many of the ideas expounded in this book were first aired.

The School of Historical Studies at the University of Birmingham very kindly awarded a research grant to enable me to make study trips to London, Glasgow and Edinburgh, and a second to cover much of the cost of the on-site inspection of the French monuments at Orange, Saint-Rémy and Carpentras. The Birmingham University Field Archaeology Unit's Research Staff Study Leave scheme importantly allowed me a short period of paid leave in autumn 1999 to revise the first draft of the book and to work on the academic notes. The Humanities Research Group of the University of Birmingham School of Continuing Studies provided a grant to pay for the commissioning of a number of line drawings for the book.

Above and beyond the call of duty, my former colleagues Lynne Bevan and Dr Roger White from the Field Archaeology Unit read and commented on various drafts of the book, much to the benefit of the finished work. Roger also provided copies of his own photographs of many sites for my reference, and also kindly allowed some of these to be reproduced here.

At Sutton Publishing I would like to thank Rupert Harding, for commissioning this book in the first place, for his forebearance while I promised chapters that did not appear until later than planned, and for his sage editorial advice once the chapters did eventually appear. Copy-editor Lucy Isenberg and editor Sarah Flight are also to be thanked for their help. I would also like to thank Dr Martin Henig for his helpful comments as publisher's reader of the first draft manuscript, although there are many arguments in the book with which he was not in sympathy.

Mark Breedon (Bambi) prepared the fine, specially commissioned line drawings with his usual skill, while Graham Norrie of the Department of Ancient History and Archaeology, University of Birmingham provided numerous photographic services which are, as always, very much appreciated. Professor John Hunter of the Department of Ancient History and Archaeology, University of Birmingham facilitated this help in kind with the photographic tasks. The Special Collections section of the University of Birmingham Library kindly allowed photographs to be taken from books in their collection. Permission to quote from 'Waiting for the Barbarians' by C.P. Cavafy came from the Permissions Department of the Random House Group Ltd, with thanks to Catharine Trippett, Permissions Manager.

For their help in obtaining illustrations for the paperback version of this book I would like to thank the following individuals and organisations: Dr Roger White; Professor Sheppard Frere; Jason Wood, Jason Wood Photographs; Marion Schroeder, Deutsches Archäologisches Institut, Rome; Ivor Kerslake and Sherry Lewis-Hartley, the British Museum; the Museo Romano, Brescia; Nanda Menconi, Cathedral Treasury, Monza; Fraser Hunter, National Museums of Scotland, Edinburgh; Sue Byrne, Gloucester City Museum; Bibliothèque Nationale de France, Paris; Dottoressa Rosanna Friggeri, Soprintendenza Archeologica di Roma; Dott. Giuliana Algeri, Soprintendenza di Brescia, Cremona e Mantova; and the Kunsthistorisches Museum, Vienna.

Finally, for her forebearance, and for allowing me to monopolise our word processor for most of the eighteen

ACKNOWLEDGEMENTS

months of evenings and weekends that it took to write this book, I must thank my wife, Lynne Bevan, to whom the book is dedicated with love.

During the preparation of the paperback edition of this book I have taken the opportunity to add a small number of new references to the notes and bibliography, but otherwise the text remains more or less the same as originally published in 2000.

I.M. Ferris,
Birmingham,
December 2003

PICTURE CREDITS

PREFACE

Much has been written in the last few years about the relationship between Roman art and imperial policy,[1] indeed about the 'power of images' virtually to define a particular emperor's reign,[2] about Roman art and propaganda,[3] and about the role of the viewer in consuming and interpreting Roman art.[4] But little attention has been paid to a possible difference between the motives and expectations of the creators and patrons of imperial art, and the perceptions and understanding of its viewers. The ubiquitous and chronologically extended use of images of barbarian peoples in the narrative and rhetoric of Roman imperial art would appear to be an area of study where such a dichotomy could potentially be identified, and where the investigation of the creation and use of stereotypical images of non-Roman peoples could penetrate to the very core of the Roman imperial mentality.[5]

Three decades ago, the academic study of the Roman world was still dominated, in Britain at least, by ideas centred on the concept of a largely benevolent Roman empire, a stance derived from the perception of the positive benefits of the British empire. This academic agenda was subsequently seen by many younger scholars as potentially reactionary.[6] Consequently, this stance gave way to studies of the Roman empire that concentrated on imperialism as reflected through the experiences of Romanisation, both positive and negative. Acculturation and resistance became the broadly driving themes of this academic agenda for Roman studies in the later 1970s and 1980s. However, the pendulum has since swung away from these themes, towards what is termed a post-colonial perspective, in which the active pursuit of 'discrepant experiences' of empire is pre-eminent. The strategies for researching these experiences are largely textual or based upon theoretical readings of material culture.[7] Art historical studies pursuing these 'discrepant experiences' within the Roman empire have been few, and there has been a discernible and perhaps deliberate move away from engagement with visual sources in the theoretical literature of the discipline. Indeed, the so-called 'new Roman art history' that has emerged in the last few years has been accused of perhaps an over-reliance of faith in the primacy of text over image.[8]

This book is not intended to be an in-depth study of the various barbarian peoples in conflict with the Roman state. Rather it is a study of barbarians as seen through Roman eyes. There will be no attempt to deal in any detail with the history, customs, appearance or material culture of the barbarians. Nor will there be any detailed comparison of pictorial representations of barbarians with those described in historical sources such as Caesar's *De Bello Gallico* or Tacitus' *Germania*. Instead, the book will consider the idea of the barbarian – of a notional, fictional barbarian who appeared in many guises in Roman art and literature. Sometimes this barbarian appeared to be almost a simulacrum of the real thing, sometimes simply a shimmering chimera, a stereotype created to fulfil a need or desire, or to help commemorate a specific event.

It is hoped that the book will appeal to readers interested in the ancient world in general, as well as to undergraduate students of archaeology and art history. The provision of academic notes and a full bibliography should allow others wishing to pursue in more depth the more esoteric and theoretical aspects of the study beyond the book's main narrative to do so with relative ease.

. . . some of our men just in from the border say
there are no barbarians any longer.

Now what's going to happen to us without barbarians?
They were, those people, a kind of solution.

C.P. Cavafy, 'Waiting for the Barbarians'
(Translated by E. Keeley and P. Sherrard. From C.P. Cavafy,
Collected Poems, Hogarth Press, 1984)

ONE

A FEAR OF DIFFERENCE

From the days of the early Roman empire to the fall of Rome, the barbarian enemies of Rome were commonly portrayed in imperial art. Images of barbarian men, women and children illuminated the commemoration of numerous military triumphs and historical events, as for instance on Trajan's Column or on the later Column of Marcus Aurelius. But many of these images were simply stereotypes that tell us more about their creators than they do about the barbarian peoples portrayed.

Fear, dislike, suspicion or mistrust of those who are not like us are unfortunately common traits in most societies, in the past as today. This fear of difference can be an individual character trait or defect, or it can be commonly shared by a number of individuals, a class, or a group. It can also be articulated at a national level, so that the prejudice becomes institutionalised, and thus more starkly defined. Vocabulary and language, gesture and action, and literary and visual images, can all be deployed to describe and maintain these real or perceived differences, and to imbue that difference with negative or ambiguous connotations. Those perceived as different become 'other', often not viewed as being real people but presented simply through reference to generalised physical characteristics or to strange habits and customs. Gender, sexuality, colour and appearance are the most common differences defined in this way. Often what appears to be a fascination with difference can also have a negative aspect if it involves the idealisation or patronisation of the 'other'.

This book aims to investigate the creation and use of such

1

stereotypical images in the Roman world, and to assess any variations dependent on time, place or context. Some early Roman portrayals of barbarians were virtually anthropological exercises in evoking nostalgia for the world of 'the primitive savage', while there was an undoubted move towards the dehumanisation of the barbarian in Roman art from the time of the emperors Marcus Aurelius and Commodus onwards. The study of these later, often quite harrowing, images may allow us to understand the perhaps deep-seated fear of the barbarian which, it could be argued, lay buried within the Roman psyche.

The chronological span of the study primarily encompasses the period from the second century BC, when a Roman art distinct from purely Hellenistic and native Italian arts emerged in the time of the late Republic, to around AD 410, when Alaric the Goth and his forces sacked the city of Rome. As with any such study though, reference will inevitably be made to works of art created both within and without this time frame.

This first chapter sets the scene by briefly looking at the barbarian in Greek, Italian and Republican Roman art. The four central chapters examine the chronological use of images of barbarians, but not by the discussion of the subject reign by reign. Rather, they concentrate on the best-documented eras, in terms of the creation and survival of relevant works of art. Thus the reigns of Augustus, Trajan, Marcus Aurelius, Septimius Severus, the Tetrarchy and the House of Constantine dominate the narrative. The inclusion of the art of Late Antiquity, the period roughly AD 250–450, allows changing imperial perceptions of power and authority to be pursued as a major theme. The study thus traverses, but obviously does not ignore, the major stylistic, perceptual and social changes of Late Antiquity. The final two chapters attempt to provide an overview of trends, and to discuss the social and political contexts of the images.

For a study of this kind, based almost exclusively on the analysis of visual material, the variety of available sources is perhaps surprisingly limited. The visual source material considered consists principally of sculptural works produced as part of the official state commemoration of Roman victories, by generals in the Republican period and, almost exclusively, the emperor in the imperial period. The majority of these artworks or monuments were created and displayed in Rome itself. Monuments on which barbarians were depicted erected elsewhere in Italy and in the provinces are fewer in number. A later and significant exception to the control of the creation and use of images of barbarians by the state is the tradition that emerged among generals of the Antonine period in which their lives were posthumously celebrated through the commissioning of what are now generally known as 'battle sarcophagi'.[1]

In addition to the major public monuments, there were particular periods when the Roman state used other artistic media to disseminate ideas about its goals and achievements. This was certainly the case at the very start of the imperial era when the courts of Augustus and the succeeding Julio-Claudian dynasty were responsible for the production of decorated luxury items, principally silverware, gems or cameos, to be given in most cases as gifts. To a lesser extent, a similar process can be said to have occurred towards the end of the period of study, when carved ivory diptychs were produced to celebrate the power and prestige of individual consuls and emperors. From the intervening period few such court-sponsored luxury items survive, though in the third century medallions can be seen to have replaced cameos as gifts.[2] The early and the later imperial periods may have represented times when it was expedient for the Roman state to use gifts such as these to help establish relationships with provincial elites and with powerful barbarian groups and individuals outside the empire, as well as to demonstrate imperial prestige to its own aristocracy. If that was indeed the case, then the images of barbarians employed on these more intimate items of artistic production could have held an additional significance in comparison to those deployed on public monuments.

The figure of the barbarian was very common on Roman coinage but otherwise does not generally appear on other types of public art, such as mosaics. Barbarians were also relatively rare figures in private art, although some consideration will be given in this study to genre art, particularly the production of small bronzes for popular consumption. It was almost inevitable that the barbarian male appeared on many items of military art, though it may be deemed surprising that though he was often depicted in scenes of combat or defeat, the number of his appearances on commemorative stones, tombstones, and on items of military equipment is nevertheless relatively small.

DEFINING OTHERS

The definition of the word 'barbarian' has some particular significance in itself. The word is of Greek origin, and is onomatopoeic – that is, when spoken it sounds like the very thing it is used to describe. In this case it was someone who, when speaking, sounded to a Greek incomprehensible, as if uttering a noise that sounded like 'bar, bar, bar' and in so doing betrayed their non-Greek origins.[3]

This initial drive to define difference in purely linguistic terms later came to encompass both real and perceived visual, cultural and psychological differences. The barbarian needed to be categorised in this manner in order to allow the Greeks, and later the Romans, to understand their own position in the world. As an attempt at self-definition, in the ancient world this exercise relied on both the study of the barbarian peoples through historical, geographical and ethnographic writings, and the examination of their psyches through literature and drama. Vocabulary and grammar were both used by the Greeks to define and subtly defile others, while the vocabulary and grammar of Roman art could also be used in the same way. Words and symbols could be deployed with subtlety and discretion, as well as with malice and necessity. That language can control and divide, as well as liberate and unite, and that the same duality of roles can be said to apply to images as well as texts, is self-evident in late and post-twentieth-century society. Manipulation of image and text was in fact as prevalent in the ancient world as in our own, although consciousness of the fact was not then stated or debated.

The original Greek definition of barbarian left no room for manoeuvre: either you were a Greek speaker or you were not. However, the Roman imperial system allowed for the possibility of a transformation, a metamorphosis. Barbarian peoples, those outside the empire, could be transformed into subjects and citizens of the empire by conquest and incorporation. Whether this incorporation gave them equality is open to question, but certainly in state art they then became invisible, unless being celebrated at death for their service to the Roman state or by self-advertisement as new citizens following manumission from slavery. To the Romans, those citizens who were non-Romans were not always defined as '*peregrini*' – foreigners – though in Rome itself the state official who dealt with legal or procedural matters involving non-Romans was perhaps tellingly called the *Praetor Peregrinus*.[4]

Perhaps the most significant academic study of the relationship between the barbarian and classical worlds is Edith Hall's book *Inventing the Barbarian. Greek Self-Definition Through Tragedy*, which, though obviously concerned with literary rather than visual sources, nevertheless provides a template for examining the place of the 'other', the outsider, in the Greek and Roman worlds.[5] The complexity of Hall's thesis is impossible to summarise succinctly here, and, of course, the situation changed over time, but to some extent her work serves to demonstrate how the Greeks felt a certain need to define the barbarians as not just 'different' to them but also, somehow, as their generic opposites and enemies. This was at first the most overt manifestation of an otherwise internalised fear of the rise of Persian power and the threat that this potentially posed to the Greek world. In the earlier writings of Homer, for instance, there can be found no overt antipathy towards non-Greek peoples, and indeed his use of the term barbarian is limited to its descriptive rather than pejorative sense.[6]

In creating stereotypical barbarian characters, Greek writers often used the description of their supposedly flawed psychological profiles and their foreign, and therefore fantastical, material attributes as a way of highlighting the admirable qualities and characteristics of the ideal Greek, both through contrast and by comparison. Thus ethnic stereotypes were created that said little or nothing about the barbarian peoples but a great deal about the Greek society which produced them.

Strategies for depicting the barbarians also began to be applied to vase painting and the other arts, if to a lesser extent, with a distinct genre of what is called 'battle painting' probably also emerging around the time of the Persian wars. The frenzied battle scenes on the so-called Alexander Sarcophagus from Sidon, dated to c. 325–300 BC, were probably derived from now-lost battle paintings.[7] The lack of a mythologising veil to depict the Greek and Persian protagonists is noteworthy, for it had previously been through the allusive depiction of battles involving giants, Amazons, Lapiths and Centaurs, as well as Greeks themselves, that such encounters and wars had been commemorated. The Alexander mosaic in Naples Museum, originally from the House of the Faun in Pompeii, again most probably derived from a Greek painted source, thought to be by Philoxenos of Eretria.[8]

The individual figure of Darius, the Persian king, seems to have gripped the Greek imagination in a way that for the Roman period can only be compared to the impact of Decebalus, the Dacian king. The remarkable depiction of Darius' preparations for his expedition against Greece on a painted krater from the Apulian workshop of the so-called 'Darius Painter', dated to the third quarter of the fourth century BC, well illustrates the ubiquity and significance of the Alexander/Darius trope.[9]

A detailed study by Brian Sparkes of images of non-Greek peoples in Athenian art of the late sixth and early fifth century BC found that four main groups were most commonly depicted: Scythians, Thracians, Persians and Africans.[10] The artists, mainly working in the popular and accessible medium of vase painting, paid greatest attention to the depiction of clothing and weaponry. However, in the depiction of the black African the Athenian artists employed a different strategy to distinguish their otherness; rather than relying on the distinctiveness of costume and weaponry to define this ethnic group, they did this through depiction of the more obvious physical difference – skin colour, facial characteristics and hair.

While Greek males were routinely depicted naked, with that state's connotations both of physical purity and heroic endeavour, non-Greeks at this time were generally shown fully clothed, as were slaves. In the case of the Scythians, a male archer was usually illustrated – the role for which these warriors were most renowned. For the Thracians, a male horseman or rider was the preferred type.

However, Thracian women were also commonly portrayed, marked out both literally and artistically by their tattoos. Many of these women were brought to Athens as slaves, so that their ethnically distinct art of tattooing also became a brand, their mark of subservience to their Greek masters, as well as perhaps an exoticised target of the Athenian male gaze. Their otherness was quite literally written on their bodies.

As has already been noted, the Persians became the most commonly depicted non-Greek characters in both Greek art and literature. Battle scenes between Persian and Greek warriors adorn many vases and kraters, obviously in the vast majority of cases celebrating Greek victories, although a few examples are known on which Persians emerge, temporarily at least, victorious.

Sparkes discusses in detail an extraordinary scene painted on a red-figure *oinochoe* or wine jug of *c.* 460 BC, in which a most explicit and implicit link is made between the sexual potency and superiority of the Greek victor and the sexual subservience, and thus implied effeminacy, of his defeated Persian opponent. The Greek male, clad only in a short, thin cloak, nurses his erect penis in his right hand as he strides towards the figure of the defeated Persian male. The Persian, his hands held up to either side of his head in a gesture of mock fright, bends over, the implication being that he is about to be buggered. An inscription by the figure of the Greek states 'I am Eurymedon' and one by the Persian, rather obviously, 'I stand bent over'. Here, otherness, through defeat in war, is being linked to femininity, or rather to the emasculation of the barbarian male. Though Roman imperialism later came sometimes to allude to defeated male barbarians as somehow impotent, and captive barbarian couples as barren, nevertheless there is no example of sexual denigration of foreigners in Roman art comparable in explicitness to the Eurymedon vessel.

ENEMIES OF ROME

ESSAYS IN NOSTALGIA

If there can be said to be any Greek works of art that encapsulate the almost schizophrenic state of both fearing and admiring the barbarian, then it would be the sculptures of the so-called Attalid Gauls and associated eastern barbarian figures. These sculptures, dating from the third century BC, were commissioned by King Attalos I of Pergamon, following his defeat of invading forces of Galatians (though they have become dubbed as 'Gauls') and their Seleucid allies, and were erected at victory monuments set up at Pergamon, Delos, Delphi and Athens.[11] Of course, the forerunners of such works must have been the Greek representations of the triumphs over the Persians by Alexander the Great; indeed, Attalos was to an extent claiming for himself some element of continuity with the victorious Alexander.[12] As well as these monuments, the Attalid dynasty also commissioned the Altar of Zeus at Pergamon, on which the victory of Attalos' son Eumenes II over eastern barbarians was celebrated in a visually powerful and stunning manner, and yet one that was totally allusive, using a gigantomachy – a battle between gods and giants – to represent the historical conflict.

There has been much debate among art historians about which of the numerous extant free-standing statues of barbarians in western European museum collections definitely belonged to, or could have belonged to, these Attalid victory monuments. Many of these statues are in any case Roman copies rather than Greek originals. Nor is it clear in what combinations or tableaux the statues were originally presented. The details of these debates need not be repeated here. Rather, discussion will be focused on two or three of these statues only.[13]

Perhaps the best-known of these works, and indeed one of the most admired Greek works of art in general, is the statue now usually called 'The Dying Gaul', though it probably can be quite convincingly equated with the work called 'The Trumpeter', attributed by Pliny in his *Natural History* to the sculptor Epigonos. This statue, now in the Capitoline Museum in Rome in the form of a Roman copy in marble of a probably bronze original, is of a fallen Gaulish combatant, sculpted at life-size or just below life-size. He lies partially on his circular shield, discarded on the ground, supporting his upper body with his braced right arm, while his left hand holds one of his legs, perhaps on a wound. His head is bowed, whether in agony or shame is uncertain, and around his neck he wears a large torque, a common Celtic attribute. Great attention has been paid by the artist to depicting his thickened or limed hair and his moustache, again elements that identify him beyond doubt as a Celtic protagonist. He is otherwise completely naked. Also strewn on the ground are a Celtic trumpet, now broken into two, which gave the work what was perhaps its original name, and a sword and belt, though these latter items may be additions to the work made during its restoration or repair.

It is impossible not to view the statue of this isolated figure left to die on the battlefield as other than a study of 'dignity in defeat'. The nakedness of the barbarian makes him seem both vulnerable – a wounded and dying body rather than a man – and yet still strong, through the expression and celebration of his physique and maleness. While the musculature of his body has not been exaggerated in the manner of other sculptures attributed to the Attalid programme, nevertheless his nakedness would have been intended to evoke nostalgia for the strength and virility of the 'primitive'.[14]

Having viewed this work previously only through photographic plates in art history books, when I eventually visited the Capitoline Museum on a research trip I was surprised at the pronounced modelling of the Gaul's genitalia which are usually discretely posed out of sight in the published plates. This detail may again have been intended to stress the barbarian's once-possessed, but now-curtailed, potency. His nakedness and that of others in the sculptural series could have been in tribute to their heroic and admired qualities.[15]

Another of the Attalid Gaul statue group is the so-called 'Ludovisi Gauls' or 'Suicidal Gauls', though it is also known in the art historical literature, rather anachronistically, as the 'Suicidal Gaul and Wife'. A Gaulish warrior is here portrayed supporting a wounded or dead woman, catching her by the arm as she slumps to the ground. Either she has been injured in battle or, alternatively, the more widely accepted interpretation is that she has just died by her male companion's hand in a suicide pact. In his other hand he holds a sword that he thrusts into his own neck, dramatically taking his own life. On the ground at their feet lie a shield and discarded scabbard.

There would appear to be some grounds for believing that there is a stylistic and compositional link between this work and the Menalaos and Patroklos battlefield sculpture best represented by the copy version known as the 'Pasquino group', the original of which could date to the end of the third century BC or thereabouts. The allusive linking of Gauls with such legendary Greek heroes would add a further layer of nostalgic admiration to the conceptual make-up of the work.[16]

As if the subject matter were not dramatic enough on its own account, the Hellenistic Baroque style of intensification in the detailing of anatomy in this and the other contemporary Attalid works further accentuates the sense of drama, action, pain and tragedy. Blood is shown spurting from the man's neck wound and this may have been further emphasised by the use of red paint on the original sculpture. He is naked apart from a short cloak draped over his shoulders and arranged behind his back, away from his sword-bearing arm. His torso and limbs are almost improbably tensed and straining, his body is wild power personified. He twists his body around and looks up, perhaps in a defiant last glance at approaching enemy forces.

In evident contrast, the woman is fully clothed, in an elaborate fringed garment. Her limbs are limp and smooth and she would already appear to be beyond life and the containing reality of her physical body. Her threatening wildness has been extinguished. The binary oppositions in this work – between male and female, naked and clothed, unfettered wildness and wildness tamed, and life and death – would not have been easy for a viewer immediately to disentangle, making the work far more complex than a simple representation of enemies in defeat.

Representations of suicide are not especially common in either Greek or Roman art, unless they refer to historically attested events. The suicides of the Dacian king Decebalus and of other Dacian warriors depicted on Trajan's Column are the best-known examples. Can the Ludovisi Gauls be seen as purely symbolic figures or do they represent specific individuals who were reported from the scene of the Pergamene victory to have ended their lives in this way? Certainly, there are references in the work of the historian Poseidonius to a Celtic custom of mass suicide in defeat, though of course this may have been nothing more than the literary construction of a narrative of difference and otherness. Even if this statue was intended to depict the strange and curious nature of Celtic customs, nevertheless its composition also suggests some degree of admiration for the appropriateness of such a finite act in the face of defeat.[17]

Suicide may be interpreted not simply as an act of pure desperation but also as one of bravery. It could have been of particular cultural significance to the Celts. This autonomous act could be seen as a rejection of the consequences of defeat, of the forcible co-option into the political and military fate of an alien power. As Elisabeth Bronfen has written in her major study *Over Her Dead Body. Death, Femininity and the Aesthetic*, there is an ambivalence inherent in suicide, making it 'a form of writing the self and writing death . . . poised between self-construction and self-destruction'.[18] Choosing biological death in this situation would allow, at least for the two individuals here, an escape from a social and cultural death. Perhaps for the woman it also represented a way of avoiding loss of sexual autonomy, either through the fear or actuality of rape or mistreatment by the victors or through being taken hostage and being transported to an uncertain future in exile or slavery. The death of the woman may also represent a wider death, a sterile future for her tribe brought about by the failure of their military adventure. Another layer of complexity is created by the questioning of whether the death of the woman, seemingly at the hands of her male companion, represents male barbarian autonomy only.

Let us now turn to a briefer consideration of some of the other statues in this series. There are further figures of dying Gauls. One (now in the Naples Archaeological Museum) is naked apart from a helmet and is depicted in a similar pose to the 'Trumpeter' but with a large wound in his side which oozes blood. Other Gauls are represented as corpses lying on the battlefield. In addition to Epigonos' 'Trumpeter', Pliny also refers to a second work in the same series, presumably by the same artist, and again probably depicting Gauls, 'an infant pitifully caressing its slain mother'. This particular group sadly has not survived, though a Renaissance drawing of a supine woman with a child has been suggested as fitting the description of this lost work, and we can only speculate as to the pathos that such a sculptor would bring to this scenario. Whether this lost work had echoes in any other barbarian mother and child motifs subsequently employed in Roman art is uncertain. Certainly, no such depictions survive today, though on a few sarcophagi of the Antonine period scenes appear in which small children try to give comfort to their grieving mothers, and these will be discussed below.

Persians are also cast in these dramas in stone, easily distinguishable from their Gaulish allies by an attention to the detail of barbarian dress and weaponry which is almost anthropological. However, these statues of Persians are not as dramatic in terms of their composition and the rendering of anatomy. Most famous is a small-scale figure of a Persian (now in the museum at Aix-en-Provence in France), partially kneeling on the ground. He supports himself with one hand, though not in quite the same pose as the 'Dying Gaul', and looks up in what could be described as abject terror at some Greek opponent, perhaps on horseback given the angle at which the Persian's head is set, about to deliver a final and fatal blow. Another Persian (in Naples Museum) lies full-length on the ground, close to death and having just relinquished his grip on the pommel of a curved-blade sword which lies beside him. His head lolls just above the surface of the ground as he prepares to take his final breath. Both the Aix and the Naples Persians are dressed in recognisably eastern garb of trousers or leggings, long tunic and cap or hat.

The dramatic effect of these battle tableaux can only be imagined. It cannot be pure coincidence that no statues of Pergamene Greek protagonists from these battles have come down to us or have been identified by art historians. It must simply be that Gauls and their allies were the only combatants portrayed, and that the victorious role of the (absent) Greeks was taken as read by each and every viewer of the artworks. Thus the viewer in this case was an active participant in an almost theatrical event. It was probably possible to walk behind individual statues or to walk between groups of statues, and to see around one the dead, dying or defeated Gauls as if one were actually present on the battlefield, observing their weapons strewn around them like so many discarded hopes and fears. Red paint to highlight the bloody nature of their despair, perhaps the use of deliberately dramatic lighting and maybe even a sensory assault on the viewer through the use of noise to recreate the din and clamour of battle could also have been employed.

And yet these particular works of art do not leave the viewer with a sense that the defeated Gauls and other barbarians were generally inferior and beneath contempt. Rather they leave one with feelings that are altogether less clear-cut, if not actually contradictory. They would seem to be essays both on victory and on regret. It could be argued that the generally sympathetic portrayal of the defeated enemies, if dignity in defeat can be read from the statues' poses and styles, was quite genuine and reflected something almost akin to nostalgia for the lost strength and innocence somehow encapsulated within these powerful defeated bodies. This primitive power could be tamed and defeated by Greek civilisation and yet, at the same time, it represented something that had been lost to the Greeks in the process of their reaching the higher plane represented by that very civilisation.

This would seem to be the same state of apparent confusion that Edith Hall isolated in her study of barbarians in Greek literature:

> The Greeks' view of the barbarian was inherently contradictory, for civilisation's view of itself as in a process of linear progression is never unquestioned; the rise, paradoxically, is seen also as a fall. The retrospective vision incorporates the idea not only of primitive chaos, but of a more virtuous era, when men were nearer to the gods. . . . This schizophrenic vision of inferiority and of utopia gives rise to an inherently contradictory portrayal of the barbarian world.[19]

There is no doubt that underwriting both Greek literature and visual art when they dealt with the subject of the barbarians, as well as the writings of certain classical ethnographers, was a dual discourse, 'a discourse of savagery' and 'a discourse of the timeless savage'. The idea of the 'primitive savage' is one that is or has been prevalent in many historical societies at many and various times, and its presence in Greek and, later, Roman society need cause no surprise. As has been noted by Carlin Barton, recourse in early Roman society to the idea of the noble state of 'primitive' peoples, coupled with a fascination with both common and exotic animals and an idealisation of the child, was a manifestation of that society's 'helplessness resulting from complexity'.[20]

Together, the Attalid dedications reveal a complex interplay between different forms of artistic expression and their related canons of traditional tropes and motifs, each representing a different mode of cultural aspiration and identification. This has been well defined by Jerome Pollitt:

the battle of the Gods and Giants celebrated the foundation of Greek religion and moral law. The defeat of the Amazons, who had been allies of the Trojans and who had besieged the acropolis in the time of the hero Theseus, commemorated the glories of the Heroic Age and the importance of Athens as a bulwark against barbarism. The defeat of the Persians celebrated the salvation of Greek culture as a whole and the consequent flowering of Classical Athens. . . . They were saying in effect that the Gallic victories of the Attalids were of the same magnitude as the earlier battles depicted in the monument because they had ensured once again the survival of Greek culture.[21]

There is another aspect to be considered when discussing the Attalid Gauls and Persians, that of voyeurism. While the deliberate overemphasis of the physical attributes of the naked Gauls may have celebrated the inherent strength and virility of such 'primitive' men, nevertheless the attention to ethnic detail in physical appearance implies, perhaps, some degree of actual observation of such types by the artist. If these works were in fact

14

based on direct observation, how could this have occurred? An artist could have been present at the scene of battle or have come on to the battlefield once fighting had ceased and victory was being celebrated by the Pergamene forces. Dead or dying Gauls could have then been drawn or sketched, providing a voyeuristic subtext to the finished works. If this was the case, perhaps this partially undermines their often-praised ethnographic qualities, since they are not necessarily tempered by pathos. It might be, though, that the evident suffering of the barbarian protagonists presented the viewer with a study in more generalised human suffering that was easier to contemplate mediated through the bodies of the barbarians than through the depiction of such agonies visited upon fellow-Greeks.[22]

DEFINING MOMENTS

There are numerous examples in Etruscan and Italian art of portrayals of battles with Celts or Gauls – Celtomachies – probably due to the fact that from the sixth century BC onwards the Gauls dislodged the Etruscans from their territories in, and to the north of, the Po Valley. Accordingly, the area was known to the Romans as Cisalpine Gaul, that is Gaul on the south side of the Alps. By the fourth century the Gauls, under their leader Brennus, had started to harry other parts of Italy and indeed even carried their expansionism to the gates of Rome, where their seven-month siege was lifted only after the payment of a substantial ransom.

The most significant and powerful surviving example of a Celtomachy is on a terracotta frieze of *c.* 160 BC, that formed part of the decorative scheme of a temple at Civita Alba, near Sentino in Umbria. It depicted the dramatic flight of Gaulish warriors after their sacking of the Temple of Apollo at Delphi in Greece in 279 BC, the Gauls fleeing before the onslaught of Apollo himself and of other deities.[23] This historic event of one hundred years earlier had probably been chosen to reflect the contemporary incursions of the Gauls which were by then reaching serious proportions in both Italy and Greece. Alternatively, it has been suggested that the Civita Alba frieze depicted a Celtic raid on the Temple of Apollo and Artemis at Didyma near Miletus in 277–276 BC, or, as is more likely, elements of both the stories of the Delphi and Didyma raids were conflated here.[24]

On the now-fragmentary frieze the figure of Apollo himself is missing, though he would certainly have appeared on the lost fragments, given the mythology behind the historic event and the presence of Artemis and Athena Pronaia. On the left of the scene Athena raises a spear against the Gauls while to the right is Artemis, armed with a bow. One of the Gauls has been wounded and has collapsed into the arms of a comrade. Other Gauls are shown in flight, one of them with what appears to be a large *amphora*, doubtless containing wine, tucked under his arm as portable booty. Another, perhaps Brennus, the leader of the Gauls, is shown attempting to escape by chariot. After the flight Brennus is known to have committed suicide, but the artist has chosen not to depict that particular incident.

The modelling of the figures on the frieze is highly detailed and obviously represents a serious engagement of the artist and patron with the necessity of portraying the Gauls in a recognisable manner. It is interesting how this historic event has been used as a metaphor for the contemporary struggle between Italians and Gauls, and yet in a form where the events at Delphi are depicted in a mythologised way, with the intervention of the gods being shown rather than the driving-off of the Gaulish raiders by Greek forces. While similar battles between Greeks, Italians, or Romans and other peoples were often depicted traditionally in Graeco-Roman art as mythological combat, involving gods, giants or Amazons, this mixture of mortal other with protective Greek deities is unusual.

The concept that it was only through the intercession of the gods that the barbarians were seen off from Delphi reflects a certain degree of vulnerability. Certainly, for the Italians and Romans the Greek victory at Delphi also became symbolic of the triumph of civilisation over barbarism.[25] In the contemporary Greek world this became what one commentator has called 'one of the most emotional reactions of the Greeks to the impact of an alien society' in terms of the artistic and literary response to the event.[26] Indeed, the writer Propertius later recorded seeing decoration on the door of the Temple of Apollo on the Palatine Hill in Rome incorporating the figures of Gaulish warriors being thrown down from Mount Parnassus in symbolic defeat. Later coin issues also linked Rome's struggles against the Gauls with that of the Greeks at Delphi, by allusion to Apollo.

The event also had some resonance in the minor arts. A bronze figure in Naples Museum probably represents the Celtic leader Brennus in the act of committing suicide after the retreat of his raiding forces from Delphi. That the theme of male barbarian suicide became quite common in Roman historical narratives, as well as in art, has already been mentioned.[27] It is likely that many small bronzes of Gauls were produced in Italy and Rome from the first century BC to the first century AD, as the Romans first traded with, and then conquered and assimilated Gaul, following their earlier encounters with Celtic mercenaries and raiders.

While the Civita Alba frieze represents public art, Celts or Gauls significantly also appeared in private art, most notably on Etruscan funerary objects. Some echoes of the Attalid victory monuments can be found in the art of Etruscan funerary urns, in particular on those numerous urns on which Celtomachies appear.[28] There may also be echoes in these battle scenes of Greek representations of the battles of Alexander the Great against the Persians, or a conflation of both these influences. It is interesting to find this kind of imagery in the private sphere, and particularly to infer that it was considered appropriate to a funerary context. On a number of the funerary urns from Volterra can be found scenes of Celtic raiders fleeing from some god or Fury, as if from Apollo at Delphi.[29] It was probably not until the second century AD that a trend again emerged for battle imagery to be used as a common form of decoration on the sarcophagi of Roman generals. The later trend may have had some connection to this much earlier Italian-Etruscan tradition, in which the scenes of barbarian defeat became perhaps symbolic of more abstract ideas relating to allegories of life and death.

A few other related and noteworthy Italian works of art can also be briefly considered here. A formalised battle scene encircles a painted fourth-century BC *stamnos* or vase, in which Etruscan or Italian soldiers take on both mounted Gauls and Gallic foot-soldiers.[30] On the ground lies the body of a dead

Gaul, on whose chest sits a vulture or carrion bird that rips at his entrails. Another bird rests on the ground nearby, either already sated with flesh or awaiting the slaughter of further Gauls. The presence of the birds lends extra emphasis to the serious and bloody endeavour of the battle that has otherwise been subsumed within its rather formalised composition.

A second instance of the carrion bird motif can be found on an alabaster sculptural frieze from Citta della Pieve,[31] on which are depicted battlefield scenes reminiscent of the Attalid Gaul tableaux. A fallen Gaulish warrior whose eyes are being pecked out by a bird first captures the viewer's attention, while a second Gaulish warrior standing nearby commits suicide with his own sword. On another fragment of the sculpture a reclining, garlanded figure is represented, who must be one of the victors and who is here shown in repose perhaps after the celebration of a formal triumph, though the paraphernalia of the triumph are not represented on the frieze. The bodies of recently slaughtered Gauls were now being portrayed, quite literally, as nothing more than dead meat, in a strategy of defamation that in its starkness and immediacy required little interpretation on the part of the viewer.

Ceramic art was a popular medium for the portrayal of battles with Gauls, as is demonstrated by a number of painted terracotta or ceramic figures from Canosa that represent warriors, including Celts, in action or falling in their death throes. These figures date to some time in the period 270–200 BC, and would have formed relief attachments to large pottery vessels known as *askoi*. Again, from the later fourth to the late third century BC onwards ceramic seals and pots were produced at Cales in Campania, some of which depicted Celts or Gauls in the act of raiding and plundering towns or villages, in a way similar to that already described on the frieze from Civita Alba.[32]

PRIMITIVE NEIGHBOURS

While Romans, Etruscans and other Italian peoples were recording their encounters with Celtic barbarians in this way, the Romans were also recording their relationships with other Italian peoples, clothed in a language of (Roman) civilisation versus (Italian) barbarism. The Romans created a discourse of primitivism and barbarism to define and guide their military, political and social relationships with other Italian peoples with whom they came into conflict in the years of Rome's struggle for dominance among the Italian cities and regions.[33]

This strategy was to some extent borrowed from Greek ideas about the primitive 'other' but was given a uniquely Roman slant by the subsequent acceptance of those non-Roman Italians who had been considered 'other' in a process of incorporation that was later to be applied to the subject peoples of the Roman empire. Roman–Italian relationships centred around the idea of natural inequality and a civilised–barbarian divide which can be reconstructed principally through historical sources. There is little comparable visual source material,[34] though a fresco from this early period makes interesting viewing on these terms. The context in which this wall painting appears is additionally interesting, in that it was painted on the wall of a tomb on the Esquiline Hill in Rome and probably represented a private commission by the family of the deceased, rather than a work intended for wider public consumption.[35]

The painting survives only in a very fragmentary state and dates to the third or second century BC. On it is a number of figures, appearing in at least four horizontal registers of design, in scenes both of fighting and of negotiation or treaty. If historical events were being depicted here, rather than mythological subject matter, then it is likely that the main protagonist was related to the deceased occupant of the painted tomb. The two negotiating generals are labelled as Marcus Fannius and Quintus Fabius, tending to suggest that the work indeed has a historical basis. It probably relates to Rome's Samnite Wars of the later fourth century BC, the depicted Roman general Quintus Fabius in all likelihood being Quintus Fabius Maximus Rullianus, one of the most renowned military commanders of the Second Samnite War.

While certain features of the two meetings illustrated between the generals Fabius and Fannius might at first glance suggest that they confront each other as equals, nevertheless the garb, pose and attitude of the figure of Fannius deliberately place him as Fabius' inferior in the eyes of the viewer. In both scenes

Fannius wears protective metal greaves, and in one additionally wears a helmet. He is dressed in a short skirt-like garment and is draped with a heavy-looking cloak; apart from the skirt and cloak his upper body is naked. He holds no weapon, nor is any belt or scabbard visible. He stands in both scenes facing the figure of Fabius to the right, one leg slightly bent and his right arm extended out towards Fabius in a gesture of greeting or address. Fabius is dressed in a white toga and stands stiff and upright, looking towards the gesturing Fannius in both scenes. In his right hand he holds a spear, its end defiantly planted on the ground as if in defence of that very patch of earth.

A small group of similarly armed and dressed figures stands in attendance behind Fabius in the central and best-preserved scene of the meeting of the two generals. Their presence here again seems to be intended further to emphasise the unequal relationship between the two main protagonists, and thus between their respective cities and peoples. These attendant figures, though, are painted at a reduced scale – only about half the height of the figures of the generals – as are those figures engaged in combat in the lowest of the surviving registers and in a truncated scene behind the figure of Fannius in the central register. This reduction in size is a compositional device used to stress the hierarchy of the various combatants and negotiators, and the scale of their individual role in the unfolding victorious conclusion of the battles and negotiations.

Thus in this particular painting the opportunity has been taken to record a historic Roman victory brought about by the personal valour of the general Fabius, and to do so not simply by the depiction of, or allusion to, the victor, but rather through the strategy of presenting both victor and defeated in a way that further stresses their unequal fates. However, in naming Fannius some recognition has been given here to the individuality of the defeated, rather than his being rendered anonymously in the way that various enemies of imperial Rome were sometimes shown in succeeding centuries. Following their defeat, the 'barbarian' Samnites could now be civilised through incorporation into the political orbit of Greater Rome.

A FEAR OF DIFFERENCE

FROM REPUBLIC TO EMPIRE

While this study of Roman attitudes to the barbarian will begin with a detailed consideration of the image of the barbarian in Augustan art in Chapter Two, there is perhaps a danger of considering certain artistic strategies of the Augustan age as innovatory, when they may simply have been the continuation or reinterpretation of earlier Roman and Italian traditions. That pre-Augustan official art does not survive to the extent of later examples should not, therefore, rule out its consideration here. Republican art can perhaps reveal certain attitudes towards barbarian peoples that may differ from the necessary rhetoric of Roman imperial state art, whose styles, processes and motivation were part of an altogether more complex discourse. There may well have been a relatively simple difference between the definition of an enemy of Republican Rome and that of an enemy of imperial Rome, but the way in which this enemy was bodied forth in art and literature, in historical texts and in the imagination of the citizens of Rome may have been altogether more stark.

In the Republican period, it is known that the Greek tradition of constructing battlefield trophies of the enemy's captured or discarded arms and armour, the creation of a temporary victory monument of sorts, was taken up by certain Roman generals. That more permanent trophy monuments were erected on the site of a number of battles by victorious Republican generals is recorded in literary sources, though the monuments themselves do not survive.[36]

Certainly, the kind of triumphal imagery represented on the four surviving reliefs from a lost Republican monument in the Piazza della Consolazione in Rome, probably of the second or first century BC, is of a kind that was to become very common on imperial state monuments in the succeeding centuries. Motifs such as winged Victories, shields and the trophy of arms and armour captured in battle and displayed at first temporarily on the battlefield, or recreated as props for a triumphal procession in Rome, were eventually to become linked to images of defeated and dejected barbarian peoples. On the Consolazione reliefs such a visual connection is not explicitly made, as no

21

figures of barbarians appear. The monument was probably erected in commemoration of the Roman general Sulla's victory in the east over Mithridates. Inscriptions bearing the names of eastern peoples were discovered nearby and may have been derived from the same monument.[37]

Another permanent Republican victory monument was erected at Delphi in Greece in or around 167 BC. It consisted of a base and partially decorated rectangular pillar supporting a statue of the dedicatee, the Roman general Aemilius Paullus, in commemoration of his victory over the Macedonians under the leadership of Perseus at the Battle of Pydna.[38] The statue itself no longer survives, but on the pillar frieze are scenes of combat between the two sides. Particularly significant is one in which a riderless horse is shown at the centre, but in the background of the action. This represents the historically attested moment when the accidental loosing of a horse started the battle. In another scene, centred on a running figure on either side of whom rear two mounted horses, there can be seen the bodies of two slain figures, presumably Greeks, lying beneath the horses' hooves. It is very significant that one of these figures is naked. If this was a purely Greek work of art he would be described as being depicted 'in heroic nudity'. Instead, that artistic convention is being usurped and undermined by the death of the hero at the hands of the Romans.

It had originally been intended by Perseus that he would dedicate his own monument at Delphi, but Paullus' victory put paid to that plan, and indeed the very site of the monument was itself commandeered, the statue of Perseus removed and the carved frieze added to the pillar, presumably by Hellenistic artists working under the instructions of the Roman commission. These all constituted audacious and unprecedented acts on the part of Aemilius Paullus, and it was not to be until the Augusto-Tiberian period that other Roman victory monuments were set up in this way in what may be described as the enemy's home territory.

Another portrayal of battle, reminiscent of the style of the Delphi artwork and presumably broadly contemporary with it, is found on a fragmentary architectural frieze from an unknown context in Lecce, southern Italy, and now in the National Museum in Budapest.[39] Roman cavalrymen, their horses rearing up at their infantry opponents, perhaps Gauls, dominate the scene both in number and by their grouping. There is no doubt that their exertions on the battlefield will shortly be transformed into victory. Unfortunately, it is not known from what kind of building or monument this frieze originated, nor whether it formed part of a more complex artistic programme. The events portrayed likewise remain uncertain and vague, given that opinions on the date of the frieze place it anywhere between 200 and 150 BC.

Detailed historical descriptions of the celebration of triumphs in Rome, both from the time of the Republic and later during the empire when the triumph became an exclusively imperial domain, suggest that there was an almost excessive, anthropological concern at these events with the accurate display or representation of barbarian types, of their ethnic dress, and of their weaponry and material possessions.[40] Though the significance of the triumph as a ritualised drama will be discussed in Chapter Six, it should be noted here that the enforced appearance of barbarian captives on the streets of the city of Rome was as much an exercise in the manipulation of the image of the barbarian as was their appearance in static works of art. The literary sources further tell us that battle paintings, probably in imitation of the Greek tradition of such representations, were also carried in the triumphal processions, as 'visual aids' for the benefit of the rapt spectators.

An apparent obsession with the minutiae of barbarian cultures may also be discerned in Pliny's description of the trophy monument erected by the Roman general Pompey in the Pyrenees, the apparently artistically unadorned structure bearing the inscribed names of the over eight hundred *oppida* that had been stormed and captured by the general in Hispania Ulterior.[41] He similarly recorded his eastern triumphs in such list inscriptions at Rome and elsewhere.

It thus became a fashion for victorious Republican generals to commemorate their victories through monumental form and media. Other known Republican triumphal monuments include those of Domitius Ahenobarbus at Vindalium at the confluence of the Rivers Sorgue and Rhone, of Fabius Maximus at the confluence of the Rhone and Isere, and a temporary monument erected by Marius at Aix in 102 BC. Lucullus set up some kind of trophy at the border with Parthia in Armenia and at Tigranocerta and Nisibis. It was deemed worthy of note that the trophies of Ahenobarbus and Fabius were considered by Pliny and Florus to be innovatory in their permanency. These two monuments apparently were decorated 'above with enemy arms'.[42]

But it is in the war commentaries prepared by Julius Caesar, the *De Bello Gallico*, that a more fully formed rhetoric of expansionism and a crafted justification for Roman intervention in the affairs of barbarian peoples can be found.[43] The Gaul described by Caesar was not a real Gaul, nor were its inhabitants real people. They were based on reality, but were removed from it by the experiences and motivations of the author. Historians and archaeologists have moved beyond a literal reading of these texts, and have questioned whether the war-like tribal societies of Gaul and Britain were so structured as an aspect of their overall barbarism, or whether in these societies warfare was somehow institutionalised within the cultures in a more complex way. It would be equally possible to view Roman expansionism as a natural outlet for the institutionalisation of militarism in Roman society. Thus, on another level, it could be argued that growing violence within Gaulish society could have been in reaction to the equally expansionist, and perhaps to the Gauls unpredictable, power of Rome, so close by across the borders. It would indeed be surprising if the growing military, political and economic power of a state such as Rome had not created considerable shock waves well beyond its borders.

Much of the 'anthropological' text in Caesar's commentaries on his wars and campaigns in Gaul represented not truth and observation but rather, in some instances, a textual image of the Gauls that allowed their cultural otherness to be presented as both primitive and threatening. In the case of their reported inherent warlike tendencies, their predilection for human sacrifice and their lax moral ways, these were presented almost as justifiable reasons for their conquest.[44]

Interestingly, it was only a relatively short time before these condemnatory accounts were written that the Roman historian Pliny was recording his memory of the practice of burying alive a Greek and a Gaulish couple in Rome as part of some curious propitiatory rite of human sacrifice. Indeed, such a rite had been carried out earlier in 226 BC when the Celts had threatened Rome, in 216 BC, and possibly also in 114–113 BC at the time of serious barbarian incursions. Again, the distinction between the reported Gaulish execution of prisoners of war and Roman practices such as the public strangling in Rome of the defeated Gallic leader Vercingetorix seems to us today a matter of semantics, and perhaps a case of special pleading. At a later period, following Trajan's victory in the Dacian wars, in the absence of the Dacian leader Decebalus' body in Rome his head was thrown down the temple steps of the Roman Forum in a distasteful mockery of his people's defeat.

Unfortunately, little in the way of Caesarian works of art has come down to us, perhaps both because of the brevity of his reign and the destruction of the civil wars that followed his death. However, a number of coin issues celebrated Caesar's victories in Gaul.[45] A coin issue of c. 48–47 BC depicted a trophy, beneath which sits a heavily bearded, bound male Gaul, possibly the defeated Vercingetorix, though the legend across the middle of the scene simply reads 'Caesar'.[46] Another issue with the same simple legend depicted a bound male and an unbound female captive seated beneath a trophy. It is interesting to see how image and name were powerfully linked here in simple juxtaposition. Without turning over the coin to view the portrait head, the ancient viewer would have made an immediate connection between inscription and image, and would have constructed his or her own narrative of Roman–barbarian relationships from this strong device.[47]

Few works of art can otherwise be attributed to the time of Caesar, and it is probably a matter of pure coincidence that from the site of Vercingetorix's last stand at Alesia in Gaul comes a small bronze statuette of a fallen Gaulish warrior. Found in the forum of the subsequently established town it is, however, unlikely to be connected to the momentous events enacted here during the Roman siege and victory of the 50s BC, but more probably dates to some time in the first century AD.[48] The figure, only a few centimetres long, is depicted sprawled on the ground in a contorted attitude indicating that he is dead rather than sleeping, as has been suggested by some authorities. His back faces upwards towards the viewer and his head lies partly cradled by one arm, as if he had been trying to protect himself. His upper torso is bare and his lower body is garbed in trousers or leggings, as so often sported by Gauls and Celts in both Greek and Roman art. The pose is particularly reminiscent of some of the dead or dying warriors in the Attalid Gauls series and it is difficult not to think that there is some element of prototype among those well-known works that has been a direct source or inspiration for the bronzesmith who executed the Alesia statuette, or for the client who commissioned or purchased the finished article.

It is now thought that the marble copies of the Attalid statues of the 'Suicidal Gauls' and the 'Dying Gaul' were commissioned by Caesar for display at his estate on the Quirinal Hill in Rome. Ancient Greek images were thus appropriated in commemoration of contemporary Roman victories in Gaul.[49]

That Caesar was aware of the personal prestige to be garnered by sponsoring impressive public buildings in Rome is evident from the list of building projects which he had initiated before his assassination in 44 BC.[50] Such munificence had to be paid for, and it was out of the spoils of his military campaigns, particularly those in Gaul, that monies were provided. Also linked to this cycle of conquest turning into creation was the more temporary drama of the celebration of a triumph, an event that actually brought the theatre of the campaign, including many of its actual protagonists – both victor and vanquished – on to the very streets of the capital. Caesar celebrated no fewer than five triumphs on the streets of Rome in the year 46 BC, including four in one month, and the routes of these triumphs would have become as much a part of the mental geography of the city in the minds of those who witnessed them as the magnificent dedicatory public buildings that rose up in the Forum Romanum in particular in the following years.

A fragmentary terracotta relief from the first century BC may perhaps depict Julius Caesar.[51] This relief, found outside the city on the Via Cassia, has at its centre the standing figure of a Roman general, helmetless and holding in his left hand a spear, its butt resting on the ground at his side. This general, who may be Caesar, faces right and holds out his right hand towards a kneeling female figure paying him homage. Her crested helmet suggests that she may be an Amazon. A globe sits on the ground by his feet and a winged Victory hovers in the air, ready to crown the triumphant general with the victor's wreath. On his left is set up a trophy, hung with the captured arms and armour of the barbarian enemies of Rome, while seated on either side of the trophy's trunk are bound barbarians, perhaps a man and a woman. Flanking these standard displays of victory juxtaposed with defeat, symbols of the power of Rome and the impotence of her enemies, are identical scenes of building construction.

In each scene a triangular timber gantry for a crane appears, a bucket load of stone, brick or mortar being winched into the air under the control of the crane's operator who stands at its side holding a wooden lever of some kind. The crane stands before a substantial portion of walling, as a temple or basilica rises phoenix-like out of the ashes of conquered lands. This explicit linking of military power and conquest with prestige construction projects in Rome is also seen later in the friezes of Trajan's Column.

Echoes of the Caesarian conquest of Gaul can be found in the artistic programme of a number of public monuments set up under Augustus at the veteran colonies established at Arles, Beziers and Narbonne, and on the private Tomb of the Julii at Saint-Rémy (Glanum), dedicated to a veteran soldier of the Gallic Wars. Other fragmentary remains of possibly Augustan monuments in Gaul, at Biot and Saint-Rémy again, whose decoration includes arms and armour and kneeling captives, could also allude to the Gallic Wars.[52] Genre art representing captured Gauls was common.

Under the Roman Republic celebration of the victories and achievements of individual generals thus became increasingly dissociated from the personal and the transient, as reflected in the erection of a temporary battlefield trophy of arms and armour, becoming instead directed rather towards the triumphal and permanent memorial. The celebration of a triumph in Rome had been an honour accorded to any victorious general, but in the Late Republic it had become a focus for the display of naked personal ambition and self-promotion. In this way militarism had become institutionalised, which subsequently allowed for the actual triumph and the iconography of victory to be declared the exclusive preserve of the emperor. The last non-imperial triumph took place in 19 BC during the reign of Augustus. After that time victorious generals had to make do with the awarding of triumphal decorations only.[53]

Trends beginning in the Late Republican period can certainly be found more fully formed in the art of the Augustan era. This re-forming was a result of the need to present the ideas behind the new imperial state in a digestible visual format that both looked back to the best days of the Republic, before the years of civil war that followed the murder of Julius Caesar, and forward to a new era of peace and prosperity under Augustus, the eventual victor in those civil conflicts. It was not really until the time of the Antonine emperors, in the second century AD, that individual generals, or rather their families, were once more to be allowed an artistic outlet for the overt celebration of their military achievements through the fashion for the so-called battle sarcophagi of this period. But even then, the iconography associated with this channel for the commemoration of individual achievement was relatively limited, while the use of such imagery in a funerary context may have harked back to earlier Italian traditions as represented by the decorated cinerary urns from sites such as Volterra.

It would therefore appear that certain aspects of the earlier Greek attitude towards barbarians were adopted, and adapted, by the Romans, firstly in relation to their own attitude towards other Italian, but non-Roman, peoples and secondly, later, in relation to barbarian peoples with whom the Roman state was in conflict. That these attitudes came to be reflected by the construction of images, both literary and visual, is not surprising. Certain Greek modes of representation and certain stock motifs from Greek art were likewise adopted by Rome to help give visible form to these attitudes, and were themselves sometimes subtly redefined in the process. Nike became Victory, the temporary battlefield trophy became a more permanent monument in stone, battle paintings influenced sculptural traditions, and personifications of peoples and places came to be signifiers of subservience rather than of cultural diversity.

Two

Augustan Images of War and Peace

An influential study by Paul Zanker has alluded to 'the power of images in the age of Augustus'.[1] Zanker has argued that a system of imperial imagery was used in both the public and private spheres to express often complex political and ideological ideas relating to Augustus' programme of consolidation, following the extended period of civil war which had bedevilled the Roman world after the murder of Julius Caesar. While the appearance of images of barbarians on a number of the defining works of Augustan art was not considered as an explicit issue by Zanker, nevertheless their appearance will be considered here as of particular significance in itself, as well as within the larger framework of the art of the period. It will be argued that images of barbarians formed a coherent part of the rhetoric and narrative of power at this time, and that, as with so many elements of Augustan art, certain novel introductions and uses of these images resonated throughout Roman art well beyond the period.

The key works of Augustan art to be discussed here include the Ara Pacis, the so-called Altar of Peace, and other works of art integrated into the overall design of the Forum of Augustus in Rome and other public buildings in the city, including the Basilica Aemilia and the Temple of Apollo Sosianus. Consideration will also be given to a number of more intimate works, including the cuirassed statue of Augustus from the Villa of Livia at Prima Porta and the so-called Gemma Augustea. Attention will then be turned to a coherent group of

Augustan and Tiberian monuments in the province of Gallia Narbonensis and its neighbouring provinces, and to the somewhat contrasting messages about the ethos of the Augustan military and political programme and its achievements conveyed by these provincial monuments when compared with those in Rome. The direct legacy of the Augustan programme will then be considered in terms of its influence on the political art produced under the succeeding Julio-Claudian dynasty.

STOLEN CHILDHOOD

The Ara Pacis Augustae in Rome was dedicated in 13 BC.[2] Its principal sculptural scenes show members of the imperial family and their retinues, in two processional lines down each of the long, outer sides of the monument. As well as the adults, children also appear in the procession. Their presence has often occasioned comment from those studying and writing about the monument. Indeed, the identities of two of these children have been matters of intense academic debate.[3] This centres around their curious dress, the oddness of which is not questioned by either side of the argument, and whether this singles these two boys out as the adopted heirs of the emperor or as non-Romans, 'barbarian princes' as they have been dubbed.[4]

The smallest child wears a torque around his neck and is therefore sometimes identified as a Celt or Gaul, while the older wears what appears to be a Phrygian cap and is therefore identified as being an eastern barbarian child. Ann Kuttner has suggested that the Gallic child was possibly a member of the Aedui tribe and that the eastern child was Antiochus III of Commagene.[5] She has also suggested that one of the women with the eastern child was his mother, herself also in exile at Rome.[6] The counter-argument is that these were two Roman youths who had been taking part in the so-called 'Troy games', and that they were wearing costumes appropriate to the game, in which case the costumes were a further allusion to the Trojan Aeneas' legendary founding of Rome and his linking in this respect with Augustus, founder of the new Rome.

If they were indeed barbarian children, then their presence on the monument serves to strengthen the overall reading of the symbolism of the sculptural programme. Their presence here, in the company of their adoptive Roman imperial family, and in scenes that set out to show harmony in both state and family, seems at first sight quite comforting, and one that throws a positive light on the attitudes of the Augustan regime. However, this may not be the case if their presence implies the end result of a process of enforced exile for these children who had been brought to Rome not as guests or equals, but as hostages. Though once there they would have been brought up in the ways of the Roman state, perhaps they were never permitted to return to their homeland or, if they were allowed to do so as adults, it would have been under the sponsorship and influence of Rome.

For their parents, their wider family and tribe, their enforced absence would have practically constituted the denial and negation of autonomy over their reproductive history and therefore, by association, of their tribal and cultural lineage. Captured barbarian children were led before Augustus' triumphal chariot on one occasion and appeared at other triumphs, their bodies being treated as little more than trophies and exhibits. The Roman historian Suetonius noted that Augustan policy was unusual in that it sometimes involved the taking of female and child hostages from defeated barbarian tribes, in order to bind them to the keeping of treaties.[7] These instances of the Augustan political strategy involving the bartering and controlling of the bodies of both barbarian women and children contrast with, but nevertheless contribute towards, social policies of the reign aimed at establishing different types of control over women and families at Rome, at least in the upper echelons of Roman society.[8]

On the Ara Pacis reliefs the images of the barbarian children may have been used to provide a contrast that accords with other such uses of this device on the monument. Firstly, there is the 'pendant' arrangement of the children, the older on the south frieze and the younger on the north frieze. Secondly, the careful presentation of their distinctly different eastern and western dress might have signified the emperor's bringing together of the east and the west under his rule. The boys are here in a family scene, a setting demonstrating harmony and peace, yet to the contemporary viewer this would obviously have been seen as part of a process of coercion and the aftermath and consequence of war. Once more, the underlying message of exile and sterility linked to the presence of the boys may have been intended to contrast with the numerous images of bounty and fertility on the monument, and in particular with the image of Tellus on the south-east frieze. Here she appears with two children on her lap and flanked by two other female figures. All around them are verdant plants, flowers and fruit and numerous animals, all obvious symbols of fertility and plenty. A similar image of Tellus, contrasted with a captive, hence implicitly barren barbarian woman, appears on the Gemma Augustea and will be discussed below.

While the processional scenes on the outer 'precinct' walls of the *Ara Pacis* were the most immediately visible manifestation of the monument's message, there were also carved figures and scenes on the altar proper, housed inside the precinct frame. These included a generic sacrificial procession and the depiction of a number of personifications of peoples or provinces of the empire, the appearance of which is of particular relevance to this study, though unfortunately this part of the monument survives only in fragments. It seems likely that the parading of such personifications mirrored, or was mirrored by, the statuary personifications of subject peoples in the Augustan 'Portico of Nations' and the caryatid personifications in the Forum of Augustus. A precedent for such displays may have been provided by those in the Theatre of Pompey.[9]

A MORAL SPACE

In the Forum of Augustus there may have been displayed or incorporated other artworks on which barbarians were depicted. Certainly, there was erected here a frieze of caryatids, a choice of image that as well as being linked to classical Athens could also have directly alluded to the original story of the capture and exiling of the women of Caryae. In the light of the known and attested Augustan practice of demanding women hostages to secure the future good behaviour of their defeated tribes, the choice of the caryatid image seems apposite.[10]

Each pair of caryatids flanked a panel on which was carved the head of a bearded male deity, either Jupiter Ammon or Zeus Ammon, in the centre of a shield. However, these bearded heads could alternatively have represented barbarians, those with a torque or neck ring perhaps being Gauls. Such a juxtaposition of 'decapitated' barbarian men and enslaved barbarian women would seem entirely appropriate to the themes of Augustan victory art.[11]

A 'lost' Augustan monument, a Portico of Nations, may also have been a version of a caryatid porch, though with statues of conquered peoples taking the place of the Caryae women, in the same way that the Augustan restoration of the Basilica Aemilia introduced Parthian captives into the design.[12] Some insight into the possible design of the Portico may be gained by looking at the surviving thirteen, out of fifty, statues of *ethne* from the Sebasteion at Aphrodisias,[13] which is discussed in detail towards the end of this chapter, a series that was perhaps itself derived from the Augustan Portico in Rome. The grouping together of personifications of a large number of conquered peoples and nations in this way at Rome would have been an overt celebration of the power of Rome, and of Augustus in particular, rather than a celebration of the diversity of peoples brought together within the empire.

It has been suggested that the Forum of Augustus was, by both intent and design, a masculine and gendered environment.[14] That is not to say that access to the forum was in any way restricted along gender lines, but rather that the structures and imagery employed there together formed a coherent construction of Roman male power, something that would have been apparent to viewers of either sex. In that case the use here of the various female personifications of defeated nations could be seen as part of a wider strategy of discourse that had as much to do with the gender of the images of defeated nations as it had to do with their ethnicity. An examination of some of the surviving sculptures from a frieze in the Basilica Aemilia, which may date to a restoration of the monument by the Aemilius family under the patronage of

Augustus, perhaps lends extra weight to the argument for a gendered intent behind much of the Augustan programme in the forum area.[15]

The themes of the Aemilian frieze were mythological rather than historical. The depiction here of the rape of the Sabine women is the only known instance of the representation of this event in monumental sculpture, and the rendering of the punishment of Tarpeia by the men of Rome for betraying the city's security to the vengeance-seeking Sabine men would also appear to be didactic. What better way was there to illustrate the Augustan policy of encouraging higher moral, predominantly sexual standards both in public and private life, and in the conduct and duties of women in particular, than by the use of such a cautionary tale? The rape of the Sabine women was an act held to be justified, in that Rome needed sons and daughters to continue the work of its men. Conquest and sexual penetration here were construed as being one and the same, while the fate of Tarpeia was also seen as somehow justifiable in that her betrayal of the men of Rome was little different to sexual betrayal, and hence deserving of the grim death she suffered in consequence.[16] There were clear and unequivocal messages here to the women of Rome, Italy and the wider empire, and to women in barbarian lands, about the psyche of the ruling Roman male.

Finally, another major lost monument depicting barbarians may have stood near the Temple of Apollo Palatinus. It took the form of three large marble statues of kneeling Parthian men supporting on their shoulders a tripod-like structure on which may have stood a statue of the emperor.[17]

RUMOURS OF WAR

With the exception of a relief from a temple in Rome and now in Mantova, and reliefs from the Temple of Apollo Sosianus, again in Rome, there is no sculptural relief of this period from Rome itself portraying battle scenes, most commonly in Roman art the setting for the appearance of the barbarian as opponent. This is probably of significance in itself, so that when images of barbarians are shown in Augustan art at Rome then they might be expected to be playing purposeful roles beyond those simply of the engaged and the slaughtered.[18]

The Mantova frieze probably comes from an Augustan temple in Rome, perhaps the Temple of Castor and Pollux which was situated in the Augustan forum, and on it is depicted a frenzied battle between Romans and Gauls.[19] In the centre of the frieze a naked, now headless Gaul – for the sculpture is damaged at this point – is shown carrying off the naked body of a wounded or dead comrade as the Roman troops bear down upon them from the right. The bodies of these two Gauls are tensed and straining, strong and muscular in a way that recalls the over-exaggerated representation of musculature on the statues of the Attalid Gauls.[20] Indeed, it is quite possible that this heroic rescue was based on the well-known Hellenistic statue of Menalaos carrying the body of Patroklos off the battlefield.[21]

To the left of this scene are two other virtually naked Gaulish warriors; one lying slain on the ground and the other, wearing only a helmet, partially fallen and supporting himself on the ground with one outstretched arm, in a pose that again echoes one of the Attalid works. The bodies of the Gauls appear in the frontal plane of the frieze, while the Roman soldiers appear in lower relief behind. Therefore both composition and content of the work deliberately conspire together to emphasise the primitive presence and otherness of the barbarians.

The Mantova frieze would seem to share with the Attalid models a sensibility with regard to the portrayal of Gaulish barbarians which both emphasised their defeat yet at the same time expressed admiration for their courage in battle and their physical prowess. Unfortunately, because the original architectural context of the frieze is unknown, it is not possible to ascertain whether it formed part of a more complex programme of sculptural works that elaborated further on Roman–barbarian relationships, and which emphatically connected the Augustan triumphs over Gaulish, barbarian adversaries with those of Attalos.

The second Augustan battle relief comes from the Temple of Apollo Sosianus at Rome.[22] This now fragmentary, small-scale sculptural frieze, which would have adorned the inside of the temple, probably dates to *c.* 20 BC. Some of the surviving fragments depict a battle between Roman and Gaulish cavalry, with a particularly striking design of rearing and crumpling horses that in terms of its composition recalls certain earlier Greek works. Two others depict a triumphal procession. On one, a bier or *ferculum*, loaded with what appear to be sacrificial offerings, is being carried in a procession. On another, sacrificial beasts are being marshalled into line, while at a given signal blown on a trumpet attendants prepare to pick up and raise another *ferculum* on which sit two bound barbarian captives, one male and one female, chained or tied to a trophy set up in the centre of the bier.

Gaius Sosius, after whom the temple was named, supported Mark Anthony in his political manoeuvrings and in the subsequent civil wars, and was voted a triumph in Rome in 34 BC following his military successes against the Jews in the east. It was monies from this campaign that were used to commission the building of the temple to Apollo, and it might have been expected that these personal triumphs and those of his mentor Anthony would somehow have been commemorated and depicted here. However, after the victory of Octavian (Augustus) at the defining naval Battle of Actium in 31 BC, giving him supremacy in the Roman world, Sosius was captured, but pardoned. Thereupon, the Temple of Apollo Sosianus was dedicated in honour of a new patron, the surviving friezes probably relating to the campaigns of Augustus against the northern, Illyrian barbarians for which he celebrated a triumph in 29 BC.

Portions of possibly Augustan sculptural friezes depicting arms and armour, with shields, helmets and spears heavily represented in the assemblages, come from Turin and Bologna[23] and probably formed part of larger triumphal structures. These may have been arches, though whether such allusive strategies to define victory and triumph were continued around the monuments, without recourse to direct scenes of battle and combat, remains unknown.

ENEMIES OF ROME

VICTORY FROM DEFEAT

The so-called Prima Porta statue of the emperor, on which he is portrayed wearing an elaborate, decorated metal breastplate or cuirass, comes from the Villa of Livia at Prima Porta, just outside Rome (and is now in the Vatican Museums).[24] In the centre of the front of the cuirass a Parthian chieftain or king returns a previously captured Roman standard to a Roman general, a scene which alludes to the famous, disastrous Roman loss of the standards by the Republican general Crassus in 53 BC and their negotiated return to Augustus in 20 BC.

On either side of the central scene sits a female figure. One holds an empty sheath, while the other holds a drawn sword. It may be that the seemingly simplistic contrastive symbolism here was meant to suggest that the armed woman (or country) represents a client barbarian people while the unarmed or disarmed woman (or country) represents the conquered. Beneath the central scene sits Tellus, holding a cornucopia and accompanied by two children. This image of bounty and fertility obviously was again used to allude to the health of the empire under Augustus. The cuirass decoration also includes depictions of various deities, and mythological and astrological figures, but these do not concern us here.

The cuirass statue type was Greek in origin and came to be adopted by victorious Roman generals in the Republican period. A significant difference in the Roman usage, particularly noteworthy in the case of the Prima Porta Augustus, was the artist's use of the cuirass surface as a zone or plane of decoration on which combinations of motifs could be deployed to enhance the overall effect of the work. Whether the Prima Porta cuirass was modelled on a real item of decorated parade armour remains open to question.

A number of other fragments of cuirass statues have been suggested as belonging to the Augustan principate, though as none of the heads of these other works survives it is possible that they could have been associated with some of the later Julio-Claudian emperors. From the point of view of this study, the most interesting of these fragments comes from Gaul – the exact provenance is uncertain – and is now in the collections of the Ny Carlsberg Glyptothek in Copenhagen, Denmark. On the few surviving lappets or flaps of the skirt of the cuirass are highly decorated panels. Depicted on one is the figure of a male Gaul holding a small child and on another a Gaul with a 'boar' standard. The man with the infant brings to mind the Augustan artistic strategy that allowed for themes linked to fertility/dynasty and infertility/curtailed future to be deployed in situations that compared the fate of defeated barbarian nations to that of victorious Rome, and which also implied some subtext of comparative sexuality to be read by the viewer.

INTIMATE MESSAGES

Less public in their display and consumption, and targeted at a small, exclusive elite audience, were luxury objects produced for the Augustan court. These were perhaps given as diplomatic gifts or to loyal servants of the empire. They nevertheless carried messages that helped create a coherent rhetoric of imperial power and mythology. Though many must have been produced, few survive, and discussion here will concentrate on the most elaborate and best-known of these items, a large sardonyx cameo known as the Gemma Augustea, dated to *c.* 10 BC.[25]

The gem is divided into two horizontal registers of design. In the upper register appears Augustus himself, seated on a throne next to a female figure, probably *Roma*, with, according to the reading by Paul Zanker, the young Tiberius and Germanicus present in the line of the emperor's forward gaze.[26] Behind the throne stands a female deity, Tellus, with a crown or wreath, holding a cornucopia and accompanied by children. An attendant, bearded male deity, presumably Oceanus, stands near. The scene balances the themes of war and peace. Victory and its aftermath, rather than the actual winning of victory through war and battle, was the image used to convey the message. The presence of Tellus, of the cornucopia and of the children suggests the benefits of peace and plenty under the new regime in both public and private spheres. The importance of fertility, of the family, was a recurring theme in Augustan art, some would say the defining theme.

In the bottom register of design on the Gemma Augustea, below the imperial victors, are Roman soldiers and either auxiliary troops or personifications of provinces in the guise of auxiliaries, erecting a trophy of captured arms and armour, while two barbarian captives, one male and one female, sit at the base of the trophy. Two other soldiers appear to be mistreating two barbarian captives, one of whom, a woman, is being pulled along by the hair by one of the troopers. At the point where the gem is now damaged a figure may be missing, so that the barbarian woman could originally have been dragging along a child by the hand.[27] The male barbarian in this scene, who crouches or kneels in submission, may also have been held by the hair, though this is less certain.

If there had been a child accompanying these two barbarians, the image of a barbarian family emasculated as a social unit and in thrall to the power of Roman may have been intended to contrast with that of Tellus in the register above. Here, as already described, she is depicted with two children, obviously present to underscore the message of fertility, as opposed to the barrenness and impotence evocatively hinted at in the scene below. It has been suggested that rather than being a mortal female, the mistreated barbarian woman could in fact be a personification, perhaps of Dalmatia, an interpretation which need not necessarily detract from the underlying meaning of the scene.[28]

On the majority of Augustan works of art on which male barbarians appeared they were usually represented either in the act of surrendering, of seeking clemency or as bound captives. They were depicted in states of impotence rather than action, and this must have been intended as comment on their political, personal and sexual status. The Augustan policy of taking women and children as hostages on certain occasions could also be interpreted as a strategy for eroding the power and potency of the barbarian men, as well as very directly affecting the future reproductive choices of these women. There was a quite appreciable over-emphasis in Augustan art on the use of images of both Roman and barbarian women and of female personifications, while real women's images within Roman society were also effectively remodelled at this time by what may be called

Augustus' interventionist policies with regard to women's fertility and their perception of the value of their own bodies.[29]

Augustan art, then, was one that wished to be seen to be about peace rather than war, yet these visions of peace were underpinned by messages about the power and authority of the emperor Augustus, winner and guarantor of this peace.[30] The art was also part of the wider rhetoric of Augustan social policy, and it is particularly in this context that the recurring images of barbarian women and children, or of barbarian families, should be seen. In the main, this social policy was targeted at the Roman aristocracy, and among other measures included a restriction against inheritance for those without children, permission for certain groups to intermarry, perhaps as a result of some gender imbalance among some sections of society at this time, and an easing of the restrictions on divorce, to allow a man to divorce a 'barren' wife, remarry and sire children, thus securing his own lineage and that of his class and ultimately of the state.[31]

The depiction of the Augustan family and the manipulation of the images of children on a number of key works of Augustan art, particularly the Ara Pacis, could also be related indirectly to the pursuit of domestic policies that verged on social engineering. This was later to find an echo in the art of the Benevento Arch and in the way that a similar rhetoric of state interference in matters of moral and sexual behaviour underlay the Trajanic alimentary scheme's partly cynical aim of feeding the children of Italy in order to guarantee healthy future recruits for the Roman army.[32] However, recent research has suggested that a strong tradition of portraying children in all media existed in pre-Roman Etruscan art, something which may imply that the Augustan use of images of children was simply part of a longer-established and more complex tradition in Italian art, here harnessed for political ends.[33]

Images of fertility, abundance and family appeared on all the surviving key monuments and artworks of the period from Rome. Many of the images of barbarians were deployed in a contrastive, almost didactic manner: fertility was contrasted with images of impotence, abundance with images of isolation, and family/secured lineage was countered by suggestions of fertility curtailed or cheated by history. Augustan policy not only turned brick into marble,[34] and war into peace, it also transformed the bodies of conquered peoples into artistic images and stereotypes. It redefined their sexual future within a Roman context, and loosed the ties that bound image to reality in a way that was both new and dynamic, as well as being rooted quite consciously in the traditions of the Republican past and concerned with the manipulation of time through dynastic inheritance.

A GEOGRAPHY OF POWER

Less attention has been paid in the now extensive literature on Augustan art to those monuments erected outside Rome in commemoration of the emperor's military achievements, that is the so-called Alpine Trophy at La Turbie[35] and another trophy monument at Saint-Bertrand-de-Comminges in southern Gaul, close to the frontier with Spain.[36] In addition to these two monuments, a group of decorated civic arches in various of the towns of Gallia Narbonensis and its neighbouring territories will also be discussed. This group has no precedent or parallel outside of Rome and Italy for its consistent and insistent artistic message. Reference will also be made to a smaller number of Italian civic arches or gates.[37] The majority of the civic triumphal arches are Augustan in date, though some may have been completed or conceived in the reign of his successor Tiberius, as in the case of the arch at Orange.

The trophy monument at La Turbie, in the hills rising up from the coast above Saint-Tropez, is notable both for its form and decoration and for its epigraphic dedicatory panels. These inscriptions listed the names of forty-five Alpine tribes defeated and conquered by Rome in the two major campaigns of 29–25 BC and 14 BC. Upon its roughly square, raised basal plinth was set a structure similar to a tower tomb, with a statue of the emperor himself being placed on the apex of the monument.

Two relief panels, positioned on either side of the inscription in the present reconstruction, both consist of a massive trophy, hung with arms and armour captured from the defeated tribes by the Roman forces. Crouched beneath each of the trophies is a pair of barbarian captives, one on each side of the trophy's trunk. Each pair is made up of a man and a woman, the men being bound with their hands behind their backs, the women with their hands in their laps, crossed in such a way as to suggest that they too are tied up. All are clothed, although one of the women has one of her breasts exposed.

The monument provides an interesting example of the marrying of very specific information about conquered peoples, as represented by the extensive listing of their tribal names, with a generalised portrayal of their defeated state, as represented by the four captives in the decorative panels. It has been suggested that the Augustan monument owed both its location and form, as well as its singular need to name quite specifically and exhaustively those defeated peoples, to a desire to emulate and surpass the similar way in which the Republican general Pompey set about commemorating his personal victories. On Pompey's victory monument in the Pyrenees was said to have been a dedicatory inscription listing the names of over eight hundred enemy strongholds or *oppida* which he had stormed or captured during his campaigns in Spain.

Nothing survives above ground of the Augustan trophy monument at Saint-Bertrand-de-Comminges, in the border area between the provinces of Gaul and Spain. Dated to 25 BC, almost one hundred and fifty sculptural and architectural fragments of the monument have been recovered by excavation and are now housed in the local museum. It is clear that the monument commemorated a triple triumph and this could have been reflected, according to one reconstruction, in the arrangement of three separate trophies: two smaller trophies, 'Gallic' and 'Hispanic', flanking a larger, central 'naval' trophy with attendant victories. However, the celebration of a triple triumph could equally well have been achieved within the 'layered' form of a tower monument like that at La Turbie. Indeed, if one were to consider these two monuments as having been pendant structures, then a similarity of form might be expected. A cuirassed statue of the emperor may have been placed on top of the monument, though there are doubts as to whether a now-headless cuirassed torso from Saint-Bertrand does date to this period and thus belong to the trophy monument.

The naval trophy consisted of a ship's prow, representing the Augustan naval victory at the Battle of Actium in 31 BC, a female marine deity, an imperial eagle and a Victory with palm frond and a laurel wreath held aloft in her right hand. At the base of the naval trophy are a dolphin and a crocodile, to represent the emperor's dominion over both land and sea. The defeated forces of Mark Antony are not depicted. It is interesting that despite a number of instances of the commemoration of victories in civil conflicts within the empire over the next few centuries, it was not until the time of Constantine in the fourth century that Romans fighting Romans were directly portrayed in state art.

No such qualms, of course, existed in the portrayal of defeated barbarian peoples, so that the two flanking trophies utilised figures who represented generic captives – Gauls and Spaniards – and some who are personifications of the pacified regions of Gaul and Spain. This denotes an unusual appearance together of these two types of representation.

The siting of the two major trophy monuments at La Turbie in the east and at Saint-Bertrand in the west had a deliberate geographical significance, in that each stood at a major node in the provincial road system and in an area where cultural, political and military concerns met and overlapped in the late Republic and early empire. The two monuments can be viewed as territorial markers, in the landscape and of the landscape, and as pendant statements on Augustan political and military achievements. The Augustan Altar of Peace at Lyons was situated almost between the two.

Geographical as well as political significance may also be attributed to the concentration of other barbarian-bearing victory monuments in the province of Gallia Narbonensis, a clustering of monuments with martial imagery that was in almost direct contrast to the emphasis on non-military matters and peace on display in Augustan art at Rome. The concept that these monuments comprised a single idea or worldview has been best articulated by Susan Silberberg-Peirce.[38] Despite the fact that at the time of the construction of this group of monuments Gallia Narbonensis was a pacified area and a Roman province, nevertheless there was both a need and a desire in the Augustan political hierarchy for the former 'barbarian' status of the area to be represented as a means of celebrating its transformation into a civilised state by the power of Rome.[39]

Nine, and possibly ten, arches were erected at the entranceways into the towns of Toulouse, Avignon, Saint-Rémy, Orange, Carpentras, Vienne, and possibly at Saint-Bertrand-de-Comminges and the veteran colonies of Narbonne itself, Arles and Beziers. The Saint-Rémy, Orange and Carpentras arches still survive as more or less intact structures and will be described in detail below, while the other six or seven monuments are represented largely by fragments of the sculptures that once adorned them. At the three veteran colonies it would appear that the arch sculptures principally comprised depictions of captured or discarded arms and armour, perhaps laid around the base of a sculpted trophy. On a fragment from Arles it is uncertain whether one of the objects among the pile of weaponry represents an elaborate helmet or the severed head of a Gaulish warrior.[40] Interestingly, some of the captured military equipment depicted is distinctively Greek rather than Gaulish in character, alluding in all probability to Julius Caesar's earlier capture of the Greek trading centre at Marseilles.[41]

At Glanum, present-day Saint-Rémy, stands a cenotaph monument erected by and dedicated to the Julii, a locally settled Gallic family, whose three sons used the monument to honour their father Gaius Julius, probably a veteran of the Roman army who had gained his citizenship through long service.[42] Sculptural panels on the monument show cavalry battles and scenes of infantry combat between Romans and Gauls, with all the panels displaying a distinctive crowded composition and a heavy outlining of individual figures that some scholars see as deriving from the conventions of Greek battle painting. Other elements apparently derived from an Amazonomachy fit in with this interpretation of the artist's influences and source materials. The monument may date to *c.* 30–20 BC and the battle scenes may allude to Caesar's historic campaigns in Gaul, in which Gaius Julius probably fought.

Right next to the Tomb of the Julii stands a small decorated triumphal arch [43] with four panels, two on each side of the arch, containing pairs of figures, one male and one female in each case. On the east face the couples are barbarians, one couple possibly German, bound and chained to the trunk of a trophy. On the west face the male barbarians are accompanied by female figures who are perhaps personifications of Roma. On the northern panel Roma is dressed in a toga-like garment and rests one hand on the shoulder of her bound captive in a proprietorial manner. On the southern panel the naked male barbarian stands with his back to the viewer, while beside him sits the cuirass-clad figure of Roma seated atop a pile of captured arms and armour.

Figures of flying Victories frame the arch on both faces. In contrast to the obvious images on the eastern face of fertility curtailed and on the western face of barbarian manhood emasculated by the female Roma, there is a great deal of fertility imagery in the form of vegetal and floriform decorative motifs on other parts of the arch. Narrow registers of design incorporating barbarian weaponry were also used here in an almost purely decorative manner, rather than being stacked up as a trophy in the more conventional manner for displaying such spoils. The use of female personifications here as 'castrating' figures is very unusual, almost an inversion of the standard Roman imperial artistic vocabulary.

The close proximity of the tomb and arch at Saint-Rémy would have allowed viewers to compare and contrast the iconography of the two adjacent monuments as being different but complementary ways of representing Roman imperial power. The Tomb of the Julii provides a rare example of a private, family commission which utilised depictions of 'public' matters connected with political and military events. It is even more remarkable and unusual in that it is a provincial monument, and one linked to a non-aristocratic Roman or Italian family, whose social status at the time of its erection owed a debt to the achievements of their ancestor under the benevolent patronage of the Roman military system and its gift of citizenship to Gaius Julius. While the structures of the Roman Republic had allowed individuals to celebrate their own political and military successes through a number of channels, most notably the celebration of a formal triumph in Rome, towards the end of the Republic this had become a means of self-aggrandisement rather than a humble honour for the leading generals of the time. Indeed,

Augustus was to bring an end to the Republican system by making the triumph a strictly imperial event, honouring and involving only the emperor and members of his family.[44]

The arch at Carpentras, dated to *c.* 9 BC, carries the depiction of a tree-trunk-like trophy, from whose forked branches a helmet hangs on either side. Weapons are piled at the base of the trophy, while to either side stand upright figures of chained barbarians, their hands bound behind their backs and the chains looped around the trunk of the trophy. An examination of the clothing and appearance of the two male barbarian figures reveals that they are probably different ethnic types, neither of them a Gaul. One looks away to the right and the other to the left. It has been suggested that each glances in the direction of their conquered homeland, one, a German, facing north-eastwards and the other, a Dalmatian or Parthian, looking to the south-east.[45] The arch probably commemorated Augustus' victories over the Dalmatians and Germans in the period 13–9 BC and its siting here may well have had a great deal to do with the use of such monuments as territorial markers in Augustus' reign.

On the arch at Vienne chained, non-Gallic captives also appeared, wearing Phrygian or eastern caps that perhaps identify them as Parthians.[46] Thus the Vienne, Carpentras and perhaps also the Saint-Rémy arches bore imagery relating to enemies of Rome outside Gallia Narbonensis.

Though the triumphal arches of Gallia Narbonensis carried much of the standard triumphal imagery that was by then part and parcel of the language of Roman imperial power, the figure of the emperor himself did not appear on any of the monuments.[47] In this way, perhaps, a generalised and generic Roman triumphalism was being celebrated, so that the figures of the barbarians became depersonalised and anonymous. The messages of the arches' sculptural programmes assured the province's people of the protective power of Roman arms. The non-Gallic barbarians portrayed on a number of the arches were enemies not only of Rome itself, but, by extension, of all those under her protection. The style and form of these monuments were later to be reflected in the architecture and artistic programme of the Antonine arch at Besançon, discussed in detail in Chapter Four,[48] though the intended messages of this monument were somewhat different to those conveyed by the Augustan-Tiberian arches.

Either of an Augustan or Tiberian date is the decorated gate into the town of Molise, Roman Saepinum, in southern Italy.[49] The outer face of the gate bears an inscription relating to the provision of town walls and gates under the aegis of Tiberius and Drusus, and is flanked on either side by a statue of a bound, virtually naked Germanic barbarian. The statues clearly alluded to their celebrated victories in Germany in 2–1 BC. Once more there was combined here the idea that conquest and victory were integral to the economy of the empire, and that financial benefits included the provision of town walls and gates. Facing out into the countryside, away from the protected and civilised urban environment, the barbarians also acted as symbols of a more generalised danger lurking beyond the walls.

At Pola, in Croatia, the Arch of the Sergii was dedicated in the late Augustan or early Tiberian period by a local woman, Salvia Postuma Sergius, in memory of deceased family members.[50] While no figures of barbarians appeared on the simply decorated arch, other more usually imperial political motifs such as winged Victories and piles of trophy arms and armour were used in the scheme. These could have alluded both to the military careers of the male Sergii family members here being commemorated, and to the implied victory over death inherent in the commemorative power of memory mediated through a lasting monument.

During the Augustan era, military engagements also took place in Africa as a result of barbarian incursions into the provincial areas. These incursions were apparently so serious that they involved the defeat of Roman forces, the capture of a number of towns, the taking of prisoners to be sold as slaves and the carrying away of statues of the emperor. The need to protect commercial concerns and trade along the Nile subsequently led the prefect, C. Petronius, to launch a retaliatory expedition beyond the southern frontier of the province. Whether retribution was as severe as the histories suggest is uncertain. However, a major town may have been sacked, thousands of prisoners taken to be sold into slavery, one thousand of whom were sent to the emperor himself at Rome, and other tributes and promises exacted.[51]

No monument commemorating these victories is known, although it has been suggested that two small bronze figurines of black barbarian captives in the collection of the Berlin Staatliches Antikenmuseum date from this time, and could therefore represent hostages taken by Petronius' forces.[52] The statuettes, very similar but not quite identical, are of seated young black male captives, naked apart from loincloths, posed with their legs crossed, their hands tied behind their backs, and their heads inclined in such a way as to suggest that they are looking up at their captor who may have formed part of the original statuary tableau.

A LEGACY OF INNOCENCE AND EXPERIENCE

Some consideration will now be given to artworks of the succeeding dynasty, the Julio-Claudian house, which relied substantially on the artistic propaganda of the Augustan era as both a source and an inspiration for conveying its own dynastic messages, many of which were linked to the stressing of continuity with Augustan policies.[53] The form as well as the content of Augustan art was revisited on occasions, and it is true to say, for example, that the so-called Grand Camée de France, of possibly AD 50,[54] was directly inspired by the Gemma Augustea.

The Grand Camée is, like its model and predecessor, again divided into three registers, the upper register bearing a scene presided over by the deified Augustus, who is being carried through the heavens by a figure wearing an Asiatic costume, with belted tunic and cap, possibly meant to denote Alexander the Great or Aeneas. The middle register of the cameo is taken up by members of the imperial family, the seated general in the guise of Jupiter usually being identified as Tiberius or, less likely, Claudius. Depending on which of these identifications is favoured, the female figure seated on his left, holding sheaves of corn and poppies which link her to ideas of fecundity and plenty, is either his mother Livia who, as wife to Augustus, united the Julian and Claudian houses and would therefore seem to be a most fitting figure to portray on such a gem, or as is less likely, is Agrippina the Younger, mother of Nero and wife of Claudius.

Whichever set of identifications and interpretations is favoured, there was nevertheless in this central scene a very strong and specific statement being made about the continuity of the political ideology of the Julio-Claudians and about the close linkage of political and family ties in the decades following Augustus. In other words, the image confirms the promise of security through guaranteeing the imperial line as suggested on the Ara Pacis and, less explicitly, on other artworks of the Augustan age. On the Grand Camée, Augustus is present to oversee the continuation of his works and policies, and to stress the idea of the family, both imperial and Roman, as a unit of security for the state. But these scenes of imperial power and harmony were contrasted with images of barbarians in defeat, as again appeared on the Gemma Augustea.

In the central register, slumped at the base of Livia's throne, is a male barbarian wearing an eastern cap, tunic and leggings. Just as the figure of Augustus in the upper register provided a link to the central scene, so this barbarian figure provides a link to the bottom, smallest register in which a number of defeated and dejected barbarian men, women and children are portrayed. These figures are crowded or huddled together, appearing mournful, most with lowered heads. The central of these, and the figure to which the viewer's gaze is drawn, is a mother cradling her child, in evident symbolic contrast to the dynastic victors above her.

On another gem, probably of Claudian date and now known as the Marriage Cameo,[55] four imperial portrait heads and busts appear, with two cornucopiae in the foreground, out of which two of the figures seem to be emerging. An imperial eagle is depicted in the lower, central part of the composition, and piles of trophy arms and armour are placed on either side of the stone. The imperial portraits were of the then current emperor Claudius, of Agrippina the Younger, of Tiberius and of his mother Livia. The message here once more was one of lineage, of the importance of the past in the present, and of the promise of a secure future under the Julio-Claudians. The trophy weapons were a form of artistic shorthand, representing conquered barbarian peoples, past, present and future.

A sardonyx cameo vase, now in Berlin in the Staatliches

Antikenmuseum, is another court luxury item of either Augustan or Tiberian date. On it can be seen the birth of an Augustan prince, attended by a trio of female deities or dynastic figures. Also present at the birth is Venus, portrayed with a shield and standing by a trophy beside a slumped, male Parthian prisoner or a personification of Parthia.[56] This contrasting of zenith and nadir needs little further elaboration, though it is worth noting that the appearance here of a bound barbarian figure with a deity represents an almost unique use of the motif of the defeated barbarian, in that for once it was not deployed in conjunction with the portrayal of an emperor but rather with that of a dynastic heir. It could therefore be said that the barbarian figure represented conquests to be made in the future rather than those already achieved.

This luxury item could have been commissioned to mark the birth of Julia to Caligula and Caesonia in AD 39, which would make it an interesting link between the image of the conquered barbarian male and female imperial power, or at least an acknowledgment of the role of the imperial women in the success of the dynasty's military and political programme.[57] However, this idea has been dismissed by Ann Kuttner[58] almost solely on the grounds that the idea of 'conquest foretold seems unapt to a female birth'.

On one of a pair of silver cups or *skyphoi* forming part of the Boscoreale Treasure, found near Pompeii, is a figured scene relating to the Augustan political and social programme,[59] though the treasure is considered to be early Tiberian in date. In an attempt to contextualise the cups within Augustan art, the most in-depth study of the iconography of the Boscoreale cups, by Ann Kuttner,[60] has operated on the premise that the political and historical scenes on them were not unique, but rather were adapted from sculptural prototypes on a major state monument in Rome, a monument now obviously 'lost' and of which no sculptural fragments have survived.

On the 'Augustus cup' the emperor is depicted seated on a stool, surrounded by army officers and officials. He holds out his right hand towards a number of bearded, barbarian men, each accompanied by a small child. The barbarian closest to the emperor kneels at his feet in supplication and seems to be pushing forward or offering his child to Augustus. The child stretches out its arms towards the emperor, almost in response to the emperor's own expansive gesture. The second male barbarian stands behind the first, waiting in line, again with his child held out in front of him. He is standing but appears to be stooping, as if in the process of kneeling. Pictured in the background, in lower relief, is a third barbarian male, this time carrying a small child on his shoulders, the child holding on to the man's forehead or his hair. This man too is presumably waiting to offer up his child to the emperor.

It is thought that what we are seeing here is a portrayal of an actual historical event, Augustus' visit to Lugdunum in Gaul in 8 BC to inaugurate the founding of a temple there. While the barbarians in this scene may be envoys or representatives of enemies defeated in battle – in other words they are here to seek clemency for their people – there is a suspicion that this scene shows something more, that the men were offering up their children to Augustus as hostages. Such ritualised and formalised acceptance of hostages was probably a relatively commonplace event in newly conquered territories and it has already been noted that historical accounts of such hostages being subsequently taken to Rome during the reign of Augustus are well known.

While this scene may be the earliest example in Roman art of what became known as a *submissio*,[61] a stock theme where barbarians were depicted in the act of surrender to a Roman emperor, it nevertheless deviates from the somewhat formulaic nature of such scenes in that on the Boscoreale vessel the emperor is shown dressed in a toga rather than being depicted in military uniform, as would normally be expected on the occasion of a surrender of this kind. The meeting would also appear to be mediated by a Roman officer who may be acting as a sponsor for the barbarians introduced into the presence of the emperor. It has been suggested that this indicates that Augustus was here meeting with friendly or allied barbarians and that the children being offered up to the emperor were either being presented for his blessing or being handed over to the care of Rome, not as hostages but rather as willingly offered pupils for a political and social education in Rome itself. It is something of a moot point as to whether children handed over like this and taken to Rome, perhaps never to return to their homeland, are to be formally and pedantically defined not as hostages but as wards of some kind, given the unequal balance of power between Rome and its client kingdoms and provinces at the time.

It is quite possible that the small, western barbarian child on the Ara Pacis could have been one of the same children being offered up to Augustus in the scene on this silver cup.[62] The taking away of children as hostages in this manner was a deeply symbolic act on many levels, both political and personal, almost instantly negating or calling into question the very memory of the act of giving birth to the child in the first place. Such institutionalised pedaphoric acts in this period seem to be part of a narrative thread emerging or created at this time that linked, or rather contrasted, family security and harmony at Rome with the disruption and dislocation of family life in the barbarian world as a consequence of opposition to Roman power.[63]

On the 'Augustus cup' there also appears, on the side opposite to the son-giving scene, a group of seven personified provinces including Gaul, Spain, Africa or Egypt, and Asia or Arabia, the others being more sketchily rendered without identifiable attributes.[64] Viewed in conjunction with the appearance of personifications on the inner altar of the Ara Pacis and in the Forum of Augustus, it is obvious that the representation of subject peoples in this allusive way was part of the overall Augustan programme of otherwise generally avoiding the direct representation of defeat of such peoples in battle.

The barbarian submission scene on the Boscoreale cup may have been a direct influence on the artist Cheirisophos in his design of one of the more or less contemporary Hoby cups, found in a chieftain's grave in Denmark.[65] However, in this instance the 'historical' event has been transformed into a mythological motif, with King Priam kneeling in submission to Achilles, perhaps in reference to Augustus' sometimes adopted role as the new Achilles. That the cups could be slightly later in date, and that Achilles could rather be representing the emperor Tiberius, need not be a matter for concern, for Tiberius was often to follow the precedents of the artistic grammar and vocabulary first articulated in the Augustan period. The masking of contemporary events behind a veil of mythological allusion was itself very typical of the rhetoric of Augustan political ideology, with its referencing of Greek artistic form and media.[66]

ARCH ENEMIES

Few Julio-Claudian victory monuments survive, with the exception of the Arch of Tiberius at Orange[67] in Gaul. Other victory monuments are now more or less lost to us, including the Britannic victory arches of Claudius in Rome and at Richborough in Britain.[68] A now fragmentary relief from Fiesole, Italy, of a trophy with bound male captive, may have related to Claudius' Thracian successes.[69]

The arch at Orange in Provence is a remarkable survival, given the nature of the events portrayed and the subject matter of the monument's sculptural programme, that is the Roman victories in Gaul under Tiberius. Dated to AD 20–6, though some scholars favour a later date,[70] the triple-bayed arch bears a profusion of decoration. Above each of the smaller bays are reliefs depicting captured Gaulish arms and armour, with highly detailed representations of swords, shields, spears and breastplates. Recessed panels show naval spoils.[71] A battle frieze encircles the arch, while on its short sides are panels containing more trophies with Gaulish captives. Cornucopiae and various deities are also present, this potent mix of earthly and heavenly victories being similar to the compositional strategies of the Grand Camée de France. It is possible that the design of the scenes of combat owed a debt to both Hellenistic battle pictures and to the Pergamene art of Attalos I.[72]

Monuments celebrating Claudius' conquest of Britain in AD 43 were set up both in Rome and in Britain itself, at the site of Richborough in Kent, but little is known about the form or decoration of these lost monuments. No sculptural panels or inscriptions from the Richborough monument have been discovered. The Claudian victory arch in Rome was erected in AD 51 or 52 across the Via Lata,[73] but again little is known about its associated sculptural programme, though various fragments have been attributed to the monument, including part of its dedicatory inscription.

Portions of the arch were almost certainly reused as *spolia* in the Diocletianic Arcus Novus monument erected nearby in the late third or early fourth century, though whether the arch was systematically dismantled at this time or whether demolition had taken place at an earlier period and certain sculptures retained in store is uncertain. These issues will be considered below as part of the overall description and interpretation of the later monument in Chapter Five.[74]

The largest fragments, now in the collection at the Villa Medici in Rome, probably made up a panel frieze. No barbarians appeared here, though one of the female figures, whether a personification of a place or of a concept such as virtue, is dressed in leggings, a tunic and cloak that rather suggest allusion to northern barbarian dress. A more fragmentary relief panel in the Capitoline Museum, on which is depicted the sideways-turned head of a long-haired and bearded barbarian man, has been assigned a Claudian date on stylistic grounds and could have come from the Claudian arch.

Another fragmentary piece of Julio-Claudian sculpture (housed in Naples' Museo Nazionale) again comes from Rome, but it is uncertain from which monument it derives.[75] The scene forms part of a larger depiction of a triumphal procession led by a bearded barbarian male who is followed by two Romans carrying on their shoulders a small bier bearing spoils of war. They, in turn, are followed by two more bearded barbarian men in the company of a small child. One of the men rests his hand on the child's shoulder in a gesture of reassurance. Once more, it must be assumed that the child is a hostage of some kind, like those on the Boscoreale Augustus cup, though it could be that a generalised motif of barbarian children in such a situation became part of a repertoire of stock motifs used to depict imperial power and triumph at this time.

A PORNOGRAPHY OF CONQUEST

The most significant surviving Julio-Claudian building complex, in terms of its relevance to the present study, is the so-called Sebasteion at the Graeco-Roman town of Aphrodisias, in present-day Turkey, centred on a temple dedicated to Aphrodite and to the imperial cult of the Julio-Claudian emperors.[76] Among the extensive sculptural decoration adorning the Sebasteion were two cult reliefs, which, though they deal with Roman–barbarian relationships obliquely, would nevertheless appear to be part of the same rhetoric of imperial power relations that underwrite the more direct representational, and less allusive, political art of the period. A number of other works here more directly involve images of barbarian subjugation in the context of the imperial cult. Building at the Sebasteion seems to have started in the Tiberian period, but was not fully completed until the reign of Nero, and to have been underwritten by two local families. It thus falls into an unusual category of monument in the context of our study in that it represents the use of imperial imagery outside the formal control of the Roman state itself, though of course official sanction for the project must have been sought.

The first imperial relief to be discussed is of the emperor Claudius, recognisable from its likeness to well-known portrait types, and confirmed by an inscription on the statue's basal plinth that names the two figures portrayed as Claudius and Britannia. Claudius dominates the scene, and is portayed in what is termed 'heroic nudity'. He towers over the female figure, a personification of Britannia, and with one hand grasps or pulls her hair. He pulls her head up in this manner seemingly to deliver a blow to her head, though the emperor's right forearm is now missing so that his original stance and attitude cannot be fully reconstructed. One of his legs is hidden behind Britannia's body, but his stance suggests that Claudius could be bracing her body against this leg which he is driving into the small of her back. With his other leg he is kneeling on her thigh in an attempt to pinion her body down. The expression on the emperor's face has been described as both determined and cruel.

Britannia, who here, according to some commentators, is also taking on the additional guise of an Amazon,[77] lies partially sprawled on the ground, apparently overwhelmed by the ferocity of the attack being made upon her, but still trying to force Claudius away with her raised right arm. Her right breast is exposed. On her face is an expression of evident pain and an almost stunned resignation to her fate.

This particular relief has become well known to those who study Roman Britain as it is the only significant extant work of Roman art that relates to the conquest of the province and is thus quite commonly used as a book illustration and lecture slide. However, as far as I am aware, there had been no questioning of the nature of the scene portrayed until I raised this particular issue myself at an academic conference in 1994, in a reading that was, in retrospect, perhaps too dogmatic, but which nevertheless still requires reiteration here, if in a modified and moderated form.[78] As with any reading of a sculptural scene, the internal consistency of the approach validates the reasoning but does not necessarily rule out other, alternative, different or contradictory readings.

The underlying theme of the Claudius and Britannia relief would appear to be as much to do with Roman male violence towards a non-Roman or barbarian woman as it is a paean to the military successes and personal glory of the emperor Claudius. While it is the case that Aphrodisias was situated away from the centre of Roman power, and that the art of the town very much reflected the marrying of Roman themes and concerns with a Greek sensibility, nevertheless the sculptural works in the Sebasteion would have been both officially vetted and approved. It is unlikely that images of the imperial family would have been displayed here without official sanction, and they would have been targeted at a particular audience, one that was probably largely ethnically Greek, though Roman state officials from outside the area may also have been expected to visit the site on a regular basis. It is therefore within this context that both the form and the style of the sculptural programme here should be judged. The so-called heroic nudity used in the portrayal of the emperor Claudius is obviously a Graeco-Roman artistic convention, but its use in the context of the overall theme of the relief scene may have gone beyond the boundaries of simple convention.

Similarly, the suggested double layer of disguise intended for the female figure, that she is both a personification and, at the same time, also an Amazon, again implies that such conventions were so ingrained in the viewers' gaze that they could not see that she was also a woman. It defies belief that the viewers' interpretation would collude with a suggested veil or gauze of such complexity. It still seems to me that in the published accounts dealing with this particular sculpture, there is a certain amount of discomfort and reticence about the nature of the material. I would suggest that no matter how many layers of allegorical and symbolic meaning are heaped upon this work in order to understand and interpret its message, once they are stripped away there remains what is a profoundly disturbing event caught *in stasis*.

A woman's bared breast can be used to suggest a lack of constraint, to evoke unfettered wildness, and indeed, to use that word once more, otherness, as has been observed by the writer and historian Marina Warner,[79] and perhaps such a state of uncivilised being, outside the control and knowledge of the Roman experience, was itself seen as a considerable threat. Women could be deemed as somehow unclean or as polluters, and yet at the same time inhabit an ambiguous position as mothers and nurturers, as sisters and wives. Such ambiguity can be seen reflected in the image of the bared breast, which is at once both comforting and yet at the same time potentially threatening in its suggestion of otherness.

The nakedness of the emperor moves beyond mere convention when it is both juxtaposed with the portrayal of the female figure and when their attitudes and poses are taken into account. If territorial conquest is shown by the action of a male figure battering a female figure, then this must surely be a statement, at once both startlingly direct and deliberately referential and oblique, about Roman attitudes to imperial actions and policies and to conquered lands and peoples, and finally, of course, about male attitudes to women. In my initial reading of this sculptural scene, I suggested that the nudity of the emperor, the dishevelled appearance of the female figure, with perhaps her breast exposed accidentally, and the momentum of the event in action, added up to the prelude to a sexual assault, in addition to a physical assault, and to the rape of the woman. Certainly, the hair pulling, the pinioning with the knee and the blow about to be struck to her head could suggest such a culmination of 'conquest'.

There was, though, a Greek, or rather Hellenistic, model for this sculpture: the group of Achilles and Penthesilea. It may be that the cultural milieu of Aphrodisias allowed for the further conceit of the portrayal of Claudius as the new Achilles.[80] There is also a conceptual parallel in an Amazonomachy scene on a relief panel from the Portico of Tiberius, again here at Aphrodisias, in which, in the mêlée of battle, a Roman or Greek warrior grasps the hair of a falling Amazon with single bared breast.

In the Aphrodisias Sebasteion, there was also found a second such 'conquest' scene, the basal inscription indicating that it portrayed the emperor Nero conquering Armenia.[81] While more fragmentary than the Claudius and Britannia relief, nevertheless it can be seen that the 'heroically naked' emperor again looms over the female personification. She is virtually naked; only the fold of a thin cloak is draped around her neck and most of her body is exposed in its nakedness. Both of her breasts are bared. She is slumped in either a faint or in death, and is partially supported by the hands of the emperor. Her head lolls to one side, though her Phrygian-style cap remains firmly in place. A bow and a quiver of arrows may have been grasped in her outstretched right hand, but at this point the relief is damaged. Armenia is naked, exposed, vulnerable and defeated. This, though, represents the aftermath of conquest and not the violence of the act caught *in stasis* as on the Claudius and Britannia relief.

Images of 'real' barbarians also appear on a number of the Sebasteion reliefs. On one a naked, 'heroic' Augustus is represented standing to one side of a trophy, with Nike on the other side of the trophy and an imperial eagle at the emperor's feet on the right. Beneath the trophy, and cropped by the bottom edge of the stone, is a naked barbarian man – his back unusually towards the viewer so that his crossed, bound hands are for once exposed to view. He is not bearded and long-haired like the standard northern male barbarian figure, nor are any clues as to his ethnicity offered by dress or weaponry as is usually the case.[82]

On another relief Augustus appears again with a trophy, beneath which crouches a female barbarian captive, and in the company of a female deity or personification, perhaps Roma.[83] The portrayal of the barbarian woman is unusual in several respects. Firstly, she is bound, with her hands tied behind her back, a constraining measure not usually applied to female captives, who in Roman art were more often equated with passivity, even though there was also sometimes a parallel fear of the potential unfettered wildness of barbarian women. Secondly, she is depicted crying out, perhaps in pain. On both the reliefs on which Augustus is portrayed the barbarian figures are slightly smaller than normal. This miniaturisation and the placing of the figures at the feet of the emperor towards the bottom of the composition further emphasised the extent of their subservience.

Other emperors appeared on the Sebasteion portico reliefs, in equally explicit triumphal attitudes. A virtually naked Tiberius, one hand holding a spear or lance and the other placed on the upper edge of a shield resting on the ground to his left, stands next to the miniaturised figure of a bound male barbarian with bare torso, a thick cloak draped over his shoulders and wearing leggings or trousers.[84] On a more fragmentary relief Germanicus, again in heroic nudity and holding an orb in his left hand, is flanked on his right by a small male barbarian who stands next to a cuirass forming part of a trophy.[85]

There was also here a series of *ethne*, personifications of various peoples of the Roman empire and, in the case of Bosporans and Arabs, outside the empire. Each of these standing, draped female figures was identified to an ethnic group by an inscription and sometimes also by the presence of some diagnostic attribute.[86] Analysis of the thirteen, out of the possible fifty, statues erected here suggests that the peoples or tribes represented were ones that had either been defeated in battle by Augustus or who had been 'diplomatically defeated', or at least outmanoeuvred, during his reign. The series may have been based on that in the Portico of Nations erected in Rome under Augustus.

The pose of one of the *ethne* figures, with her hands held crossed in front of her, is derivative of that of a captive. This suggests that this gallery of *ethne* formed a kind of embodied map of the empire, a didactic device that acted both to illustrate diversity and at the same time to highlight difference from a position of civilised detachment, as may be said to be partly the Greek tradition of personifying countries and cities. However, the Roman version stressed the commonality of these diverse peoples by reason of their defeat at the hands of Rome, and while each was seen to be different, nevertheless that difference was simply here a device to illustrate the sameness of their historic fate and the almost infinite boundaries of an empire that could incorporate and overcome such diversity.[87] This was part of an overall artistic rhetoric of Roman power that also included the drama, ritual and theatre of the triumph, where images of real and imagined barbarians often appeared together and where personifications would also often play a role, thus further blurring the boundaries between the real and the imagined. The same process is seen in the erection of the trophy of captured arms and armour, with its ritualised manipulation of the fragments of defeat in lieu of the presence of the defeated, maimed, dead and putrefying bodies of the foe.[88]

That this rhetoric of power permitted the galleries of defeated peoples seen at the Aphrodisias Sebasteion and in Augustan Rome at the Portico of Nations to be represented by exclusively female personifications must pose further questions in terms of a gendered analysis of this phenomenon. This would appear not to be a simple evocation of the caryatids of fifth-century BC Athens.

The female gender of the personifications made the images particularly potent in the context of imperial and military imagery. The conquest of Britain by Rome, represented in the form of an emperor (male image) battering a personification (female image), and the display of the submissive peoples of the empire as represented by personifications (female images), were gendered constructions that added another layer of meaning to the discourses of Roman imperialism.

The Roman worldview was not that of the Greeks. The Roman use of personifications was not benign and neutral, and there are many examples of the calculated Roman manipulation of the idea of the personification in state art.[89] In the Augustan forum caryatids of conquered female personifications appeared, and later in the reign of the emperor Hadrian a similar gendered geography of Roman dominion was to reach its artistic apotheosis.[90]

In summary, Augustan and Julio-Claudian political art shared many common traits. The agenda was set by an immediate need to establish legitimacy for a new regime and to stamp the authority of that regime on the very fabric of Rome itself, by the transformation of the city into a politicised space. In the provinces a similar situation occurred, though different artistic strategies were employed to achieve this aim.

In Rome, political imagery generally avoided direct reference to war and battle, though figures of defeated enemies were routinely depicted on monumental and luxury art. The celebration of victory had now become the sole preserve of the emperor, as had the setting of moral rules for the conduct of the women of Rome. The use of images of barbarians and personified peoples was also, therefore, now extended to encompass issues relating to their gender, that is curtailed fertility in the case of barbarian women and impotence in the case of the men.

A number of large trophy monuments, arches and decorated gates were erected in Italy and particularly in the province of Gallia Narbonensis under Augustus and his immediate successors. On these monuments many images of defeated barbarians were portrayed, while on the arch at Orange numerous battle scenes were depicted. This building programme would have left few viewers in doubt as to the unforgiving nature of Roman military power, the consequences of its wrath, and the advantages of its protection. Viewers of the sculptures in the Sebasteion complex at Aphrodisias would have had a further opportunity to contemplate the underlying Roman imperial attitude towards the peoples of the empire and those beyond.

THREE

THE TRAJANIC BARBARIAN

It is from the reign of the emperor Trajan that perhaps the largest body of artworks portraying barbarians has survived. While to some extent this is a reflection of an element of chance in historical survival, it may perhaps also reflect the sheer importance of contact with the barbarian world in the political and ideological make-up of his reign. This contact was principally through the policy of imperial expansion, pursued by war. In particular, images of the emperor's wars against the Dacians came to dominate the state art of Rome at this time and during the reign of his successor, the emperor Hadrian, who pursued the completion of some monuments started or conceived under Trajan. Indeed, it is probably true to say that the Dacian prisoner became the defining image of the age.

By examining the four key surviving monuments associated with the reign of Trajan – Trajan's Column and the Great Trajanic Frieze in Rome, the Arch of Trajan at Benevento in southern Italy, and the so-called Trophy of Trajan at Adamklissi in present-day Romania – common themes emerge in the way that seemingly simple and easily understood images of barbarians were used to convey quite complex messages within the overall schema of each monument and of the reign as a whole.

CONQUEST AND COMMERCE

In Rome, Trajan's Column,[1] still standing today, would have dominated the new forum complex in which it was erected. The column was intended to be an integrated element within the forum's design, the grandiose scale of the overall works being intended as a statement of the economic benefits of the emperor's costly and, in some quarters, heavily criticised Dacian wars. Indeed, even the dedicatory inscription on the basal plinth of the column refers to the quarrying and removal of vast quantities of rock and soil from the site before building works could commence, as if further to stress the sheer effort put into urban regeneration during Trajan's reign rather than it simply being an era of war and crisis.[2]

For those who had doubted the wisdom of the Dacian enterprise, such misgivings would now have been alleviated not only by the military victories but also by the economic benefits to Rome that accrued from the spoils of those wars and which were used to finance the new building schemes in Rome. The most explicit link between conquest and commerce was made by the construction of the huge new market complex to the north of the Forum. Trajan's Forum was the last of the great fora here at the heart of the empire, and with an overall area of some 26,000 square metres, the largest. Inaugurated in AD 112, though not fully completed by then, it was intended as both an architecturally and artistically integrated programme. The Roman viewer could also at the same time still visit the other adjacent and nearby fora, and ponder the significance and message of the historic artworks there.

Three sides of the pedimental base of the column are carved with captured Dacian weapons and armour, piled up as trophies, with some carvings of weapons also appearing on the fourth side, the front of the base, and perhaps representing an actual temporary victorious display of such material here before the dedication and building of the column. But it is the spiral relief sculptures around the column that are of particular interest to the present study. While it was probably not originally intended that the column shaft would be decorated, nevertheless the addition of the decorated sculptural frieze was achieved relatively harmoniously, and would have given the column an extra filip of originality in its use as a medium for conveying its intended messages to its viewers.

Many of the sculptural scenes would not have been visible from the ground below, and the viewer would have had difficulty in following the action in scenes that twisted around the column's shaft. Such concerns, however, do not seem to have troubled the sculptors, either in coming up with the design of the column friezes in the first place or in the manner of the execution of the sculptures themselves; those at the top of the column are as detailed and well executed as those at the bottom. Of course, the viewer would have been aided a little by the original appearance of the column friezes as they would have been painted and accessories crafted in bronze, iron or wood would have been held by some of the figures. This would have emphasised certain scenes that today might be difficult to see in their present unpainted and unadorned state. Again, the presence of contemporary two- or three-storey buildings nearby may have provided access in the form of balconies or viewing platforms for those wishing to see certain of the upper spirals of the column.

Nevertheless, it would have been impossible for any Roman viewer to 'read' the column in the manner that can be achieved today by reference to the full photographic surveys of the monument – undertaken when the provision of scaffolding for repair work and conservation was available, for instance – and to casts of the reliefs taken on a number of occasions, including those prepared for the great Fascist-sponsored Augustan exhibition of Roman Culture of 1937 and now on display in Rome at the Museo della Civilta Romana.

It must be assumed that the column was intended to make a direct appeal to the eye of the viewer through its daringly original form and dense decorative scheme. If the viewer were then to take away an impression of the artworks as a suitable commemoration of the victories and achievements of the emperor Trajan, then it would have served its fundamental purpose. To achieve this, the scenes in which the emperor himself appears are very clearly positioned, almost in a vertical plane, to stress his centrality to the unfolding drama of the campaigns in Dacia. Closer inspection would have provided additional insights into the artistic programme, and repeated viewings would have allowed for further revelations and detail to emerge through the reading of individual scenes. The sheer density of the artwork and the great number of scenes presented, with hundreds of human figures playing out the incessant drama, allowed for as many readings to be made as there would have been, and continue to be, viewers of the column.

The reliefs tell the story of Trajan's two Dacian wars. Various scholars have attempted to match events on the column reliefs to historical accounts of the emperor's campaigns.[3] But the reliefs cannot truly be called historical documents, nor can they be viewed strictly as war reportage. However, they do provide the most detailed statement on the nature of Roman imperial power at the peak of the empire's expansion.

Despite first impressions, battle scenes do not dominate the column, nor when shown do they dwell upon the bloody realities of war. However, the artists did not flinch from including one or two jarring scenes that do not sit well with modern sensibilities, but which would not perhaps have been seen as out of place by the ancient viewer. While not intending to pre-empt discussion of some later monuments, it is true to say that, in comparison with these, the portrayal of war on Trajan's Column is perhaps surprisingly sanitised. It has been suggested that the relatively few, and somewhat formulaic, battle scenes reflected the deliberate desire in the conception of the monument to address and allay a fear of the army – its soldiers, its independence and its power – among the population of Rome, by playing down this aspect of the column.[4] That is, it was a monument to the Dacian wars of Trajan but not to the army itself.

Turning now to the column reliefs themselves, one of the first things that strikes the viewer is that there was a concerted effort by the artist to represent the Dacians as a distinct ethnic group rather than as undifferentiated, generic barbarians, as was often to be the case in Roman art. However, there is little individuality among the basic Dacian types, whether male or female. So many reams have been written by archaeologists and ancient historians on the detailed depictions of Roman military equipment, arms and armour on the column that it is easy to overlook the fact that the same attention to detail was not expended on the attributes of the Dacians, though the spoils in the sculptural trophy pile on the pediment of the monument are clearly and recognisably Dacian armaments. In earlier times Roman art had established a distinct and direct engagement, in terms of veracity of representation, with the depiction of the

Gaul or Celt and with their distinctive weaponry, something that may reflect a different attitude to these peoples to that harboured for the Dacians at the time of Trajan. This may merely be an impression, but it would certainly be of great interest in academic terms to verify or deny such an impression through a detailed chronological catalogue and synthesis of trophy monuments in Roman art.[5]

As a general observation, on the column the figures of the Dacians are often used in a purely contrastive way, dismantling their fortresses before the arrival of Roman forces, in contrast to an almost exaggerated concentration on the building and construction work being carried out by the Roman troops. Perhaps significantly, these troops are almost exclusively legionaries rather than auxiliaries. This seems to be part of an overall narrative thread that stresses a sense of overwhelming order among the victors and disorder among the defeated barbarians. This is also something that will be noted in the discussion of the Great Trajanic Frieze, but there the contrast was achieved by a different compositional strategy.

Dead and dying Dacians were represented quite routinely. Dead Romans were not, though in one scene doctors notably give aid to a wounded Roman soldier. The Dacians were also quite commonly depicted in forests and woods, or up in the mountains, as opposed to in their towns or fortresses, thus possibly creating in the viewer's mind a visual opposition between nature, as represented by the Dacians, and culture, as represented by the Romans, and hence between barbarity and civilisation respectively. This is quite possibly another example of the 'nostalgia' trend, a longing for a purer and simpler state of being, previously noted as occurring in Hellenistic Greek and some Roman portrayals of Celts or Gauls.[6]

Though important, attention here will not focus on the numerous scenes of skirmish and battle on the column, but rather on some of the more unusual scenes in which barbarian protagonists appear. The numbering system used to locate individual scenes is that devised by Cichorius, and followed by most subsequent researchers.[7]

One scene in particular (Scene XXXVI) would appear to be significant in its contrasting of civilisation and primitive barbarity. Here, the emperor Trajan himself, on his way to the war, is depicted with his entourage, entering a provincial, probably Moesian town. He is shown being greeted by the enthusiastic local populace – men, women and children. This is a scene of inclusivity, with not just male officials being represented, as was so often the case, and is of interest for that very reason. To paraphrase Natalie Boymel Kampen, who first made this observation, the presence of women and children in this scene stresses the importance of a civilised and protective environment for this community, for these families, provided under the rule of Rome.[8] It suggests a guarantee of future prosperity in both the public and private spheres. The lives of these people had been transformed under Roman patronage and imperialism, an important point which must not be lost sight of in concentrating on the issue of barbarians; a barbarian could be transformed into a citizen or a proto-citizen from a legal point of view, if not necessarily into an equal in the minds of those at Rome.

One of the most extraordinary scenes (Scene XLV), set in a fortress or town, is of Dacian women torturing Roman prisoners. In the upper part of the scene, two Roman captives have been stripped naked and appear to be bound, their hands tied behind their backs. Four barbarian women stand by, two to either side of the prisoners, each somehow striking or prodding at the helpless men, each of whom has his head turned away from the women, perhaps in pain. Beneath the walls, in the lower part of the scene, a third, bound Roman captive sprawls on a rocky outcrop while a Dacian woman stands over him and appears to be jabbing him with a stake as he recoils in agony.

The very unusual nature of this scene – it is unique in Roman art – may mean that it is a representation of an actual event from the wars, though one that has not come down to us in any historical account and which has not been illustrated on any other Trajanic monument. On the other hand, it could be a fictional scene, one created by the artist to make a particular point about the cruelty inherent in the Dacian people, even among the women, and in some way to be part of a justification for the wars. As already noted, there was some opposition to this venture from certain parties in Rome, and such a scene may have served to counter any residual criticism there. The torture scene may have been intended both as an indicator of barbarian cruelty in general and of the otherness of barbarian women in particular. It has been suggested that the women, rather than being Dacian, are in fact Moesian women taking revenge on these men, who are themselves Dacian and not Roman, for their incursion into the Moesian province and for the slaughter of the women's husbands or sons who were loyal to Rome.[9] This seems unlikely.

The torture scene was positioned relatively low down on the column's shaft – being part of the seventh spiral up from the start of the base – suggesting perhaps that it conveyed a particular message that was important to get across to all viewers. Even if other incidents elsewhere on the column could not easily be seen, this particular scene would be clearly discernible even from the ground.

Certainly attested by the historical sources, and depicted on other works of art, is the suicide of the Dacian leader, Decebalus, following the successful storming of his mountain-top stronghold of Sarmizegethusa by the Roman forces and their pursuit of the fugitive king (Scene CXLV). On the column we see the moment of Decebalus' death, literally seconds before the arrival on horseback of the mounted Roman officer Tiberius Claudius Maximus, who was subsequently to behead the body of the Dacian chieftain and cut off his right hand as trophies to present to the emperor. The actual scene of the mutilation of Decebalus' corpse was, unsurprisingly, not depicted on the column.

While Decebalus' suicide could be seen as a brave act, a final flourish of defiance which would rob the Roman victors of his participation in a stage-managed triumph in Rome, it can also be viewed as an act of self-authorship, an attempt to regain in death some form of control over his own destiny, if no longer over that of his people. But Maximus' act of beheading inverted the act of self-authorship in a most macabre fashion, with the Dacian leader's severed head being represented as a trophy in another scene on the column. Such a portrayal of victory – even over death – may itself have been used to provide further testament to the superiority of the Roman forces and of Roman imperial power.

Elsewhere on the column (Scene CXL, for instance) there are depicted the suicides of other Dacian leaders. This narrative of the death of the power and lineage of the Dacian male aristocracy, together with the forced transportation of female Dacian noblewomen into exile, tells a powerful story of the ending of Dacian elite lineage in its present form and of an uncertain future for the surviving women of this elite, relocated in the political, social and sexual framework of Roman society.

Nor did the column artist flinch from portraying some particularly bloodthirsty acts by the Roman forces. The beheading of the dead Decebalus towards the end of the second war was not the only instance of this practice depicted on the column. In Scene XXIV, in the midst of a hectic skirmish between Roman and Dacian infantry forces outside a wood, stands a Roman trooper with his short sword in one hand and a shield in the other. He prepares to fight off a Dacian opponent who raises his own sword to strike a blow at the Roman. The Roman soldier has already taken a battlefield trophy, a Dacian head, and this he grips in his teeth, by the hair, in order to keep his hands free for battle.[10] As it hangs down in front of him, blood drips from the severed head, this blood perhaps being originally rendered in paint when the column was inaugurated. In Scene LVI, outside a Roman encampment, two bearded Dacian heads are displayed mounted on posts, and in Scene LXXII two heads are offered as trophies to the emperor himself by Roman troopers.

A BITTERSWEET REVENGE

The other monument of the Trajanic era that directly portrayed the wars, rather than simply alluding to them, is the Tropaeum Traiani – the so-called Trophy of Trajan at Adamklissi in present-day Romania, in what would have been the Roman province of Moesia Inferior.[11] This massive trophy took the form of a stepped monument rising up from a stone-faced circular drum or mound of earth, some 34 metres in diameter, around the outside of which and below whose cornice were set fifty-four sculptural panels or metopes. The uppermost part of the drum was crowned by a series of sculptural crenellations. On top of the mound there was an actual trophy – a branched tree, or a sculpture of this, hung with captured equipment. At the base of the trophy were twice life-size statues of chained barbarian prisoners, both seated and standing, though these are now fragmentary and heavily weathered. A remarkable, full-size reconstruction of the monument has been built around the ruinous remnants of the original structure and helps in the visualisation of what would have been the original impact of the monument on the surrounding landscape.

Though the form and siting of the trophy harked back to the Augustan use of such monuments as geographical markers, in some respects it would seem to have been more simply a war memorial and victory monument. It was also symbolic of revenge achieved, of a historic wrong being righted. It is known that the trophy was one of three monuments erected in, or near, Adamklissi at one time or another in the Roman period. The two earlier monuments were a mausoleum and an altar bearing a list of names of Roman war dead, presumably from a particular battle in the Dacian wars of the emperor Domitian. The siting of the Trajanic victory monument here was obviously a way of declaring that the defeats of the past reign had been avenged and that the military honour of Rome had been reclaimed.[12] The sheer scale of the trophy monument, in contrast to the relatively small scale of the other two monuments, would have further emphasised this point. One might also ask for whom the Adamklissi monument was constructed and who were the intended viewers. Given the sensitive location of the site, it is most likely that it was intended to be a purely military memorial, by soldiers for soldiers.

Turning now to a discussion of the actual artistic embellishment of the monument, it will be seen that the conception, style and execution of the sculptures here were very different indeed to those of the other Trajanic monuments discussed in this chapter. It is provincial work in all respects – though provincial is not being used here as a pejorative term – which can be seen as reflecting quite precisely its geographical location, the requirements of the commission and the intended audience.[13] As with the discussion of the column, no attempt

ENEMIES OF ROME

will be made here to describe systematically each sculptural scene or to try and relate individual depictions to literary accounts of the Dacian wars.

The crenellations of the monument each bear, in relief, the figure of a single male barbarian captive, not always a Dacian since also included are some of their allies against Rome, principally Germans and Sarmatians, with the captive's hands tied behind his back. A tree usually appears in the background, once more probably to act as a device linking the Dacians and the other barbarians to the woods and the mountains, that is to the natural and thus uncivilised world, a link that was also made on Trajan's Column, though in a somewhat less explicit manner. The single bound captive represents not a particular individual but rather a nation in defeat, something that would have been further emphasised, and temporally extended seemingly to infinity, by the repetition of this depiction and motif right the way around the circuit of the monument. An eternal return to a state of perpetual subjugation.

The scenes on the metopes are mostly of one-to-one combat, as representative of the larger battles and the Dacian wars in general, something that the art historian Diana Kleiner has viewed as being 'in the long tradition of metope design, which can be traced back to such Greek examples as the metopes of the Parthenon'.[14] Nevertheless, these scenes are not entirely symbolic, and one or two individual scenes have a greater significance. For example, the emperor Trajan is present on one metope in *adlocutio* and, on another, on the march. On a third a horseman, thought to be the emperor again, rides down a Dacian chieftain, doubtless a metaphor for the defeat of the Dacian nation by the power of Rome, though such a scene is both in a broader tradition of rider and fallen foe motifs and could also allude to the exploits of the Roman cavalryman Maximus as also portrayed on Trajan's Column.

On metope XXXIV a naked, beheaded Dacian lies at the feet of a Roman soldier whose attention is focused on a naked archer perched up in a tree and poised to loose an arrow. Rather than being a recently fallen enemy, it has been suggested that the body on the ground is actually the partially decayed corpse of a Roman soldier killed in an earlier engagement on this spot, and able at last to be present at this scene of retribution. This interpretation would perhaps fit in well with the motive for siting the monument here at Adamklissi, if it were also the site of funeral monuments linked to tragic Roman reversals in Domitian's Dacian wars.[15]

BONES AND BREAD

A very different type of monument is the so-called Arch of Trajan at Benevento, in Campania, to the south of Rome. Its artwork was intended to convey a series of messages about the emperor's social policies, especially his alimentary programme designed to distribute corn to poorer Italian families, as well as about his political and military achievements. The two strands of policy were in many ways indissoluble, in that the food relief programme might cynically be seen as helping to guarantee healthy recruits into the Roman army for some future date. However, there may also have been more openly triumphal monuments set up in Italian cities after the Dacian wars. A relief fragment depicting a bound male captive standing beneath a trophy may come from one such triumphal arch at Pozzuoli, near Naples.[16]

The Benevento arch is one of the few monuments or artworks considered in this book on which the figure of the barbarian, in the form either of a direct barbarian image or alluded to through the use of personification, appears as part of a complex artistic programme in which military and political achievements are presented as inextricably linked to social and economic ones in the imperial ideology of the time. Furthermore, the fate of the barbarian peoples defeated and conquered by Rome is presented as an inevitable, and thus acceptable, prerequisite for the well-being of the people of Rome and Italy. The bodies of dead barbarians, arguably metaphorically converted into marble and bricks in the Forum and market of Trajan in Rome, were here metaphorically turned into bread to feed the needy children of the wider Italy.

The arch reliefs, of course, also commemorated triumph in the Dacian wars, but did this not by direct portrayal of scenes of war and battle but rather more subtly by stressing the concrete benefits that such imperial conquests had brought not only to Rome, but also to Italy in general. Nevertheless, the significance of the Dacian and German wars to the emperor was made clear here by the assumed titles of Dacicus and Germanicus appearing in the dedicatory inscription. Trajan was also later, after AD 114, to assume the title of Parthicus, again emphasising the importance of these campaigns and victories to the emperor's psyche. The arch displayed Trajan's concern to rule a well-fed Italy, achieved through road building and the construction of harbours, the establishment of colonies and a targeted social programme.[17] Well-fed young Italian males were also, of course, the future soldiers of the empire. Attention to their health and general well-being might have been considered to be a good investment on the part of the state, a view that might appear overly cynical but which may yet have been one of the motives behind the *alimenta* scheme, as was suggested by some contemporary Roman observers, including Pliny.[18]

In the same way that examination of the Ara Pacis immediately drew attention to the unusual depiction of numbers of children on the monument – and their presence was seen to be of a particular and deliberate significance – so this is also the case with the Benevento arch.[19]

The scenes in which barbarians or personifications of conquered peoples appear are admittedly few, and may be considered to be generic, alluding to the nature of imperial power and authority in general, rather than being specific to the theme of the arch. The overall artistic programme of the arch has been read by art historians as being easily subdivided, principally into what have been termed the 'country facade' and the 'town facade'.

On the country facade, that is the face of the arch that looks away from Benevento into the countryside and still much further beyond, out towards Dacia and the rest of the northern parts of Trajan's empire, are found scenes most relevant to this position, with military affairs predominating. On the town facade, looking into the town and, more widely, into the heart of Italy and towards Rome itself, the same artistic strategy applied, with social and political matters being mainly alluded to here. For example, on the attic reliefs on the country side the emperor Trajan is seen being greeted by a deputation of deities or personifications, principal of whom is a female figure kneeling in both greeting and submission to the emperor, a figure who is generally interpreted as representing Dacia itself.

On the frieze which runs right round the top of the monument, beneath the attic, is depicted a triumphal procession – probably that celebrated in Rome in AD 107 at the end of the second Dacian war – in which walk numbers of Dacian captives, including men, women and children. The latter group appears in evident contrast to the numerous Italian children on the arch who receive the benefits of the war against Dacia and of Trajan's reign in general, in the scenes depicting the alimentary system in operation. While this frieze girdles the whole arch, it is evident that Trajan in his triumphal chariot is placed on its town side, while that part of the triumphal procession in which the Dacian prisoners walk is on the country facade. Two young Dacian children, each clinging on to their respective mothers, and a third mother with a babe-in-arms, appear in the line of paraded captives, though in smaller numbers than the male captives, among whom is a prisoner of some importance, who, though evidently bound, rides in a carriage or open cart.

The linking of barbarian mothers with their children may be intended to contrast with the Italian fathers and their children depicted elsewhere on the arch and, of course, with the overall message of the monument which stressed the paternal blessing of Trajan – the father of his country – for the well-being of children in both Rome and Italy.[20] The supposed exaggeratedly small size of the barbarian children has been read as a further artistic strategy for emphasising the depth of their future despair, again in contrast to the better future laid out for the children of Italy under the aegis of Trajan, in a striking phrase that places the Dacian offspring as 'frozen in the perpetual childhood of slavery'.[21]

The barbarians depicted on Trajan's arch at Benevento could be viewed as more or less minor figures in the overall artistic programme of the monument. Indeed, it could be argued that they appear purely and simply to play their allotted role in the scene of the emperor's triumph, in which barbarian captives would have been paraded as at virtually every other such event in Rome. The very fact that the monument most often elicits

ENEMIES OF ROME

from art historians comment on the unusual preponderance of
images of children makes the appearance of the barbarian
children something more than simply as actors in the drama of
a Roman triumph. Indeed, such a concentration on the
representation of children in state art had not been evident
since the appearance of the imperial children, and perhaps also
of barbarian children, on the Ara Pacis Augustae.

EMPEROR AND ARMY

The most complex monument of Trajan's reign, in terms of its
composition and allusive subject matter, is the Great Trajanic
Frieze which was erected at the north end of the Trajanic
Forum in the reign of his successor Hadrian, probably as part
of the complex around the Temple of the Deified Trajan.[22] It is
thought that the Great Frieze was about 30 metres in length, a
scale that, combined with the size of its figures – they are 3
metres high – would have had a significant impact on the
viewer even when contrasted with the other great building
works of Trajan's reign, such as the column and the markets.

Unfortunately, none of the frieze remains *in situ*, and indeed
parts of it were taken down in the Roman period, to be
incorporated as *spolia* into the fourth-century Arch of
Constantine, where they remain to this day, while other
portions of the frieze are now to be found in museums and
collections in Rome, Berlin and Paris. The significance of the
reuse of these particular fragments will be considered in
Chapter Five.[23]

A cast of the various fragments has been made and a
reconstruction of the whole frieze attempted. We will consider
below whether there may have been any particular process of
selection of images for reuse on the Constantinian monument
that has a bearing on the present study, to determine whether
any of the images of barbarians had a particular emotional
currency that transcended the period of their creation.

The subject of the frieze was again the Dacian wars of Trajan's
reign, tying in this later monument with the already completed
column, though, as will be seen, doing so in a more allusive and
less direct manner. Battle scenes between Romans and Dacians

appear, as do scenes showing Dacian prisoners and the final surrender of the Dacians to the power of Rome. The composition of the battle scenes creates an immediate contrast between the Roman forces and their Dacian opponents, a contrast that is not simply that between victor and defeated, or between power and impotency against the might of Rome. Rather, this contrast is between order and chaos, and therefore, by extension, between civilisation and barbarity.[24]

The sculpted forms of the Roman soldiers in the lower and upper registers of the frieze are executed in a repetitious style, in repetitive themes, and the figures of the soldiers are often grouped together in such a way as to reinforce the unity and order of their depiction. In contrast, the Dacians are rendered in a great variety of poses, the majority of these involving the contorting of their wounded and dying bodies as they fall to, or lie on, the ground, more or less confining them to a churning sub-register of the frieze. This compositional effect creates a sense of disharmony in the work and links the Dacians with the impression and idea of chaos and disorder. In turn, this seems to break up the cohesion of the battle scene and to draw the viewer's gaze immediately on to one twisted, dying barbarian body after another, the ordered Roman figures above rendered almost invisible through the anonymity of presentation and style.

But, in seeming contradiction to this anonymity, there is a very significant difference in the way that the artist has rendered highly detailed and varied military dress and equipment for the otherwise undifferentiated Roman forces but has noticeably restricted the portrayal of Dacian accoutrements to a minimum. It has been suggested that rather than being contradictory, this difference reinforces the order–disorder dichotomy by suggesting efficiency, represented by the provision of good and necessary equipment, opposed by inefficiency.[25]

One of the most important scenes depicts Trajan himself, not masterminding the campaigns from behind the lines of battle as he was shown on the column, but rather as an active participant in a scene of combat.[26] The mounted emperor rides down a Dacian who is shown being trampled beneath the horse's hooves, while another Dacian male kneels before the emperor seeking clemency. Behind the kneeling figure a dense skirmish between Roman and Dacian forces takes place, as two Roman soldiers at the very back of this mêlée make their way back towards the Roman lines, each holding aloft a Dacian's severed head, in a scene that has direct parallels with one on Trajan's Column.

While the depiction of the mounted emperor could be taken simply as artistic licence on the part of the Hadrianic artist, it could also have been an attempt to link the person of the emperor more closely with the victory of the army than had been done by the artists of the column and, more especially, with the defining horseback charge of Maximus in his attempt to capture Decebalus. There are other possible explanations for this scene. On the one hand it could be argued that the representation was never intended to be read in such a literal manner as is being undertaken here, and that the viewer would have taken the scene simply as an allusion to the emperor's pivotal role in winning victory in the Dacian wars, though this might more usually have artistically been rendered by the figure of the emperor overcoming a female personification of a people or country, as used, for instance, at the Aphrodisias Sebasteion. It could be that the type of the barbarian foe being ridden down by a Roman cavalryman, and to be discussed in Chapter Six, was such a popular and particularly well-known military image that Trajan, that most military of emperors, could have seen fit to appropriate it for himself or to have it appropriated on his behalf by the Hadrianic artists.

Such an exchange between what could be called vernacular military art, principally appearing in certain contexts in the western provinces, and state art at Rome would be extraordinary, although not altogether impossible or unthinkable. A more mainstream view is that an equestrian statue of the emperor trampling a Dacian stood in the Forum, and that though there are no literary references to such a work and no remains of such a statue have been found, nevertheless its existence may be inferred from certain coin types of Trajan's reign which show such a scene and which may have been designed with reference to a well-known forum statue.

There is, indeed, in the works of Statius reference to a now vanished colossal equestrian statue of the emperor Domitian standing in the Forum Romanum.[27] The emperor's horse was posed with its foreleg resting on the prostrate body of a defeated barbarian. The emperor apparently held one arm outstretched in a gesture said to be designed to bring a formal end to a battle. The Domitianic statue, dismantled following his *damnatio memoriae* in AD 96, could have been the prototype of what was subsequently to become a common imperial motif on both statuary and coinage. Such intertextual cross-referencing seems to have been particularly common in this period, as has already been seen in the case of the presentation of trophies of severed heads to the emperor on both the column and the frieze.

It is interesting that the frieze and the column, although ostensibly at first glance utilising the same repertoire of subject and imagery, were in reality very different in the way in which they presented the subject and deployed imagery to different ideological ends. In the whole of the period under consideration in this book there is no better illustration of the subtlety and nuance sometimes inherent in the use of images of barbarians in imperial art and rhetoric.[28]

While the column is not strictly historical commentary, nevertheless it was quasi-documentary in content. The frieze, on the other hand, was in a tradition of heroicising art, more commonly associated in the Hellenistic tradition with mythological representation, in the form of battles between Greeks and Amazons, or involving giants, centaurs or Lapiths. The emperor Trajan on the column was one with his army; he addressed his troops, he was on campaign with them, he observed their labours and battled against the Dacians, and so on. Indeed, the column perhaps somewhat exaggerated his direct involvement in the campaigning, for he was in all likelihood well behind the lines for much of the time. However, on part of the frieze, as described above, the mounted figure of Trajan was to be seen in the very thick of frenzied battle.

Unlike the Augustan and Julio-Claudian courts, there does not appear to have been any significant production of luxury court items of silver plate or gems by Trajan, something that may be of significance itself in terms of the way in which imperial ideologies and mythologies were created, disseminated and maintained. An exception lies in a set of carved ivory panels, possibly originally set as inlays in a box or casket or in furniture, which comes from Ephesos in Asia Minor.[29] The scenes on the ivory panels are complex, and depict variously Victory and defeated peoples and provinces. In a 'historical' scene on one long-side panel the emperor meets barbarian chieftains and a crowd of their followers. The main barbarian protagonists are bearded and are dressed in tunics and trousers.

In the other cities of the empire there may have appeared other, obviously smaller-scale and less ambitious statues which linked the person of the emperor Trajan with his victory in Dacia, such as one now fragmentary example from the Agora in Athens which depicts him in military garb with a cowering barbarian at his feet.[30]

As already noted, it is true that for the reign of Trajan, more than for any other previous or subsequent reign, the figure of the defeated barbarian, in this case the male Dacian, was to become virtually a representative symbol of the reign itself, particularly on coinage. A number of the emperor's coin issues displayed features or motifs that first came into use or prominence at this time.[31] One reverse type bears a bound male Dacian which echoes many of the well-known sculptural images. On another type Dacian prisoners appear as what have been dubbed 'attributes' of the emperor – that is, accepted as belonging to, or being representative of his post or person. In one instance, two exaggeratedly small barbarians kneel in submission on either side of the figure of Trajan.

Echoes of the artwork on the frieze and trophy can be seen in coin issues which depicted the mounted emperor thrusting a spear at a fallen Dacian. More explicit than the monumental sculpture of the reign are issues illustrating Trajan standing with his foot on Decebalus' severed head. On another coin issue the emperor stands with his foot planted on the back of a cowering, prostrate male barbarian, the composition on some examples of this type cropping the barbarian figure dramatically so that only his head and shoulders remain visible on the coin. It is possible that the origin of this type lay in the coin issues of the mid-70s BC, and was variously reinterpreted, with Roma and Augustus appearing with their feet planted on a globe, to provide overt symbolism of Rome's dominion over the whole world.

THE TRAJANIC BARBARIAN

AN ICON OF THE AGE

It can therefore be seen that the principal monumental relief sculptures of the reign of Trajan place the defeat of the Dacians at the very core of his achievement and make the Dacian barbarian the symbol of the age. There is a number of massive individual sculptures of single male Dacian prisoners, dating to the Trajanic period, surviving in museum collections in Italy and elsewhere, as well as, more tellingly, eight such figures reused in the fourth century and incorporated into the overall artistic scheme of the Arch of Constantine in Rome.[32] Positioned on top of each of the projecting columns of the arch, four on each side of the monument, most of these figures stand upright and proud, with their hands clasped together in front of them. They appear not to be bound. Another stands with one arm crossed over his chest. Most of the figures are bearded and some wear Dacian caps. All wear leggings or trousers, with a long over-tunic and cloaks that reach down to the ground.

While elsewhere in the book a certain amount of discussion will focus on the strategy in later Roman imperial art of miniaturising figures of barbarians in some instances, to emphasise their abject and inferior position in relation to the Roman state, it should be noted that Trajan's reign sees a perhaps much more surprising artistic strategy, one of overemphasising some free-standing figures of male Dacians.

These male figures are powerful and commanding studies, of which a few variations are known, though it is not likely that any of them was intended to be a portrait of any particular Dacian individual. With their mixture of pathos and pride they bring to mind the somewhat contradictory strains of reading inherent in the figures of the dying Attalid Gauls. Apart from one or two poignant scenes of vulnerable barbarian children that appear in the sarcophagus art of the second and third centuries, this is really the last period in Roman art of which it can be said that tempered admiration for a barbarian foe is conveyed in a work of art.

It could also be the case that within the overall artistic programme of Trajanic Rome there was a need further to stress the achievement of the emperor and of the Roman army in defeating an enemy as feared as the Dacians, by placing these enormous statues of the enemy within the very heart of the complex funded and built from the economic benefits of this struggle. It is likely that all of these statues were originally set up in the Forum of Trajan and that they formed part of the overall, insistent message mediated through the artworks there. Figures of Dacians could also have adorned the facade of the Basilica Ulpia, as well as having been placed around the porticos of the forum.

A precedent for such a display could have been the Forum of Augustus in which, as has already been discussed in Chapter Two, was to be found the so-called Portico of Nations, though the Dacian sculptures were obviously not intended to be caryatid-type figures. Nevertheless it is an interesting echo of the earlier example of portraying subject peoples or nations, and a connection that would probably have been made by the Trajanic viewer who would still have been able to visit and admire the Augustan forum. It is also possible that a similar tripod monument to an Augustan one on the Palatine Hill, using marble figures of kneeling eastern barbarian men to support the superstructure of the monument, could have been set up in or near the Trajanic Forum.[33]

Finally, one might ask whether for the fourth-century Roman viewers of the Arch of Constantine the historic Dacian opponent still had some residual significance in himself, some particular significance in what could be termed the demonology of Rome's struggles against barbarian opponents over the centuries.

POTENCY BY PROXY

As well as being portrayed on works of art as the most military of emperors – on campaign with his forces and controlling the military manoeuvres against the Dacian enemy himself on Trajan's Column; in the thick of battle and riding down a Dacian chieftain (by allusion obviously Decebalus) on both the Great Trajanic Frieze and the *Tropaeum Traiani* – Trajan also appears on the Benevento arch as the 'father of the country', in an artistic programme in which masculine potency is further stressed by the absence of women and the presence of children.

Through their study of the portraiture of the emperor throughout his reign, several art historians have noted that the 'official' portrait types did not age at all over this period, even though the emperor was sixty-four when he died in AD 117.[34] This latter fact suggests a concern, perhaps it may even be said an over-concern, with physical appearance and aesthetic–erotic appeal on behalf of the emperor, if one accepts that overt masculinity as expressed through power, military prestige and potency by proxy can be read from his portrayal in the overall artistic programme of his reign, and through the completion and dedication of Trajanic monuments in the reign of his successor Hadrian.

Indeed, such a combination of an ever-youthful portraiture throughout his reign with his appearance in a succession of overtly masculine roles can also be found in the art of the court of Augustus. He, too, played the part of soldier, father figure, dutiful husband and loving son, though the latter two are visually expressed by the pendant appearance of the imperial women in Augustan art. It is likely that the creation of the ever-youthful Augustan portrait grew out of a similar trend among figures such as Sulla, Pompey and Caesar fighting for influence and power in the dying days of the Republic and was itself a direct and bitter reaction against the popular late-Republican, so-called veristic type of portrait of mature or elderly senators and time-serving bureaucrats, portraits that may have been viewed by these younger, dangerously ambitious men as mirroring the decrepit state of the nation.

A SEVERED HEAD

As noted earlier in the chapter, the graphic depiction of the death of Decebalus is also found on a second artefact, one that is both a public monument, so momentous was this event in the history of the period, and a private monument: the tombstone of Tiberius Claudius Maximus, the young cavalryman hurtling towards the crumpling Dacian leader on the column relief.[35] Found in 1965 near Philippi in northern Greece, the surviving part of the huge tombstone stands over 3 metres high. Towards the top is a small inset panel showing a remarkably similar, though not strictly identical, scene to that which appears on the column and, below that, a second panel depicting what are thought to be decorations for bravery awarded to Maximus for service in both the Dacian and Parthian wars.

In the 'capture' scene Decebalus has already slit his own throat and is shown in the process of falling to the ground as Maximus gallops towards him at speed, holding in one hand two spears and a shield, while in the other he holds aloft or brandishes his sword. The rest of the tombstone is taken up by an extended inscription which provides a remarkably detailed biography of the soldier commemorated, though one that must reflect the fame and renown that came to him in his lifetime through his exploits and deeds undertaken in the service of Rome. The death of Decebalus and his symbolic 'capture' by his subsequent beheading more or less ended the war, and the subsequent displaying of the severed head to the army on the column marks the start of a gruesome journey for this bloody trophy to Rome where, along with his chopped-off right hand, it was thrown on to the Gemonian Steps for public inspection and vilification.[36]

That Decebalus is one of the few barbarian leaders whose individual portrayal in Roman art has come down to us is of note. That he appears on a number of works of art – on Trajan's Column, on the Adamklissi Trophy and on the tombstone of Maximus – is more remarkable still, and suggests that he held a particular place in the 'demonology' of Roman–barbarian relations. This, once more, probably accounts for the excessively cruel treatment of his severed head when it was brought back to Rome after the war.

Trajan's reign also saw the emperor initiating extended military campaigns against Parthia. It is therefore somewhat curious that these dangerous enemies of Rome were not represented in the celebratory artworks of his later reign, or posthumously in the reign of Hadrian, with the degree of attention given to the Dacians. The barbarian captive clutching the skirts of a colossal standing figure of Trajan from Egypt may be one of the few examples of the portrayal of the defeated Parthians. The statue comes from the palace of Trajan at Ranuleh, Alexandria, the site of a legionary fortress.[37] Captured Parthians did, though, appear on coin issues.[38]

A TIME OF RETRENCHMENT

Almost as a footnote to this chapter, it is interesting to consider the surviving sculptural works associated with the emperor Hadrian, Trajan's immediate successor. It was in Hadrian's reign that the idea of constant expansion of the empire was laid to rest, and while some of the martial monuments which commemorated the expansionist ventures of Trajan were possibly completed, if not actually conceived, under Hadrian's supervision, nevertheless there is an unusual dearth of monuments in this era associated with military and triumphal matters.

This perhaps calls into question the previously proposed theory that the very idea of imperial power was routinely visually represented by a number of artistic tableaux or combinations of motifs that included Victories, trophies and defeated or captive barbarian foes. Hitherto, the attention of scholars has focused on the common use of provincial personifications of peoples and provinces as a Hadrianic phenomenon.[39] A dominant symbol of the emperor Hadrian's heroic qualities was also to be the depiction of his role in the hunt, a pursuit of which he was particulary fond in reality.[40] Apparently equally common was his portrayal dressed in military cuirass. This was part of a wider strategy to underline his aesthetic predilection for the culture, art and traditions of ancient Greece, where the cuirassed statue type had its origins.

The most astonishing single piece of artwork from the reign of Hadrian is an imperial statue portrait type, represented now by just the one surviving example, though it was undoubtedly a widespread type that would have been found throughout the cities and military bases of the empire. The emperor stands with his left foot on the back of a prostrate barbarian male on the ground beneath him. This statue, from Hierapytna in Crete,[41] uses a marked and obviously highly exaggerated difference in size between the figures of the emperor and the barbarian, the latter being the size of a small child who if stood upright would scarcely come up to the emperor's knees. The cuirassed Hadrian looms over his symbolic, defeated foe, and looks ahead into the distance rather than down at the man below.

This miniaturisation of the barbarian makes him unreal as well as symbolic of the real. In tandem, some overemphasis of the size and sheer physical presence of the emperor – for his honed solidity appears equally unreal – creates a power dichotomy which it might be thought scarcely needed stressing in the eyes of the contemporary viewer. Such miniaturisation was later to become a much more marked trend in imperial coin and statue representations of barbarians, and indeed the image of the single, prostrate barbarian male beneath an emperor's foot was set to become in some instances simply an imperial attribute and signifier.[42] It would certainly seem that this trend emerged during the Trajanic-Hadrianic period, though isolated earlier examples can be cited.

Hadrian then, and to a large extent the succeeding Antoninus Pius, did not continue the expansionist and aggressively military policies of the earlier emperors, and this is strikingly reflected in the architectural monuments and artistic strategies of the imperial programme at this time, if with some exceptions. It has been written that they declined to embrace 'the theology of victory' – a most appropriate phrase – created by their predecessors.[43] However, the reign of Hadrian has been identified by art historians as one in which the use of figures of personifications was unusually common. An explanation is required for this, though it is nevertheless recognised that less pronounced precedents exist for the linking of provincial personifications to a programme of imperial ideology in earlier periods, as in the Augustan and Julio-Claudian eras. It has already been suggested, during the discussion of the *ethne* statues from the Julio-Claudian imperial cult building of the Sebasteion at Aphrodisias, that while the process and model for the personification of peoples or places came from Greek art, the way in which the personified images were perceived and used was very different indeed in the Roman world, particularly in an imperial context.[44]

The Hadrianic provincial personifications consist of a series of twenty-five coin issues, each with a different type represented, and, growing out of this, the sculptural programme of the

Hadrianeum or Temple of the Divine Hadrian in Rome itself, conceived and built as a monument to Hadrian by his immediate successor Antoninus Pius, in or around AD 145.[45] Despite the fact that the building no longer stands to any extent and its sculptural decoration is no longer *in situ*, enough of the sculpture has been recovered and preserved in the Museo del Palazzo dei Conservatori to allow a discussion of its content and significance.

There survive twenty-one depictions of personified provinces, the figures being modelled almost life-size and frontally posed, some with their heads inclined to one side, as if viewing some particular object or person in that direction, in all probability a statue of the deified emperor himself. Other relief panels from the Hadrianeum bear images of 'barbarian' arms and armour, though not displayed as a 'trophy', and these weapon panels were probably placed between the personified figures. Of these panels nine survive.

An extensive literature exists on the identification of the individual personified provinces through careful analysis of their attributes, but details of these scholarly investigations need not be reproduced here. Suffice it to say that the figures are all female – such is the vocabulary and grammar of the personification process – the conquered and possessed lands being transformed and metamorphosed into compliant female forms.[46]

If, as seems likely given the relatively unweathered appearance of the reliefs, the personification and weapon panels were set around the interior of the temple *cella*, their positioning being focused upon the cult statue of Hadrian himself, then the conception of the overall artistic scheme might conceivably be viewed as one in which the provinces were not simply present here to represent the conquests of Rome. Under Hadrian the empire was consolidated with no new conquests being undertaken, hence the gallery of personifications could have been designed to be understood as a gathering of the provinces of the empire presided over by the benevolent figure of the emperor whose cautious and wise stewardship had helped guarantee an era of general peace and prosperity. Certainly, if contrasted with the bound *ethne* from the Aphrodisias Sebasteion and the tableaux there representing the active conquest of Britannia or Armenia, there is something almost anodyne and reassuring about the Hadrianic conception of the family of empire.

In summary, it was between the time of the Julio-Claudian emperors and the reign of Trajan that there emerged new ways in which ideas relating to Roman imperial ideology were expressed in art. A distillation of these trends can be found in the art of the Trajanic era.

In Rome itself, a previous avoidance of portraying war by the direct depiction of battles was startlingly reversed by the programme of sculptural friezes on Trajan's Column, on which numerous scenes of battle during the Dacian wars were executed. Nevertheless, the overall message of the column frieze was that war brought prosperity to Rome, a message not unlike that of Augustan art. Numerous images of subjugated Dacians and, to a lesser extent, Parthians were to be seen around Rome and on coinage.

Trajan's arch at Benevento conveyed a slightly different message about the riches accrued from the wars, and suggested that such wealth would be used to build roads and harbours, and to feed the children of Italy. At Adamklissi, a trophy monument depicting the defeat of the Dacians in a simple and direct manner was very much in the tradition of the Augustan trophy monuments at La Turbie and Saint-Bertrand-de-Comminges and the Tiberian arch at Orange. Thus similar images of defeated barbarians were intended to be read in different ways.

Trajan's reign marked the furthest expansion of the Roman empire. Under his successor Hadrian retrenchment followed, and there are consequently fewer depictions of barbarians from this time. However, the Augustan and Julio-Claudian strategy of using personifications of conquered peoples to stress the concept of limitless empire was revived under Hadrian and on monuments commemorating his reign. The cuirassed figure of Hadrian in a statuary group from Hieraptyna looms over the miniaturised figure of a sprawling barbarian held in place beneath his feet. Hindsight perhaps allows this to be seen as a metaphor for an empire that had over-reached its limits.

FOUR
THE TIDE TURNS

The reign of Hadrian's successor, Antoninus Pius, was on the whole one of peace and prosperity for Rome. However, this was relatively short-lived. Marcus Aurelius and Lucius Verus, the adopted heirs of the Antonine dynasty, reigned over an era of uprisings and major wars against the Parthians in the east and the Marcomanni in Germany. Lucius died in AD 169 and Marcus died on campaign in AD 180. This period saw a fundamental change in the way in which art was used to express political necessity and uncertainty. This was best reflected in the friezes on the Column of Marcus Aurelius in Rome, though consideration will also be given in this chapter to other Antonine monuments away from Rome, principally the Great Altar at Ephesos and sculptures from the Antonine Wall in Scotland. It was also evident in a significant, though temporary, move away from the imperial exclusivity of the use of images of victory to a situation in which senior military men of the era celebrated their achievements through the commissioning of what are now known as 'battle sarcophagi'.

While the Column of Marcus Aurelius in Rome might be dismissed as a debased copy of Trajan's Column, in both form and content, a close analysis of the artwork on the later column shows that the two monuments could not be more different in terms of the political and social ideologies represented. While the problems inherent in viewing the middle and upper portions of the frieze on Trajan's Column would have been alleviated by the original appearance of the sculptures as painted and enhanced by the addition of metal or wooden fixtures, and those with access to the libraries on either side of the column would have been afforded an easier and more privileged viewing, nevertheless much of the dense and detailed frieze would not have been visible. On the Column of Marcus Aurelius the size of the individual figures was increased, less background was created and there were fewer spirals to the frieze, all doubtless deliberate strategies to make the artwork more readable, even if still somewhat difficult to follow in sequence around the shaft of the column.

The column was commissioned by Marcus' son Commodus shortly after his father's death in AD 180 and was completed in or shortly before AD 192. Standing to roughly the same height as Trajan's Column, its shaft was decorated with a spiral frieze depicting Marcus Aurelius' military campaigns against the Marcomanni of Germany in AD 172–3 and the Sarmatians in AD 174–5. The column base no longer stands, though drawings of its sculptural programme survive from the Renaissance, while the bronze equestrian statue of the emperor that once stood on top of the monument was removed at some time during this period.[1]

As with the discussion of Trajan's Column in Chapter Three, it is not the intention here to deliver a scene by scene analysis of the column, nor to try and relate its scenes to historically attested events. Rather a general description of the column's programme of decoration will be given, and then attention will turn to a number of scenes where the interaction with barbarian protagonists is of particular importance in terms of what it tells us about changing trends in military, political, social and imperial ideologies.

The drawings of the column base show relief panels very similar in composition to contemporary sarcophagus art, though only two sides of the base were recorded. On one side appear four Victories, standing in front of a hanging swag which is draped over their shoulders. Each figure holds out an arm to grasp a wreath with the Victory next to her. On another side of the base the emperor himself is portrayed, dressed in military uniform, in company with two officers and other soldiers. A riderless but saddled horse stands to the right. On the left-hand side of the relief is a number of male barbarians being escorted into the emperor's presence by a guard. Two of the barbarians kneel in submission. These two scenes are typical ones of imperial victory and imperial *clementia*.

The column reliefs begin with the Roman forces crossing the River Danube at the start of the Marcomannic campaign, there being a break in the spiral narrative at the end of this campaign and before the depiction of the Sarmatian wars, marked by the figure of a Victory writing on a shield, as also appeared on Trajan's Column between the depiction of the first and the second Dacian wars.

Almost entirely absent from the relief narratives on the Aurelian Column are the types of camp and fortification construction scenes that played such a large and significant part in the artistic scheme of Trajan's Column. It has been suggested that such scenes were included in such large numbers there, and in such an exaggerated manner, in order to stress the importance of the army and its soldiers to Rome. The army was not only a fighting force, winner of wars and guarantor of the empire's security, but it was also an economic force in terms of its indirect contribution to the financial dynamics of empire, its labours away from Rome and Italy being transformed into bricks and marble back in Rome itself. It would be taken as read by the Roman viewer that the army's victories would also lead to the shipping to Rome and Italy of numerous captives as slaves. Slaves were part of the very fabric of the city, which had relied upon a regular supply and influx of slaves following foreign conquest since the time of the Republic.

A TROUBLED PSYCHE

It is therefore analysis of the battle scenes that must lead any reading of the Column of Marcus Aurelius.[2] In the numerous battle scenes on the column – many more than on Trajan's Column – there is often almost a sense of panic and frantic endeavour on the part of the Roman forces that seems to be at odds with the clinical precision of many of the military manoeuvres depicted on Trajan's Column. While the composition and style of the Trajanic column's battles suggested a sense of order, underscored by the general uniformity of many of the figures of massed troops, on the Aurelian column disharmonic forms, awkward figural poses and jagged composition together create almost the opposite effect.

The Roman forces have no sooner crossed the Danube than they destroy an abandoned German village (Scene VII) and bring before the emperor two mounted barbarian male captives who had evidently not been able to flee the environs of the sleighted village in time (Scene VIII). In the same scene appear two other, dead barbarians, perhaps executed prisoners, whose inert bodies sprawl one on top of the other in the foreground of the scene. In the background, a Roman soldier pushes his shield into the back of another, semi-naked barbarian prisoner, the posture of the Roman suggesting that he may be about to kill the prisoner with his sword. The barbarian, his bare back to the viewer, reaches up one arm, perhaps in a gesture of pain or despair, and seems almost to brace himself against the frame of the relief space.

One battle scene (Scene XI) includes the denouement of a German siege of a Roman fortification that is guarding a strategic river crossing. The German attackers are defeated not by the staunchness of the Roman defenders alone but rather by what is known as 'the miracle of the thunderbolt'. A thunderbolt strikes the German siege engine, killing many of its operators, thus bringing relief to the sore-pressed Roman troops. A later battle scene (Scene XVI), where Roman victory is only gained through what is generally referred to as 'the miracle of the rain', includes the shocking portrayal of a vast heap of barbarian corpses, weaponry and a slaughtered horse. This motif, a pile of bodies, also recurs during the depiction of the second campaign (Scene CIX).

That these victories were won only through the miracle of divine intervention indicates a lack of certainty about the military capability of the Roman forces to overcome their barbarian opponents in this war, a lack of confidence and a vulnerable side of the Roman imperial psyche that had not been seen before in Roman art and one that must have reflected a wider social and political crisis of confidence.

Following the Roman victory after the rains, barbarian women and children are shown being rounded up and herded together (Scene XVII). Indeed, the brutal treatment and routine execution of prisoners are also starkly portrayed elsewhere on the column, most tellingly by a scene of execution (Scene LXI) where the beheading of barbarian male prisoners is overseen by Roman troops while the actual act of holding the bound male captives and striking the blow is carried out by their compatriots. It is not entirely clear whether they are being forced to do this, or whether the complicity of these particular barbarians has been bought by Rome. The bound prisoners, their faces in some cases contorted with terror, stand in line awaiting their fate while crumpled bodies lie nearby, their severed heads resting on the ground beside them.

The severed head of a barbarian is presented to the emperor some time later (Scene LXVI), this kind of grotesque trophy being familiar from its occurrence also on Trajan's Column. At the emperor's feet stand a number of other Roman soldiers with a live barbarian captive, though his immediate guard holds him by the hair in a violent mimicry of the head held above. A few scenes later there occurs another horrific scene of execution (Scene LXVIII). A group of six Roman footsoldiers, with shields held in one hand and lances in the other, is caught in the act of spearing and killing a number of unarmed barbarian men. One barbarian already lies dead on the ground and another, as a spear is thrust deep into his shoulder, lets out a scream of agony that is captured on his face by the artist in a pornography of violence. Being herded towards this killing field (Scene LXIX) are four more male prisoners and a number of barbarian women, two of them holding babies and another touching her young son or daughter who nestles up close to her body. This woman holds one arm protectively across her breast. Whether these men and women are being brought to watch the executions taking place in the adjacent scene or whether they are being led to their own deaths is unclear.

Elsewhere, a larger group of women captives is being led away into exile, along with captured flocks of animals (Scene LXXIII). One woman grasps the arm of another in a gesture of comfort, while a third woman turns her worried face round towards the woman behind her, as if seeking reassurance. Women prisoners are also shown in some distress (Scene LXXXV) waiting for a group of Roman soldiers to cross over a pontoon bridge, presumably before they are led over themselves. One soldier, having just crossed the bridge, bundles a woman and child ahead of him or out of his way: she turns her head around towards him, frightened and uncertain. A bullock cart, on the back of which sit two further women captives, perhaps more important prisoners or hostages than those forced to walk, forms part of the column of refugees and prisoners. One can only guess at the eventual fate of these groups of women, but in portraying groups of exclusively female barbarians in these instances a very specific point was being made about the gendered nature of conquest and Roman imperialism.[3]

One of the most shocking scenes is that of the sacking of a German village (Scene XX), with the emperor and his attendant officers being shown as spectators at the event. Roman troops slaughter the barbarian men. One soldier is depicted about to bring his sword down on to the figure of a barbarian man already partially stunned and on the ground on all fours, his bare back to the looming figure of the Roman. Another Roman soldier grabs a woman by the hair as she attempts to flee the village with her child. Her garment has fallen away from her right shoulder to expose her bare breast, a rendering that may itself be laden with symbolism. A slaughtered barbarian man lies dead on the ground behind the woman and it may be assumed that he was her husband and the child's father. If so, this image of a family split asunder by reason of their resistance to the power of Rome was deployed here quite cynically and in a context where there is no pendant motif celebrating the security and happiness of the Roman family, as had been seen in other, earlier examples of state art.

Women and children, including a babe in arms, are shown being captured and manhandled in other scenes (Scenes XCVII and CIV), while a female barbarian prisoner is shown being killed (again in Scene XCVIIB). In Scene XCVII, following a battle, a woman is dragged off by the hair, a motif that was employed in an earlier sequence relating to the first campaign, and her child is led away by two Roman soldiers. Ahead of them another woman, her arms down at her sides, is manhandled by a trooper, while behind them a soldier stabs a female barbarian in the breast with his sword as she attempts to raise up one of her arms in futile self-defence. Given that captured women would have been valuable to the Romans as slaves, the killing of women in these scenes is surprising.

In Scene CIV a group of women prisoners and their children is herded together, with one Roman soldier shown pushing an evidently terrified mother and her clinging, equally terrified son towards the main group of prisoners, while a second soldier drags a young, childless woman away from the group. He pulls her by the left arm while she holds up her right arm in evident protest. The nature of her imminent fate is uncertain. These scenes seem to be suggesting that war is inevitably something that affects all society, that women and men are equally affected, even if victims rather than active protagonists. In many ways, the dehumanising view of war displayed on the column is more true of the consequences of war than is the case with the representation on any other monument erected in Roman times.

It is unfortunately the case that the objectifying process of war has a numbing effect on the maintenance of sexual codes and prohibitions, and that the breakdown of these vital social constructions, or their deliberate suspension as a policy of conquest, leads to the kind of violence against women in war shown so blatantly on parts of the column. Portrayal of such events without the masking and filtering gauze of allegory or allusion was something quite new and revealing in Roman art. A comparison with the scenes involving women on Trajan's Column is instructive. There, barbarian women were captured or taken as hostages. They were present at scenes of siege and to the rear of battle, but nowhere were they shown being mistreated or killed as part of the general routine of war, as seems to be the message on the Aurelian column. The only jarring scene involving women on Trajan's Column was one showing Dacian women torturing captured Roman soldiers, a scene so extraordinary in that context that it can be interpreted as probably relating to a recorded, notorious incident from the Dacian wars or as an allusion to the inherent barbarity of Dacian and barbarian women in general.[4]

The final, upper reliefs on the Column of Marcus Aurelius portray barbarian peoples going off into exile with their belongings and their animals. Most are on foot, some on horseback, a few ride in bullock carts. The exiles include both men and women, but no children are depicted, which may be of significance. Such a scene of the defeated, impotent enemy leaving the arena of combat is quite a traditional trope in the context of Roman imperial art and brings to mind, in particular, similar scenes on the Trophy of Trajan at Adamklissi.[5]

This brief, selective discussion of the Column of Marcus Aurelius may appear to be biased towards the discussion of battle, cruelty and death. However, it nevertheless represents a true reflection of the overall message of the monument. It was, of course, a victory monument, a war memorial; but while such monuments concentrating on war alone had been set up in the provinces, for example at Orange and at Adamklissi, the appearance of one here in Rome requires further discussion. It might perhaps have been expected that a Roman monument would endeavour to convey other more subtle and complex messages relating to imperial policies or aspirations.

Given that the inspiration for the form and decorative style of the spiral friezes on the Column of Marcus Aurelius came directly from Trajan's Column, it might be informative to compare the artistic programmes of the two columns. On the Aurelian column, the barbarian has simply become a body, dehumanised pieces and fragments of bleeding and battered flesh,[6] whose fate was dictated by Roman imperial authority. These bodies are stabbed or hacked at, they are pushed and herded like beasts being brought in from the fields, they are pulled along by the hair, they are beheaded and their bodies piled up in heaps for the edification of the viewer.

A shying-away from engagement with the bloodiness of the column's content, or attempts to view it as debased, almost degenerate, classical art sullied by the acceptance of trends of portrayal prevalent in military and plebeian art of an earlier period would represent a failure to come to terms with the reality of the imperial psyche at this time.

THE TIDE TURNS

A CONTRASTING CLEMENCY

Another major monument, a triumphal arch or, quite possibly, arches, was set up in Rome under Marcus Aurelius but is now 'lost', apart from a very few sculptural panels attributed to it, some of which were reused, with the emperor's head recarved, in the fourth-century Arch of Constantine.[7] The eleven surviving decorative panels date to between AD 176–80 and relate either to the emperor's campaigns against northern barbarian peoples, as on the column, or to the evocation of his virtues. The scenes move from the leave-taking of Rome, through religious rites, to the addressing of the troops on the eve of battle. Actual battle scenes were either not included on the arch, which would be surprising considering the almost obsessive interest in their detailed portrayal on the column, or none has survived.

A scene of *clementia* may be assumed to be taking place after a battle, with two barbarians being brought into the presence of the emperor to learn of their fate. As Roman soldiers stand around them, standards at the rear of the depiction, the emperor sits on a stool set on a raised dais or podium, with one of his generals standing behind him. The emperor gazes straight ahead, into the distance, and does not seem to be paying any attention to the pleading of two barbarians standing at the foot of the dais. One of the barbarians is a bearded old man, presumably a chieftain of some sort, here to plead for the fate of his people, the other a youth or boy who physically supports the old man, possibly his father, who may have been wounded in the battle. The old man looks up at the emperor and appears to be speaking, his right arm held out in supplication while his left arm is around the shoulder of the youth who is buckling slightly under the weight. The young man holds his head against the old man's breast and looks down in seeming resignation.[8]

Another *clementia* scene is much more conventional in its composition and takes place on the battlefield, rather than off it as in the previous example. The emperor is shown here on horseback, attended by troops. Two barbarian captives have gone down on their knees in supplication before the victorious emperor. They reach up their arms towards him and he, in turn, gestures to them with his right arm that clemency is granted.[9]

A similar composition, on the so-called Torlonia Relief, perhaps from an arch in the Via di Pietra in Rome, shows a bearded emperor – probably the co-emperor Lucius Verus – with two members of his entourage in the background, receiving the submission of a group of four barbarians, three men and a youth. However, in contrast to the presumed father and son pairing on the Antonine arch *clementia*, where the son physically supports the father, here the youth stands upright behind the kneeling figure of the man who appears to be the leader of the barbarian delegation. All the barbarians extend their arms in gestures of supplication while the emperor likewise gestures, but in clemency after hearing their pleas.[10]

The remarkable survival of a bronze, life-size equestrian statue of Marcus Aurelius, now housed in the Palazzo dei Conservatori on the Capitoline Hill in Rome, is the only extant example from antiquity of what was a relatively common type of Roman imperial representation.[11] Though the equestrian statue derived from a Greek type, it was used in the Roman period in a subtly different manner – to demonstrate both individual and state power and authority rather than simply to honour an individual person, as in the Greek manner. As already noted, the earliest Roman type may have been Domitianic, and the influence of the mounted figure types of Roman military art may have entered the mainstream of state art at this time.[12]

The equestrian statue shows the emperor holding one arm and hand in such a position as to suggest that leather reins were originally affixed to the statue and that they were held here, while his other arm is outstretched in a gesture of *clementia*, remarkably similar to his pose on horseback on the arch relief. He looks ahead, rather than at the ground or at any other specific point of reference. The horse is vividly modelled, its mouth open, its mane bristling and its right foreleg either placed on or trampling some now-vanished object or person, probably originally the figure of a cowering barbarian. There is a twelfth-century reference to the presence of the barbarian, as there had been with the Domitianic forerunner of the work.[13] However, the overall composition of the Aurelian work very much reflected the inherent contradictions of his reign, in that here both power and military might were being celebrated in the traditional manner through the trampling of a foe, yet at the same time a generalised gesture of clemency was being extended to the peoples of the barbarian lands. The individual messages of the column and of the arch were here brought together in a powerful way.

A somewhat more hybrid compositional scene of imperial triumph, thought to date to the time of Marcus Aurelius though it could possibly be slightly later, appears on a ceramic mould from Aquincum in Pannonia – modern Hungary.[14] Thought to have been used for the baking of celebratory cakes, perhaps for official functions, this object bears decoration conflating military and triumphal events in a manner that suggests the artist's reference to a number of monumental artistic schemes in Rome.

The bearded emperor rides in a chariot or *biga*, progressing under a triumphal arch which is heavily decorated with spoils of war in a manner that suggests its identification as the Porta Triumphalis in Rome, the chariot being preceded by the figure of Mars. Riding in the chariot with the emperor is Victory who holds a wreath over his head. While he guides the progress of the chariot with one hand, with the other the emperor thrusts a spear at a bound male barbarian, dressed in tunic and trousers, seated on the ground behind the chariot. Thus battle and triumphal progress are conflated, and the emperor is unusually himself shown in combat with the enemies of the empire, though the symbolic nature of that combat is indicated both by the fact that the barbarian is already bound and defeated and that the emperor 'fights' from a triumphal chariot. The manipulation of time and space inherent in the composition of the Aquincum mould is reminiscent of the similar strategy used by the sculptor of the Bridgeness legionary distance slab from the Antonine Wall in Scotland, discussed in detail below.

A MESSAGE TO THE PROVINCES

Away from Rome, monuments commemorating the achievements of the Antonine emperors Marcus Aurelius and his co-emperor Lucius Verus were also erected, those at

Besançon in Gaul, at Ephesos in present-day Turkey, and at Tripoli in Libya being of interest here.

The decorated municipal arch at Besançon was most probably constructed in the reign of Marcus Aurelius. Its dedicatory inscription does not survive, and while it may be post-Antonine in date its sculptural programme's allusions to campaigns against both northern and eastern barbarian foes suggest the correctness of its attribution to the time of Marcus, when wars against the northern Marcomanni and the eastern Sarmatians and Parthians took place. Urban monuments elsewhere bearing friezes of captured arms and armour, as at Parma, Italy, were probably also erected at this time.[15]

The arch is very much in the tradition of the erection of decorated civic arches in Gallia Narbonensis that occurred under Augustus and Tiberius, when the martial imagery employed on them was more provocatively resonant within its Gallic context. Again, as was the case with the earlier arches, the Besançon arch was also a geographical marker, the town being sited on a major road route to, and from, Italy.[16] Roman troops are depicted in battle against both eastern and northern barbarians, while Victories and bound captives also appear, very much as on the earlier monuments. But, just as the intervention of the gods on the side of the Romans was shown on the Column of Marcus Aurelius in Rome, so here too on the Besançon arch does Jupiter appear scattering giants with his thunderbolt. The gigantomachy, the battle with giants, is used here as an obvious allusion to the battle of (Roman) civilisation with the other (barbarism), a battle whose outcome can no longer be guaranteed.

The Great Antonine Altar at Ephesos was a monumental structure which included a huge sculptural frieze, about 30 metres in length.[17] A complete reconstruction of the frieze cannot be made with certainty, as many of the individual panels are now lost, but hypothetical reconstructions suggest that the overall theme of the decorative scheme was a celebration of the triumphs and achievements of Lucius Verus, rather than of the achievements of the joint reign. The three strands of the work are Verus' adoption into the imperial house, his military triumphs against the Parthians, those old enemies of Rome, in the campaigns of AD 163–6 and his apotheosis following his death in AD 169. The panels featuring the Parthian campaigns unflinchingly addressed the bleak realities of war as did those on the Aurelian column in Rome, though there was here at Ephesos no attempt at narrative or at a wider contextualisation beyond the battlefield. Battle scenes may have alternated with depictions of dead or dying Parthians.

One of the battle scenes portrays a Roman cavalryman riding down a Parthian foe, while a second cavalryman towards the front of the scene tramples another Parthian who is trying unsuccessfully to fend off the attack by holding his shield up over his back. In another, a Roman foot-soldier tenses himself, and draws back his right arm in preparation to strike a swingeing blow with his sword against a Parthian who kneels on the ground before him, his back to his Roman assailant. Though armed, the Parthian makes no attempt to move or defend himself. A rearing horse in the background and other figures to the left are incidental to the actions of the main protagonists.

Three bearded and long-haired Parthians figure to the forefront of another panel. One is slumped either wounded or dead on the back of his horse, a second stands and looks back at the Roman troops in a confused, perhaps frightened manner, while a third Parthian kneeling to the left of the panel reaches to pull an arrow or spearhead out of his back. The figures of two Roman soldiers in the background are here incidental. A self-composed fate is achieved by two kneeling Parthians who, elsewhere on the frieze, commit suicide by plunging their own swords into their breasts.[18]

Parthian men also appear, as captives rather than combatants, on one face of the Arch of Marcus Aurelius and Lucius Verus at Tripoli.[19] Here they are in the company of Parthian women and children in family groups posed beneath battle trophies. In the best-preserved of these groups the man stands upright facing out towards the viewer, seemingly alone with his thoughts, while his wife sits on the ground at his side and offers comfort to their child who clasps her in return. The barbarian family as symbol of a whole nation in defeat, used to stress the totality of that defeat, was by now a familiar motif of Roman state art. There was, however, a certain element of pathos and sympathy in the portrayal of the captives on the Tripoli arch which was absent from the major Antonine monuments in Rome.

It has been suggested that two decorated black limestone herms – generally a form of boundary or conceptual marker – found in the Baths of Antoninus Pius at Carthage represent fragments of a lost triumphal monument, commemorating perhaps a victory over barbarian forces that had entered the Roman North African territories.[20] On one of the herms is the head of a black African, and on the other the head of perhaps a Libyan barbarian, each representing the ethnic make-up of the defeated forces.

Dated also to the Antonine period, to some time around AD 146–50, is a unique example of the representation of barbarians in mosaic art. In the basilica at Tipasa, in Mauretania, was laid a pavement whose central panel or *emblema* depicts three barbarian prisoners.[21] The three figures, a seated man and a woman in the foreground of the scene and a child standing behind them, appear to be ethnically Berber in origin. The bearded man is completely naked and is bound with his hands behind his back. The woman wears a dark cloak, but the child, a boy, is again naked. All three figures appear downcast. An oval shield lies discarded on the ground behind the man. Although the image of the bound prisoner, and of the family in defeat and captivity as representative of a tribe in defeat, was common, as has been evident throughout this study, the context is certainly unique and difficult to account for.

In the largely decorative border surrounding this central panel are twelve almost portrait-like heads or busts of individuals who may also be barbarians, to judge from their appearance, though this identification is uncertain and, were it to be correct, difficult to relate to the fate of the three prisoners, the mosaic's main protagonists. It is more likely that the twelve individuals, eleven men and one woman, were members of the local elite who both supported the military exercise and provided funds for the provision of the dedicatory mosaic, though it might have been expected that such dedicatees would have been named either individually or collectively in an accompanying inscription.

That such a mosaic adorned a public building makes it

necessary to interpret its significance in terms of its potential relationship to public events. It is known that Tipasa was the main base used by the emperor Antoninus Pius for a military campaign against the Mauri, and it is thought most likely that the mosaic was linked to the commemoration of that event. However, there is no typical imperial imagery present on the mosaic, and it must therefore be seen as perhaps a local, municipal commemoration, though one presumably accorded official state sanction and approval.

IN DEATH AS IN LIFE

Of particular interest to this study is a very distinct group of highly decorated battle sarcophagi, of which about twenty examples are known, dating from the mid- to later second century, on which dense scenes of Roman–barbarian warfare were executed.[22] In addition to the main group, there is the later Ludovisi sarcophagus which will be discussed in Chapter Five, though it should be seen as part of the same genre of artistic commemoration. These sarcophagi represent the first real instance in this study of the widespread use in Roman aristocratic circles of what might be deemed 'official' artistic themes in a private context. They perhaps suggest that imperial and aristocratic concerns about political instability and compromised security on the frontiers merged at this time in a way that had not previously occurred.

The best known example of the type is the Portonaccio sarcophagus, of a late Antonine date, c. AD 180–90.[23] This consists of the main body of the sarcophagus, which is carved on three sides only, and a flat, decorated lid. The main scene on the carved long side of the body is a fraught and frenzied battle scene, between Roman forces and Germanic barbarians. The sheer density of the composition, with fighting troops almost intertwined one with another, is quite striking and claustrophobic.

The central figure, on whom the viewers' eyes eventually alight once they are able to make sense of individual representations among the seething mass, is a Roman cavalryman at the centre of a squadron of riders who are battling fiercely with the barbarian footsoldiers all around them. Other Roman infantrymen take part in hand-to-hand combat, depicted principally towards the bottom third of the sarcophagus. Barbarian bodies fall to the ground or are contorted into awkward shapes as they lie in their death throes, many trampled under horses' hooves in the confused mêlée. The faces of the barbarian protagonists variously display looks of pain or of horror, while their Roman opponents remain largely impassive. Roman soldiers spear the enemy, stab or hack at them with their swords in a seeming frenzy. The battle scene is flanked by two trophies, beneath each of which stands a pair of barbarians, one male and one female in each case. They are not bound, but their distress in defeat is quite evident.

On the two short sides are scenes of prisoners being led across a pontoon bridge and another of barbarians surrendering. On the sarcophagus lid are various scenes of both public and military life and of the deceased's private life. The lid is book-ended by two large masks. Looking from right to left are represented first what appears to be a scene of the bathing of a child, a marriage being celebrated in the central scene, while the final scene shows barbarians begging a seated Roman general for mercy. Behind the general's stool, a Roman soldier stands guard over barbarian prisoners huddled around, and sitting beneath, a trophy. A dejected-looking barbarian mother and her child are at the forefront of the group of captives, in quite evident contrast with the young Roman woman and her child at the other end of the lid. These three scenes can be considered as obliquely biographical, in that they do not necessarily relate directly to the life of the deceased, but rather refer to qualities and virtues that would have been, at least in theory, personified in the actions and life of the dead man. The marriage would relate to *concordia*, while the scene with the pleading barbarian related to *clementia*.

This sarcophagus was obviously commissioned for a high-ranking military officer, perhaps Aulus Iulius Pompilius, a general under Marcus Aurelius, although this identification is circumstantial.[24]

Natalie Boymel Kampen in her study 'Biographical Narration and Roman Funerary Art',[25] has discussed the move away in this type of art from the use of a visual narrative framework towards the use on sarcophagi and other types of funerary monuments of abstract representations of concepts of virtue as reflections of the life and personal qualities of the deceased. These concepts of virtue themselves became less relevant in this type of art from the later second century onwards, a trend not altogether coincidental in the date of its occurrence.

Among the abstract virtues were *virtus*, represented usually by a battle motif, and *clementia*, represented by a scene of submission by a barbarian family. Changes in attitude brought about by political crises and the perception of the breaking down of traditional roles in society were factors in the questioning of the relevance of the old perceptions of virtue. In art, these changes are best seen reflected in the decoration on the Portonaccio sarcophagus, on which the small scenes of what may still be called biography are relegated to the lid while the sarcophagus itself is dominated by a complex and harrowing battle scene like those on the Column of Marcus Aurelius, although on the sarcophagus the scene is of an entirely symbolic nature. Representations of the old virtues are nowhere in evidence, and in the battle it may be surmised that victory must be won at any cost, and that such striving is now simply an end in itself. This contrasts, of course, with the celebration of the old Roman virtues by the emperor himself in his book, the *Meditations*.

Both direct and oblique biographical references were to become less common from the mid- and particularly later second century onwards as the previously admired and chronicled virtues themselves became less valued in Roman public life. These abstract virtues in art were replaced by what has been dubbed 'a new and transcendent ideal of spiritual superiority'.[26]

The so-called 'Clementia Sarcophagus' in the Vatican Museums dates to *c*. AD 170.[27] Its decoration consists of a scene in which a military commander, bearded and portly in what must have been a portrait representation, gives audience to a large group of heavily guarded barbarian men, women and children seeking clemency. One man goes down on his knees before the victorious general, a second and third remain standing. Each has an expression of pain or anguish on his face, but particularly striking, and surprisingly poignant in the context of the art of the period, is a kneeling woman and her small child who rubs at his eye with one hand while touching his mother's arm with the other. She reaches out her arm to comfort the crying child. At the same time as giving the barbarians an audience, the general is being crowned by Victory. The scene is flanked at each end of the sarcophagus face by figures of bound male barbarian captives seated beneath a trophy, each of these figures looking up, with their heads turned away from the central scene.

On the short sides of the sarcophagus are depicted further barbarians. On one side, a cart or waggon is shown carrying prisoners, though it is not clear whether this is intended to represent captives being escorted away from the battlefield or being paraded in a triumphal procession in Rome. The prisoners consist of a woman and her child, perhaps in echo of the two figures on the sarcophagus's front, the woman seated facing the back of the cart, with her head in her hands in what is generally known as the 'mourning captive' pose, while the unattended child rests one arm across his mother's shoulder and with his other reaches out to, and touches, the spear held by the Roman soldier who accompanies the cart. This mixture of a sorrowful scene tempered by the playfulness of the small child is unusual. On the other short side of the sarcophagus are seated captives guarded by Roman troops. Two women and a man appear here, one of the women again depicted in a huddled, 'mourning captive' pose.

The overall decorative scheme of the Clementia Sarcophagus was both traditional and at the same time novel, in that the artist introduced elements of both playfulness and pathos into the depiction of the barbarian peoples here who are otherwise portrayed as defeated, dejected and pleading. That these elements were introduced through the medium of the image of a child, in one case to elicit sympathy and in the other to raise a smile at the child's wilfulness, rather than through that of an adult, perhaps alludes to the fact that the *clementia* of the general, and by association of the Roman state, had positively affected the future of those children and the overall future of their people or tribe. It may be that the tribe's defeat led to their incorporation within the empire and that all the benefits of *Romanitas* became theirs as a result.

It has been argued in earlier chapters that the use of images of barbarian families in state art has usually been to suggest a curtailed future rather than a secure one, and indeed this would have been the impression received by the viewer of the main sarcophagus scene. It is only when the right-hand side is examined that the child's playfulness introduces a more nuanced element into the reading of the overall message, a message which was slightly out of step with much of the ideological art of the period.

A sarcophagus of *c*. AD 150 from a site on the Via Appia in Rome is taken up almost entirely by a battle between Romans and Gauls.[28] The mid-second century was obviously a period far removed from the era when the Gauls were the major barbarian enemies of Rome, and it must be assumed that the decorative scheme was deliberately anachronistic in both its choice of protagonists for the symbolic battle, and in its style and composition which harked back to Hellenistic models.

The Gauls all display the exaggerated physique of the Attalid Gauls,[29] and some of their poses – one supporting himself with outstretched arm on the ground, another holding off a Roman soldier who grips him by the hair – were stock motifs from the long-established Graeco-Roman tradition of battle pictures. However, in contrast to this is the narrow register of decoration on the sarcophagus lid which depicts a seated line of defeated and highly dejected barbarian captives, with captured arms and armour filling in the background, in echo of the trophies which flank the battle scene below. The three male captives are all bound, and of the three barbarian women, one holds up her hand to her head in pain or anguish while the other two are shown with children, one child comforting its huddled and brooding mother and the other child being held by its mother protectively. Both the action of the defeat of the barbarians, and the consequences of that defeat, are juxtaposed to dramatic effect. Given that the Gauls were a historic, rather than a real, enemy at this time, this motif of a barbarian foe successfully overcome may have been chosen as a reassuring reference point at a time of Roman uncertainty over the eventual outcome of their wars and battles against newer and different barbarian foes.

Another example of a sarcophagus adorned with scenes of the life of a Roman general is now in a collection in Mantova,[30] its original provenance being uncertain; here a marriage (*concordia*), a sacrifice (*pietas*) and a barbarian family begging for mercy (*clementia*), with the barbarian child tugging at the general's garment in supplication, represented the qualities that he was thought to have brought to his life of service.

It is hardly surprising, given the extended period of time spent by the emperor Marcus Aurelius at war and on campaign, that an over-preoccupation with military affairs and martial concerns should also have been the lot of a large sector of the upper echelons of Roman society at this time. It is not, therefore, surprising that their involvement in the wars of his reign should have been commemorated in a dramatic and original way, by the commissioning of the battle sarcophagi. These were executed in a style that is both part of an overall tradition of Italian and Roman funerary art, and yet at the same time highly original in terms of its evident stylistic and narrative links with the state art that commemorated those same wars.[31]

However, it should also be noted that other types of decorated sarcophagus were just as common, if not more so, in this period, including biographical sarcophagi.

Also popular on sarcophagi was mythological decoration, which again could be used to allude to victory and/or a military career in its own way. Such allusive strategies were more in keeping with the legacy of Hellenistic art. Fictive battles between Greeks and Amazons made perhaps the most obvious of these links with real struggle and real heroism in contemporary times. In particular, the encounter on the battlefield between Achilles and Penthesilea, the queen of the Amazons, is strikingly portrayed on a sarcophagus of *c.* AD 250 now in the Vatican Museums. The Greek hero is captured in the midst of the mêlée of a battle that rages all around him and yet from which he appears strangely isolated, holding the dying Amazon in his arms, her body gently slumping towards the ground. His attraction to the woman he has just killed is yet to register on his face.[32]

Sarcophagi portraying the Indian Victory of the god Bacchus could be taken as alluding on the part of the deceased or his family to an adherence to the Bacchic cult and its associated ideas of salvation, or as a reference to the idea of victory and triumph in the abstract, a victory over those who were not of the Graeco-Roman milieu and whose mythological exoticism could be taken to denote a generalised 'other'. One particular example, in the collection of the Capitoline Museum in Rome, shows the procession of the triumphant god and his companions of the *thiassos*, and his attendant beasts, while in the background of this busy and lively scene two bound prisoners, seated back to back, are being transported along in the procession on the back of a camel. Here mythological captives play a reluctant part in a triumph that could be read as alluding to the real thing.

The final sarcophagus type, and one whose popularity related to artistic and social trends that were particularly marked in the Hadrianic period, was the hunting sarcophagus. The hunt was again allusive rather than real, and acted as a metaphor for heroic achievement in general and thus could be said to be the same as, though somewhat different from, the battle-type of sarcophagus in its celebration of manly pursuits. The hunt or chase could also itself represent the course of a human life, with death lurking suddenly and inescapably at its end.[33]

The screaming and contorted faces of barbarians on the Column of Marcus Aurelius and on some of the Antonine battle sarcophagi represented a new mode of artistic depiction that went hand-in-hand with the brutal realism of the fate of these peoples. This can also be seen reflected on the tombstone of the Roman legionary soldier C. Septimus who died in Pannonia some time in the later second century.[34] The tombstone is now in the collection of the National Museum in Budapest.

In the scene above the dedicatory inscription, an armed legionary, either Septimus himself or a generic figure, stands to the right of a group of barbarians with whom he is engaged in combat. One barbarian already lies dead on the ground. A second kneels next to him, his body and head turned away from Septimus who appears to be reaching out one hand towards him, perhaps to grab his hair before despatching him to the same fate as his fallen friend. The kneeling man holds up one of his hands in an open-palmed gesture which may represent either acceptance of the blow about to be struck or his dismay at the death of the other barbarian. He looks up to the heavens with an anguished expression on his face that catches his suffering in stone for eternity. A third barbarian combatant moves away from the group to the left. It is the pain and suffering of the central barbarian protagonist that immediately catches the viewer's gaze, and indeed even places the figure of Septimus, the man whose life and career were here being celebrated and commemorated, in a supporting role.

TO THE FRONTIER

Attention will now be turned to a remarkable group of sculptural reliefs from the very frontier of the empire, from the Antonine Wall in Scotland. Generally known as 'legionary distance slabs', these decorated stones were set up at regular intervals along the frontier earthwork by legionary work parties building the wall, in order to commemorate their efforts. Of these distance slabs, twenty have so far been discovered and though they probably do not represent the full complement of slabs erected, nevertheless they constitute a remarkably coherent group.[35]

The slabs are usually discussed in terms of their immediate context, and of their epigraphic content and significance. The overriding theme of the series is commemoration of conflict and conquest, the physical expansion of the boundaries of the Roman empire and the manifestation of that expansion by the building of a frontier earthwork. They also provide a snapshot of a harsher, more clinical attitude towards barbarian enemies than has been seen elsewhere through the study of earlier state-sanctioned works of art. It has already been discussed how on Trajan's Column there were celebrated the physical labours and construction works of the Roman army, as well as the army's martial power in achieving victory over the Dacians, both strands being elucidated exclusively through the medium of the artwork of the spiral frieze. In the case of the Antonine Wall reliefs, the artwork alludes only to the subjects of victory, legionary power as celebrated through display of individual unit symbols, and the fulfilment of religious and military duty. The matter of the construction of the wall is commemorated only in the inscriptions.

Out of the twenty Antonine distance slabs, only four will be discussed in detail here, as these four bear images of barbarians alongside other commemorative motifs and inscriptions. The largest, most elaborate and most significant slab comes from Bridgeness, West Lothian, towards the eastern end of the wall.[36] This consists of a central panel bearing an inscription, citing its dedicators as the Second Legion Augusta, flanked by two sculptured scenes, one of which portrays a Roman cavalryman and four barbarian figures. The cavalryman rides at a gallop, with a spear raised in his right hand, while in the foreground of the scene are the barbarian men in various poses, one seemingly ridden down by the charging horseman, a second falling to the ground with a broken-off spear shaft sticking out of his back, a third seated on the ground to the left. He looks away from the field of battle and gazes towards the viewer, while the fourth figure, a headless, evidently bound torso, sits to the right, his severed head lying on the ground next to his body.

It soon becomes apparent that rather than being a representation of a single cavalryman attacking four enemies, it may in fact be recording the fate of a single barbarian man who appears four times: the first time being overcome by the Roman cavalryman, and in his fourth and final appearance being shown as an executed prisoner. This is artistically very bold, with its startling juxtaposition of three separate scenes, linked thematically but temporally dislocated.[37] The battle scene quite obviously owed its inspiration to the horseman-and-fallen-enemy type of auxiliary cavalry tombstone of the first and second centuries which will be discussed in detail in Chapter Six.[38]

The second distance slab, from Hag Knowe in Dumbartonshire, survives only in part, the surviving fragment depicting a kneeling and bound male barbarian captive.[39] It can safely be assumed that a second, or pendant, barbarian would have occupied the same position on the other side of the slab, the central portion probably having borne an inscribed panel and possibly other figures or symbols. These barbarian figures were presumably symbols of a whole group or tribe in defeat rather than of individual captives.

The third slab bearing engravings of barbarians is from Summerston Farm, Lanarkshire.[40] Dedicated and erected again by the Second Legion, it bears two sculpted scenes, one on either side of the dedicatory inscription, and barbarians appear in both. In the right-hand scene a cavalryman, in an almost identical pose to that of the horseman on the Bridgeness slab, rides at a foe who stands or lies out of scene, while in the background a winged female deity, in all probability Victory, waits to crown the Roman victor with a wreath. In the foreground sit two male barbarians, both with their hands tied behind their back. Their shields lie discarded on the ground behind them. Presumably the pair are depicted to represent the final outcome of the cavalry charge and battle. In the left-hand scene a single barbarian male, again trussed up as a captive and with his shield behind, sits beneath the emblems of the victorious Roman army units.

The fourth distance slab comes from Hutcheson Hill, Bearsden, and was set up by the Twentieth Legion.[41] It shows an elaborately designed architectural setting, either a temple or, more likely, a triumphal arch, with figures placed in the central arched space and in the pedimented spaces on either side. The central scene depicts Victory once more crowning a member of the triumphant Roman forces, in this case a standard-bearer, while looking on from the sides are two bound barbarian captives, the line of their gaze suggesting that they are viewers of the victory ceremony.

Analysing these four slabs as a group, it is true to say that the rhetoric of victory and triumph represented makes no allowances for the humanity or honour of the defeated foe. There appears to be no magnanimity displayed towards the enemy nor any hint of respect for them either as a group or as individuals. In comparison to the auxiliary cavalryman tombstones discussed in Chapter Six, the Antonine Wall stones do not seem to tell of victory over worthy opponents, victory achieved by bravery, craft and guile, by individual skill and resourcefulness. Rather the slabs represented communal achievement, and thus the subsuming of the part or individual within the whole, and a victory that was in no way in doubt, something alluded to perhaps by the appearance of deities with the army in two scenes, and on the Bridgeness slab by the portrayal of the soldiers communing with the gods through sacrifice.[42]

On all four slabs barbarians figure as bound captives, while on the Bridgeness stone one is shown as having been subsequently executed by beheading. The captives are afforded no element of dignity, they are shown as less than men, objectified and exposed naked in their indignity. It could be argued that the curiously posed barbarian at the forefront of the Bridgeness slab, described by one authority as 'resigned and contemplative' and by another as being a stock image derived from the well-known 'mourning captive' motif, is in fact attempting to cover his nakedness and somehow to hide his shame and vulnerability.[43] The creation in this way of a visual narrative which objectified the barbarian men through the depiction of their dead, bound or mutilated bodies exiled them to a space more usually thought of as occupied by objectified women. Imperial power relations were here being written on the bodies of barbarian men as we have already seen them being written on the bodies of women.[44]

There may be some significance in the fact that these slabs were set up at the very fringe of the empire, on a newly established frontier, where Roman and barbarian relationships were brought into stark contrast. At this location, bodying forth the barbarian in a way that sealed and controlled his destiny would seem to be quite appropriate. With the abandonment of the Antonine Wall frontier in the AD 160s, it would appear, from what is known of the circumstances of the recovery of a number of the distance slabs, that they were each carefully taken down from their position on the earthwork and buried in a large pit nearby. Perhaps the potent symbolism of the distance slabs, a discourse of military might, of victory and of the debased nature of the peoples of the newly conquered territories, was too painful to contemplate in the light of the circumstances of the abandonment of the still relatively recently established frontier.[45]

A CONVENIENT CANVAS

It has been demonstrated how from the time of the emperors Marcus Aurelius and Commodus onwards there is a very significant trend in Roman imperial art towards the growing dehumanisation of the barbarians, through the graphic depiction of their fate at the hands of Roman forces. The extraordinarily harrowing scenes of battle, slaughter and carnage on the Column of Marcus Aurelius in Rome have been analysed in some detail above for the information that they provide on the manner in which these changes occurred and were manifested. The direct representation of battle on monuments in Rome itself was rare in the Augustan and Julio-Claudian eras and it was probably first and most significantly attempted on Trajan's Column.

The development of this trend reflected wider changes within certain sections of Roman society at the time, and changes in the value system of many of those involved in public life and affairs of state.[46] This trend can also be seen in military art, such as that from the Antonine Wall in Scotland discussed above, and some authorities would argue that this debasement and dehumanisation indeed had their origins in the military rather than the political sphere.[47] This may well be so, but the influence and operation of the army were part and parcel of the working of the state, particularly in that its operations and influences were cross-provincial. There would seem to be almost a kind of special pleading inherent in an argument that seeks to separate imperial policy from the actions of the guardians of that policy. These changes in attitude can also be seen reflected in private funerary art probably associated with senior military figures in the army of the time.

From the very heart of the city of Rome to the furthest frontier of the empire, in Scotland, the crisis within Roman society in the Antonine period was reflected in the art of the military and political spheres. The figure of the barbarian became a convenient canvas on which the fears and neuroses of the Roman state were indelibly drawn. While it would be somewhat naive and simplistic to describe this as a sign of the loss of innocence in Roman–barbarian relationships at this time, nevertheless the dramatic refocusing of the ways in which it was deemed acceptable to portray the enemies of Rome that took place in the seventy or so years between the

1 'The Dying Gaul'; Capitoline Museum, Rome. (*Photo: Author*)

2 'The Suicidal Gauls'; Museo Nazionale Romano, Palazzo Altemps, Rome.
(*Photo: Soprintendenza Archeologica di Roma*)

3 Battle between Romans and Gauls; Tomb of the Julii, Saint-Rémy. (*Photo: Author*)

4 The suggested Western barbarian child on the Ara Pacis, Rome. (*Photo: Author*)

5 The suggested Eastern barbarian child on the Ara Pacis, Rome. (*Photo: Author*)

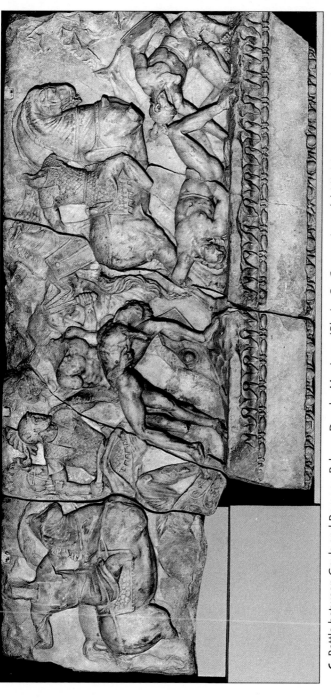

6 Battle between Gauls and Romans; Palazzo Ducale, Mantova. (Photo: Su Concessione del Ministero per i Beni e le Attività Culturali, Soprintendenza di Brescia, Cremona e Mantova)

7 Barbarian captives on a bier, Temple of Apollo Sosianus; Museo del Palazzo dei Conservatori, Rome. *(Photo: Deutsches Archäologisches Institut, Rome, 71:45)*

8 Gemma Augustea; Kunsthistoriches Museum, Vienna. (*Photo: Kunsthistoriches Museum*)

9 Barbarians bound to a trophy. Detail from the Alpine Trophy of Augustus, La Turbie. (*Photo: Jason Wood Photographs*)

10 Barbarian captives bound to a trophy, on the arch at Carpentras. (Photo: Author)

11 The Grand Camée de France. (*Photo: Bibliothèque Nationale de France*)

12 Claudius and Britannia relief from the Sebasteion at Aphrodisias. (*Illustration: Mark Breedon*)

13 Dacians retreating into a forest; Trajan's Column, Rome. (*Photo: © F.A. Lepper and S.S. Frere*)

14 Dacian women torture Roman prisoners; Trajan's Column, Rome. (*Photo: © F.A. Lepper and S.S. Frere*)

CXLV

384 385 386 387 NW22

15 The suicide of Decebalus; Trajan's Column, Rome. (*Photo: © F.A. Lepper and S.S. Frere*)

16 Roman soldier with Dacian's head grasped in his mouth; Trajan's Column, Rome. (*Photo: © F.A. Lepper and S.S. Frere*)

17 Scene of combat; Tropaeum Trajani, Adamklissi. (*Photo: Author, after Richmond 1967*)

18 The mounted Trajan in the thick of battle on a panel from the Great Trajanic Frieze, Rome; reset in the Arch of Constantine, Rome.
(*Illustration: Mark Breedon*)

19 Hadrian crushing a miniaturised barbarian, from Hieraptyna, Crete;
Archaeological Museum, Istanbul. (*Photo: Roger White*)

20 Pile of slaughtered barbarian bodies, Column of Marcus Aurelius, Rome.
(*Photo: Graham Norrie, after Petersen et al. 1896*)

21 Execution of prisoners; Column of Marcus Aurelius, Rome.
(Photo: Graham Norrie, after Petersen et al. 1896)

22 Woman pulled by the hair; Column of Marcus Aurelius, Rome.
(*Photo: Graham Norrie, after Petersen et al. 1896*)

23 Equestrian statue of Marcus Aurelius; Campidoglio, Rome. (*Photo: Author*)

24 The Portonaccio Sarcophagus; Museo Nazionale delle Terme, Rome.
(*Photo: Deutsches Archäologisches Institut, Rome. 61.1399*)

25 Clementia Sarcophagus; Vatican Museums, Rome. (*Photo: Author*)

26 The Via Appia Sarcophagus; Capitoline Museum, Rome. (*Photo: Author*)

27 Detail of the Bridgeness Legionary Distance Slab.
(*Photo: © National Museums of Scotland*)

28 Roman soldiers and barbarian prisoners on a column base on the Arch of Septimius Severus, Rome. (*Photo: Author*)

29 Barbarian prisoners on the Arch of the Argentarii, Rome.
(*Photo: Deutsches Archäologisches Institut. 59.749*)

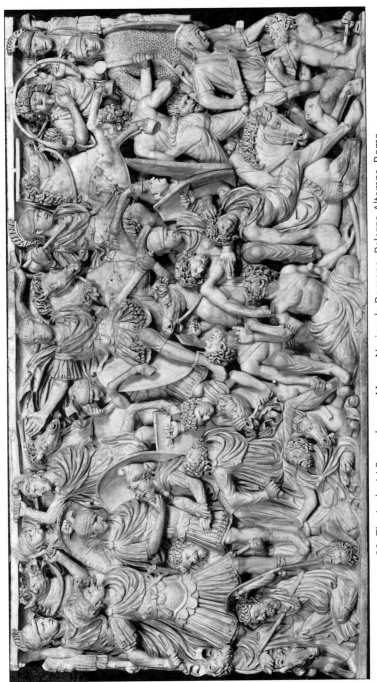

30 The Ludovisi Sarcophagus; Museo Nazionale Romano, Palazzo Altemps, Rome. *(Photo: Soprintendenza Archeologica di Roma)*

31 Victory and barbarian captive; from the Arcus Novus, Boboli Gardens, Florence. (*Photo: Roger White*)

32 The Arch of Constantine, Rome. (*Photo: Author*)

33 Sarcophagus of Helena; Vatican Musuems, Rome. (*Photo: Deutsches Archäologisches Institut. 63.2339A*)

34 The Stilicho Diptych; Cathedral Treasury, Monza.
(*Photo: © Museo del Duomo di Monza*)

35 Base of the Obelisk of Theodosius, Istanbul. (*Photo: Roger White*)

36 Campana Plaque showing barbarian prisoners in a triumph. (*Photo:* © *British Museum*)

37 Decoration on a gladiator's helmet from Pompeii.
(*Illustration: Mark Breedon, after Petrikovits 1983*)

38 Column base depicting chained barbarian prisoners, Mainz Landesmuseum.
(*Photo: Roger White*)

39 The Smaller Ludovisi Sarcophagus; Museo Nazionale Romano, Palazzo Altemps, Rome. (*Photo: Soprintendenza Archeologica di Roma*)

40 The tombstone of Rufus Sita; Gloucester City Museum. (*Photo: © Gloucester City Museum and Art Gallery*)

41 A *balteus*; Museo Romano di Brescia. (*Photo: Museo Romano di Brescia*)

42 Tile depicting a Gaulish captive; British Museum.
(*Photo: © British Museum*)

43 'The Prisoner', probably a Gaul; Museo Romano di Brescia. (*Photo: Museo Romano di Brescia*)

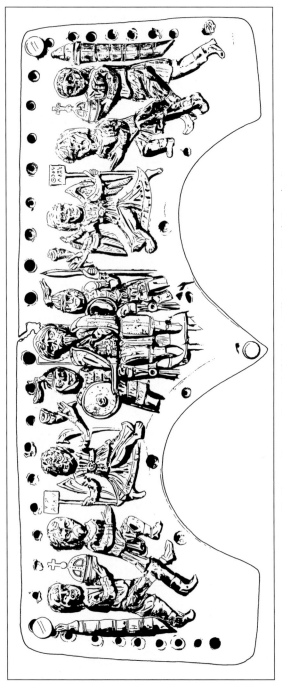

44 Decoration on the Agilulf Helmet. (*Illustration: Mark Breedon*)

erection of Trajan's Column and the Column of Marcus Aurelius must have echoed political realities, imperial expediency and a perceived public need for reassurance. There was to be no overall return to the ambiguity of previous eras, nor was the idealisation of the barbarian again to be part of the Roman imperial rhetoric of power.

FIVE

THE ENEMY WITHIN

Although the second-century crisis on the frontiers of the empire was resolved by the wars pursued by Lucius Verus and Marcus Aurelius, this solution was to prove only a temporary one. Two new large confederacies of German peoples beyond the Rhine and Danube frontiers, the Franks and the Alamanns, and other expansionist tribes, the Goths and the Vandals, exerting pressure on the Danube, from the third century were to become increasingly threatening to the stability of the empire. In the east, the Parthian menace was replaced by that of Persia under the Sassanid dynasty.

Together with this, the increasing barbarianisation of the Roman army in the later third and fourth centuries, with extensive recruitment of troops from beyond the frontiers of the empire, provided a new context for the use of barbarian imagery in Roman imperial art. The state now needed the aid of certain barbarian groups to bolster its power and to defend its very existence. It could be said that this study now comes full circle, with the enemy without now becoming, by invitation, the enemy within. The external pressures on the empire also contributed towards internal disharmony that created an arena in which, at best, intrigue and plotting took place among the military and political elites of Rome and the wider empire, but which at worst led to the rise of usurpers and civil conflict.

In order to pursue these themes of external threat and internal instability, attention will be paid in this chapter to the art of the Severan dynasty, including the arches of Septimius Severus in Rome and Leptis Magna, of the Tetrarchy, and finally of the era of

116

Constantine. Some consideration will also be given to a resurgence of the commissioning of private battle sarcophagi in the Severan period and the production of luxury items utilising political imagery at the imperial courts of the fourth and fifth centuries.

ORDER FROM DISORDER

At the very end of the second century, following a period of civil war, Septimius Severus came to power, his rise not only being connected with his victory over his rivals for the imperial purple but also with his resounding successes over the Parthians, historic adversaries of Rome in the east, that led to his adoption by acclamation of the title Parthicus. These victories were commemorated at Rome by the dedication of a victory arch in the Forum in AD 203 which also celebrated the founding and legitimacy of the Severan dynasty.[1]

Most of the decorative programme of the arch was relegated to four relatively small relief panels, two on each side of the monument. These panels depicted the siege and capture of the four Parthian cities or strongholds of Nisibis, Edessa, Seleucia and Ctesiphon, and were composed in such a way as to suggest that they may have been based upon battle paintings, such as were carried in triumphal processions in Rome, and whose use was part of a long tradition stretching back to Hellenistic times.[2] An *adlocutio* scene concludes the portrayal of the capture of Ctesiphon.

Though now quite badly damaged, partly as a result of a fire in the Forum in antiquity, the relief scenes display many of the stylistic traits of a state art that had to some extent moved away from the tradition of grand narrative in the commemoration of historic events. The figures are very small, while no attempt was made either to produce a continuous story-line or to create linking scenes.

In Scene III one register of decoration depicts an event during the siege of Seleucia when a body of Parthian cavalrymen flees the area, the leading horseman who turns back to look at the now-condemned city probably intended to be their leader Vologases, retreating to fight on elsewhere. Soon afterwards, the city surrenders, its defenders holding up their arms in submission, while one man bravely attempts to get away from the city by swimming across the River Tigris.

Beneath the four panels is a narrow, band-like register inhabited by low-relief figures taking part in a triumphal procession, these figures being even smaller and less well realised than those in the panels above. The scene has a desultory, rather than triumphalist, ambience which is emphasised further by the wide spacing of the figures. Included here are Parthian captives and paraded booty from the wars carried in carts or waggons, but the emperor is nowhere to be seen. At the culmination of the procession, a Parthian prisoner kneels before a seated Roma, larger in scale than the human figures, and begs for clemency. In the centre of the band, and seemingly blocking the route of the procession, sits a slumped and dejected personification of Parthia, again depicted at a larger scale than the tiny human figures traipsing along in the parade.[3]

On the bases of each of the eight free-standing columns of the arch, four on each side of the monument, are carved Roman soldiers leading bound or chained male Parthian captives, dressed in their distinctive traditional costume. A single captive appears on the base's sides and a pair of captives on the front, one of whom carries a small child in his arms. This image may have been deployed here for its relevance to the Severan reverence of children which was reflected in the emperor's relationship with his own sons and the linked desire to recreate dynastic stability, and in his alimentary programme targeted at the children of Rome and Italy.[4]

It is difficult to see, though, how the perhaps motherless barbarian child was intended to be a symbol of the emperor's benevolent attitude towards the young, unless it was in a contrastive way. Women were conspicuously absent from the sculptural programme of the Trajanic arch at Benevento and indeed on that arch a specific link was made between fathers and children, and between the role of the emperor as both father of his country and provider for its children. Women were equally and probably deliberately also absent from the Severan arch, aside from the personified figure of Parthia.

The inscription on the arch raises interesting questions about the relative importance of visual as opposed to textual images at this time. The lengthy text occupied virtually the entire attic of the arch, in a position that on earlier monuments would have been occupied by relief panels. The inscription established the legitimacy of Severus and his sons, before the alteration of the inscription as part of the *damnatio memoriae* of Geta, and praised their role in restoring order against internal enemies, and in extending the empire for the benefit of the Roman people.[5]

Another monument in Rome celebrating the Severan dynasty, though in this case not a state-sponsored dedication, is the so-called Porta Argentariorum or Arch of the Argentarii in the Forum Boarium.[6] This monument was really a gate rather than an arch, and was erected by the guild of silversmiths in AD 204. The decorated panels on the arch largely concerned themselves with the secular and religious duties of the imperial family, but on one panel two Roman soldiers are depicted with two male captives, probably Parthians. Victories appear elsewhere on the monument, as does a decorative panel depicting military standards and trophy arms and armour. The use of images of defeated barbarians here perhaps acknowledged that such figures were seen as being indivisible from the person of the emperor, whether specific historical victories were being celebrated or not.

The location of the arch in Rome itself was significant. The symbiotic relationship between imperial action and economic well-being at Rome, in Italy and across the wider empire, could account for the inclusion of such motifs in this context, an implicit link that had not really been made in state art since the time of Trajan.[7] That such a link was suggested on a monument like this, and that some sanction or co-operation from the imperial family can be assumed, is intriguing.

During the French occupation of Pavia in northern Italy in 1797 there is recorded the destruction of an equestrian statue of Severus, known as the Regisole.[8] This statue type, including apparently the figure of a defeated barbarian crouching beneath the front hoof of the emperor's mount, probably derives from a Domitianic prototype, as discussed in Chapter Three, and it is highly likely that the Pavia statue was a copy of a Severan work in the Forum at Rome.[9]

Outside Rome, perhaps the grandest of the state monuments of the Severan period was erected in the emperor's home city of Leptis Magna in Libya, probably in or around AD 203 or AD 207 on the occasion of an imperial visit to the city.[10] This quadrifons arch, that is in the form of an open square with an arch through each of the four sides of the square, was embellished with a programme of sculptural adornment that celebrated the emperor in a style befitting both his local origins and his political office. In contrast with the decorative scheme on the Severan arch in Rome it was archaic in style and composition and in its sheer lavishness. In addition to two groups of relief panels, the outer facades of the monument also bore decoration in the form of captive barbarians, trophies, Victories, garlands and mythological scenes. However, only some of the historical relief panels, now in Tripoli Museum, will be considered in detail here.

A scene of triumphal procession of Roman army units, with the emperor and his two sons depicted standing in a *quadriga* or four-horse chariot, was juxtaposed with a pendant procession of captives in eastern garb to the right. In the Roman military procession are soldiers carrying a bier or litter in which sits a captive woman, perhaps someone of importance, and a small child who tries to attract her attention. Another child is being dragged along in the procession of captives.[11] It is likely that this is a generic triumphal scene rather than the depiction of a specific triumph, which some authorities at one time believed to have taken place in Leptis Magna as part of the ceremony of the imperial visit. However, the presence of the children and the artist's strategy of drawing the viewer's attention particularly to them does add a distinctly emotional subtext to what was otherwise a relatively standardised scene of imperial triumph and power.

On another relief panel from the Leptis arch, Julia Domna, second wife of Septimius Severus and mother to Caracalla and Geta, and thus in this context to be viewed as the mother of the Severan dynasty, appears together with a male figure in the guise of Hercules, mounted Roman soldiers and, once more, captive barbarian women being carried on litters. Perhaps there was some specific significance here in terms of returning to the traditional contrastive roles of the fertile Roman woman and the barren barbarian woman, or it may be one of only a few instances in which martial imagery was linked directly to a female member of the imperial family and where military success underwriting the well-being of a particular dynastic house was presented as being also good for Rome and for the empire as a whole. This would certainly have agreed with her role as *Mater Castrorum* (Mother of the Fort), a title which the Severan women often adopted. This would allow barbarians to become attributes of other members of the imperial family and not just the preserve of the emperor alone.[12] As we shall see when the sarcophagus of the empress Helena is discussed, the presence of martial scenes on her coffin has led some art historians to question the significance of the iconography in the context of the burial of an imperial woman.[13]

A frieze depicting Severus and his sons doing battle with eastern barbarians comes from Cyrene, again in Libya, but it is uncertain from what kind of monument this fragment may have derived. An elaborate architectural facade at Corinth, Greece, with colossal figures of male barbarians as caryatids and bases decorated with standard scenes involving captives, men, women and children, probably also commemorated Severus' Parthian victories,[14] but in a more dispassionate Greek style.

On a relief of uncertain provenance, now in Poland, the emperor Caracalla appears in company with his mother Julia Domna in another scene that married imperial themes of victory and dynastic celebration in an unashamed manner.[15] The bearded Caracalla reaches an arm out towards a trophy at the foot of which cower two miniaturised, bearded barbarian male captives, both of whom look up towards the figure of the emperor towering above them. In one hand Julia Domna holds a palm frond and is here portrayed in the guise of a wingless Victory. With her other hand she places the victor's laurel wreath on her son's head. Given the special relationship between the imperial women of the third century and the Roman army, it is not especially surprising to see Julia Domna appearing here in this role, particularly given the stress laid on dynastic stability in Severan art in general.

REPOSITORIES OF MEMORY

There was also in the Severan period a resurgence in the popularity of battle sarcophagi, previously particularly favoured in the Antonine period. This, perhaps, should not be surprising, given the prevalence of martial imagery in Severan state art, though the portrayals of battle scenes on the Severan arches in Rome and at Leptis Magna were not as obsessively concerned with the nature and outcome of battle and war as those on the Aurelian column or on contemporary battle sarcophagi.

It is interesting that the Severan battle sarcophagi, rather than taking as their principal theme the wars between Rome and Parthia, as might have been expected, largely employed mythological subject matter. On one of the best examples, a sarcophagus in the Vatican Museums, Achilles is depicted slaying Penthesilea,[16] among a tangled and intertwined battlefield scene that looked back to the type of dense compositional mêlée that was to reach its apotheosis with the Ludovisi sarcophagus. Dated to the second quarter of the third century, the Achilles and Penthesilea sarcophagus is also noteworthy in that the faces of the two main protagonists would appear to be portraits of a couple, perhaps a husband and wife who commissioned the work, he in all probability having served in the army at some stage in his career. This was perhaps a strange choice of subject for a couple to make, given the fact that Achilles had just killed Penthesilea, a deed that he himself is about to come to regret by looking into her dead face, but a deed that nevertheless he cannot undo.

An unusual, later example of a battle sarcophagus is the Ludovisi sarcophagus, probably dating to *c.* AD 260.[17] Found near Porta San Lorenzo in Rome, the whole body of the sarcophagus is taken up by a crowded battle scene involving Roman cavalry and infantrymen, though the composition is less claustrophobic than that of the Portonaccio sarcophagus discussed in Chapter Four. The mostly bearded, long-haired barbarian adversaries are either Goths or a generalised, non-specific barbarian group. They are largely confined to the lower portions of the scene, as fallen and wounded bodies.

Two of the barbarians wear soft, Phrygian-style caps. One of these men is being attacked by a Roman soldier, his body twisted around in an uncomfortable and unrealistic pose, who appears to be pulling his beard. However, it is not this oddity that first captures the viewer's eye, rather it is the figure of a mounted Roman officer, his horse rearing up in the centre of the mêlée as the officer faces towards the viewer and holds up his right arm, palm extended, in some kind of command or gesture. This man appears to be both at the centre of the action and yet outside of the scene by reason of his dress – he wears no helmet and carries no weapon – and of his stance, which seems curious in the context of the battle. His facial expression also suggests a lack of engagement with the events unfolding around him, and indeed his distant gaze would well fit the description of a state of transcendent spirituality assigned to many imperial personages in the art of Late Antiquity.

The identity of the deceased military man for whom the sarcophagus was commissioned remains uncertain. While claims that he was an imperial figure are not widely accepted, it is possible that he could have been Hostilianus or Herennius Etruscus, two brothers and high-ranking military figures who both died, coincidentally, in AD 251.[18]

The body of the sarcophagus and its lid somehow became separated, and it is thought that a lid now in the Römisch-Germanisch Zentralmuseum in Mainz, Germany probably belonged with the Ludovisi sarcophagus.[19] However, the sarcophagus lid likewise offers no clues to the identity of its occupant, as the panel that would have carried a painted inscription is now blank. Beneath this panel are four mourning captive barbarians before a trophy, two seated and two standing, while to the right a group of six male barbarians and two children, placed towards the front of the composition, are being marshalled into the presence of the military commander to seek clemency. One child looks up to, and holds the hand of, the man behind him, while the other looks towards the Roman general seated on a raised podium. A Roman officer who has accompanied the barbarians into the presence of his commander places his hand on the top of the second child's head in a protective gesture that adds to the poignancy of this particular *clementia* scene.

The seated general holds out his arm in a gesture virtually identical to that of the equestrian figure on the sarcophagus body below. To the left is a large portrait of a Roman woman holding a scroll or will and standing before a drape being held by two servants. She must have been either the wife or mother of the deceased. It has been suggested that this is not a representation of a traditional, generic *clementia* scene. The events on the sarcophagus lid do not appear to relate to the pleading of a group of dejected and defeated barbarians, as the individuals depicted are not in the bedraggled state so typical of such scenes in imperial art. Rather what is represented may be a diplomatic scene, in which friendly barbarian envoys are being formally introduced into the general's presence, in order to complete some pact or treaty, and the children may be present here in the role of hostages, as has been suggested was the fate of the Gaulish children portrayed on one of the Boscoreale cups.[20]

Such an interpretation of the scene on the sarcophagus lid would account for the relaxed and accommodating attitude of the Roman officer towards the small child standing next to him. Even if accepted as a diplomatic scene, and one comparable to the Lugdunum event on the Boscoreale cup, it should not be forgotten that the giving of hostages in this manner nevertheless was something that, even if not taking place under direct threat or duress, was the result of a severe imbalance of power between barbarians and Romans.

SAFETY IN NUMBERS

For much of the third century, crises on the frontiers, civil wars and the resulting instability and uncertainty at Rome were reflected in a virtual moratorium on public building in the capital and on the erection of commemorative monuments there. Indeed, this period was one in which few significant state monuments were built. It is therefore not until much later in the century that the subject of this study can be returned to.

The establishment of a new, innovative form of imperial rule –

the Tetrarchy – under the emperor Diocletian, was commemorated, along with that emperor's own individual achievements, with the erection of the monument known as the Arcus Novus in AD 293. Set up on the Via Lata in Rome, the actual form of the arch is unknown, for unlike many other such Roman monuments it was not depicted on coin issues of the time and it was taken down in the fifteenth century without any record being made.[21] However, the new era of political stability brought about in Rome at this time was reflected in a return to the creation of artworks capable of putting across to the populace the ideas and ethos behind the new regime.

Of those surviving fragments that can be confidently assigned to the original monument, it is two pedestal bases that were eventually reused as landscape decoration in the Boboli Gardens in Florence that are most germane to this study. The monument also incorporated sculptural and building fragments from other, earlier structures – such reused pieces generally being referred to as *spolia* – most probably including some from the first-century Britannic Victory Arch of the emperor Claudius, which had stood quite close by on the Via Lata.[22] The selection of these pieces would not have been a random exercise, nor would it have been undertaken on purely aesthetic grounds. The ideological motives behind the selection, as far as they can be tentatively reconstructed, will be considered below after a description of the monument's overall appearance and sculptural programme.

One pedestal has on two of its faces scenes with barbarians. In one scene, a bound, male barbarian captive is depicted walking ahead of his Roman keeper. From a stylistic and compositional point of view it is interesting to note that the captive's state of imprisonment is further emphasised by his being positioned in the very centre of the scene, confined by the frame of the pedestal face, while the figure of the Roman soldier, the captor, is only partially in the scene. He bleeds into the frame.

On an adjacent face, the figure of Victory, in flowing dress and holding a palm frond in her right hand, is depicted standing next to a trophy of arms and armour, beneath which kneels a diminuitive figure of a male barbarian, again with his arms tied behind his back. Here the small stature of this figure was a compositional device to suggest the general subservence of this particular barbarian. He was simply an attribute of Victory in this particular case, and was as unreal as the disembodied artefacts that made up the trophy above him. Similar figures appear on the second pedestal, though there are some relatively minor variations in the physiognomy and appearance of the barbarians shown there.

The reused Claudian fragments have been described in detail in Chapter Two, and consideration will therefore be given here to the matter of their selection, in terms of how it may have represented an ideological repossession of their imagery, and of concepts connected with that imagery. As Diana Kleiner has pointed out, the very fact that one of the Tetrarchic rulers at the time of the erection of the Arcus Novus was the emperor Constantius Chlorus, who had himself gained significant military victories in Britain over the breakaway state of Carausius and Allectus, establishes a conceptual link between the two emperors.[23] That the emperor was indeed subsequently to die in Britain, at his military headquarters in York during a further campaign, adds poignancy to the link.

Obviously it is not possible to offer any overall interpretation of the Arcus Novus's programme of sculptures based on the few fragments which are known today. As with any imperial monument it would have carried a propaganda message connected to the policies and achievements of its sponsor, as well as itself being symbolic of a return to stability in Rome under the rule of the Tetrarchy. Indeed, in order to celebrate ten years of joint rule by the four Tetrarchs, the so-called Decennalia relief was set up in the Forum at Rome in AD 303.[24] Again, little of this monument survives, just the basal plinth of one of five columns, one face of which is decorated with figures of Victories holding up a shield which bears an inscription commemorating the anniversary. Under the shield crouch a male and female barbarian, while trophies are depicted on either side of the figures of the Victories.

Another Tetrarchic commemorative monument of considerable size and significance was set up in Thessalonica, in northern Greece.[25] The Arch of Galerius was built to celebrate both the successes of the emperor, particularly his spectacular victory over the Persians in AD 297, and the stability and revitalisation brought to the affairs of the empire by the rule of the Tetrarchs. The arch was part of an extensive, palatial complex in Thessalonica that recalled the large-scale integrated architectural schemes of earlier days in Rome.

Galerius was a military man who rose through the ranks of the army and received due recognition of his outstanding martial qualities by his selection first as Caesar in the eastern empire and then by marriage alliance and military triumph to become Augustus there upon the abdication of Diocletian. The victory over King Narses of Persia, after an initial reverse in fortunes in the field earlier in the same year, was of major significance for the empire as a whole and led some commentators, perhaps somewhat unimaginatively, to hail Galerius as the new Alexander the Great.

Discussion of the arch will concentrate on the sculptural scenes on the faces of the two surviving, out of four original, piers. These scenes are self-contained and 'stacked', one above the other, on each face of the piers. A scene of the equestrian emperor crushing or trampling his foe[26] is in the tradition of Hellenistic battle painting, so familiar by now from numerous earlier Roman monuments and on coin issues of earlier reigns. The scene had a purely symbolic value and set the emperor's victory over the Persians into an unbroken line stretching back to Trajan's trampling of Decebalus on the Great Trajanic Frieze.[27] There are also echoes here, though doubtless unconscious ones as it is highly unlikely that these works were known to anyone in the west, of Shapur I's Sassanian victory monuments, with the emperor Valerian depicted in shame and defeat. These monuments will be discussed in detail in Chapter Six.[28]

One, and possibly two scenes make reference to the historically attested capture of the harem of Narses, an act that is loaded with symbolism and which again evokes earlier episodes when the women of a particular tribe or country became virtual pawns in the actions of imperial policy. Generally accepted as linked to this incident is a scene of supplication where a delegation sent by Narses appears and kneels before Galerius and a contingent of his troops, probably in the hope of securing the release of the women. Curiously, and perhaps significantly, the emperor is also accompanied by the figure of a female deity, perhaps Roma, who herself leads a number of other female figures who may be personifications of other Italian or provincial towns or cities. The appearance of these symbolic women, in thrall to the power of Rome, cannot have been anything other than a juxtaposition of these now 'civilised' women with the foreign 'barbarian' women from the harem of Narses. Reference may also have been made here to the fate of the Sabine women in the early mythology surrounding Rome's foundation.[29]

The scene in which Galerius and his three co-tetrarchs appeared is also worthy of note. Galerius is shown in combat, possibly with Narses, while the other three are depicted with small barbarians either crouched at, or under, their feet. This was a scene of symbolic triumphalism. The miniaturisation of the barbarian so that his appearance was simply as an attribute of an emperor probably had its origins in the Trajanic period. The line-up of three emperors in such a pose was particularly emphatic and striking, this tripling of the motif perhaps further emphasising the united power and solidarity of the tetrarchs.

RECLAIMING THE PAST

In the discussion of the Great Trajanic Frieze in Chapter Three, mention was made of the fact that portions of this monument were subsequently reused in the decorative scheme of the Arch of Constantine in Rome. Dated to AD 312–15, this arch was erected both to celebrate ten years of Constantine's reign and to commemorate his significant and crucial victory over the usurper Maxentius at the Battle of the Milvian Bridge.[30] The Trajanic sculptures were not the only reused monumental fragments in the arch, and consideration needs to be given to whether the selection of sculptures for reuse and incorporation in the new work took into account any aspect of the presence of barbarians in these scenes, and, if so, what this choice and recontextualisation can tell us about these images or about Roman–barbarian relationships in the age of Constantine.[31]

The reused Trajanic Frieze fragments included two pieces

that depicted the emperor himself, in a scene of *adventus* and on horseback trampling a Dacian warrior. The portrait head of Trajan in both cases was recarved to become the head of Constantine. At first this seems easy to understand. The commission simply required some generic imperial scenes, scenes of *adventus* and victory being more than satisfactory in this respect, though the contemporary emperor needed to be in these scenes. But was this just a pragmatic strategy of reuse of readily available sculptural material? Frieze fragments depicting battles between Roman troops and Dacians were also reset in the attic of the arch.

The process of the selection of the material for reuse would have involved considerable ingenuity on the part of the supervising artist, and indeed the tradition and technique of reuse and incorporation of such *spolia* must have been viewed as an element as significant as the carving of new images in the art of Late Antiquity, something which has already been discussed in relation to the same process being employed in the construction of the Diocletianic Arcus Novus using fragments from a Claudian monument. They represented an establishing of links not only with times past and with past imperial figures or triumphs but also, in this case, with an art of the past – for the Trajanic fragments were more or less classical in style and execution – and with a past way of viewing and perceiving the world through motifs, imagery and symbolism.

Was the Trajanic monument still standing *in situ* at the time and was it therefore now deliberately dismantled in order to obtain the required fragments? Had the monument been previously taken down or so damaged that it needed to be dismantled? If the latter were the case, then had the frieze been in storage somewhere in Rome, awaiting some future decision to be made on its fate, or had the intention been to store it in perpetuity?

In addition to the Trajanic frieze fragments, a number of free-standing statues of male Dacian captives, four on each of the long sides of the monument on top of its projecting columns, are also almost certainly of a Trajanic date, and derived most likely from the Forum of that period.[32] As the Dacians were, by the time of Constantine, historic enemies rather than any longer posing a real or contemporary threat to Roman power, it is probably in this historical context that their appearance on the arch should be understood. They would seem here to represent generic barbarians rather than ethnically specific barbarian figures, or they were simply being employed as visual mnemonic devices to link Constantine with Trajan. Their presence must also have been a cautionary one, to remind the Roman viewer of the fact that, due to pressures on the empire in the later third century, the Romans had been forced to evacuate Dacia in AD 271, and that the need for vigilance against the barbarian foe was as real in the era of Constantine as it had been at the time of Trajan.

Roundels from a Hadrianic monument were also reused on the arch, but as none of these portrays barbarians they will not be discussed here. Also reused were eight relief panels from a lost, major second-century Antonine monument, possibly a triumphal arch, as suggested by the nature of the scenes on the reused fragments. These included barbarian submission scenes. One, described in full detail in Chapter Four, involved an aged barbarian man physically supported by a youth. Another was a more traditional portrayal of imperial *clementia* towards two kneeling male barbarians.[33] Again, the emperor's head was recarved to become that of Constantine.

Of the newly commissioned Constantinian artworks, the most significant is a frieze that encircles the monument and both commemorated contemporary historical events and alluded to the virtues of the emperor. The style of the frieze, with its small, awkwardly posed figures in most instances appearing in scenes devoid of background and lacking in depth or perspective, is that of the art of Late Antiquity, in contrast to the style of the earlier, reused classical pieces. The frieze depicts the emperor's troops marching out of Milan, the siege and capture of Verona, the Battle of the Milvian Bridge, Constantine's victorious entrance into Rome, his address to the Roman people in the Forum, and finally his distribution of largesse to them. These six major scenes are not in the form of a continuous narrative but are broken up into small scenes of individual footsoldiers or mounted troops.

The other Constantinian elements of the arch are spandrels

portraying Victories and seasons, river gods and various pagan deities, and pedestals containing variously Victories, Roman soldiers, trophies and barbarian captives, and planetary figures in roundels. The pedestals are not thought to be exact copies of the pedestals on the earlier Arch of Septimius Severus and on the Diocletianic Arcus Novus, but rather to be adaptions of these exemplars.[34] This could again be construed as a direct and deliberate allusion to past emperors and past monuments, though ones that on this occasion were not stripped for *spolia*.

The three visible faces of each of the eight Constantinian pedestals are variously taken up by Victory standing over the small figure of a kneeling male barbarian, Roman soldiers escorting a captive and bound male barbarian, and trophies beneath which sit barbarian families. Both northern and eastern barbarians are represented here. The presence of barbarian children is probably highly significant. A certain stressing of the appearance of the captive and tamed barbarian, or enemy in general, again further emphasised by the redeployment of the free-standing statues of the full-size Dacian prisoners on the upper part of the arch, could relate to the freeing of Maxentian supporters by Constantine as one of the acts of *clementia* to celebrate his *decennalia*.

The sculptural programme of the Arch of Constantine, consisting as it does of both old and new carvings, cannot simply be dismissed as a hotchpotch of easily available, suitably sized and shaped fragments reset around a poorly executed, post-classical historical scene, along with badly copied and misunderstood motifs from earlier times. If, as is argued here, selection and composition were integral to the message of the monument, then the message must be uncovered.

In looking backwards in time, by direct use of past sculptures and by indirect allusion and reference represented by the copying and adaptation of motifs and images, the arch was being used to make a statement about its own time. It may be that Constantine wished to be seen as heir to an imperial tradition that predated the Tetrarchy, a tradition that linked him with Trajan, Hadrian, Marcus Aurelius and Septimius Severus, rather than with a system that had ultimately encouraged usurpers, and indeed had brought civil war to the very gates of Rome. While Constantine was celebrating his victory over a Roman, Maxentius, on the monument – and undeniably that remains its main theme and purpose – this is diluted by the profusion of other images and devices on the arch and by the relatively small scale and size of the historical frieze depicting the winning of that victory.

References to the past here may have been intended as a tribute to the Roman army. Constantine had been hailed as Augustus by the army in Britain, following the death of his father there, and it was the continued loyalty of his troops that brought him victory in the civil war and ensured that he entered Rome triumphant. Establishing legitimacy for these forces could have been achieved by reference to Trajan, that most military of emperors, to Hadrian with his vast frontier work in Britain still partially intact, to Marcus Aurelius whose reign was largely taken up by campaigning, and to Severus who like Constantine's father died on campaign in Britain. Certainly, the presence of numerous barbarians, historic enemies from both the east and the north, attested to the victory of Rome against her previous enemies in general. Maxentius, while not obviously a barbarian, could nevertheless now be defined, like the barbarians, as an enemy of Rome, if only in the eyes of the new Constantinian regime. Such a conclusion is reinforced by the language used in contemporary panegyrics.

While in his earlier career Constantine had accompanied the emperors Diocletian and Galerius on a number of military expeditions, his own reign was not marked by campaigning against barbarians on any significant scale, which makes their appearance in such numbers on the artwork of the arch all the more puzzling and in need of careful consideration.

This leads on, particularly in the light of the fact that Constantine's reign saw the adoption of Christianity as the official religion of the Roman imperial house and of the state, to a brief consideration of whether the imperial iconography that employed the images of barbarians in such a complex way was able to adapt these images for use in an altogether different religious milieu. From now on, the state's attitude to those who were deemed to be 'other' must also take account of 'other' as including non-Christian peoples. Having discussed so many examples of barbarian peoples kneeling in obeisance and submission to Rome, images dating from the first century up to the fourth, it is hardly surprising to note that this motif was in all probability the inspiration for that of the submission of the three kings or magi to Christ.

Indeed, it is not just the form of the motif that links it to the imperial iconography of barbarians. There is also the fact that these 'three wise men' were from the east and were therefore usually portrayed in Roman art as Persians. Such a scene is found on the base of Theodosius' obelisk in Constantinople, though perhaps the most striking and visually sumptuous example of the motif is to be found on one of the sixth-century wall mosaics in the Church of Sant' Apollinare Nuovo in Ravenna, northern Italy.[35] Seated on a throne and attended by angels sits the Virgin Mary with the infant Jesus on her lap. From the right comes a procession of the three Persian magi, clearly identifiable from their eastern headgear and dress, each bearing gifts and followed by a line of gift-bearing female virgins. Here, the homage of the barbarians is not directly within the context of submission to Roman imperial authority, nor is there any conflating of Roman imperial earthly power and that of Christ in heaven, an example of which will be discussed below. However, given the imperial connection with the foundation of this church under Theoderic and the administrative status of Ravenna, perhaps viewers would be expected to make such a connection for themselves.

ON FEMALE POWER

The issue of gender-related imagery, and the potentially differing expectations, experiences and perceptions among Roman viewers of particular works of art depicting barbarians, whether male or female, may have had a significant bearing on the reading of these images, and on the motives behind their creation. This issue has already been touched upon in the discussion of the appearance of Julia Domna on the Severan arch at Leptis Magna, in scenes that also include images of barbarians.[36]

Discussion will now turn to the porphyry sarcophagus of a female imperial figure, thought to be Helena, mother of the emperor Constantine, who died in AD 329 and whose sarcophagus was placed in an imperial tomb on the Via Labicana in Rome.[37] The heavily restored sarcophagus is enormous, the carved figures on it being about a quarter life-size. It is interesting to consider in this case whether the iconography of the sarcophagus, which includes martial scenes with barbarians, was in any way related to the gender of its occupant or whether her gender was submerged or subsumed within her imperial persona and position, something that was already hinted at by the very material – 'imperial' porphyry – out of which the sarcophagus was made.

The two long sides, and both short sides of the sarcophagus are decorated with a battle scene that consists of two registers of widely spaced figures, the upper being charging or parading Roman cavalrymen and the lower being barbarians, the majority of whom are unarmed and in many cases bound, and who seem to be being ridden down or trampled by the horsemen. On one of the short sides are five bound or chained male barbarian captives accompanied by a mounted escort of two Roman cavalrymen. Other carved figures on the sarcophagus include male and female busts, putti holding swags or garlands, reclining female deities and a lion on the lid, but these will not be considered further here as they do not appear to be anything more than purely decorative funerary motifs in the classical tradition.

The placing of the decorative scheme around all four sides of the sarcophagus, with the Roman and barbarian figures seemingly thus engaged in an unending and continuous struggle, may have been both symbolic and compositional, with the sarcophagus being placed standing in a central position in its mausoleum where it would have been viewed in the round. This message of eternal conflict and eternal victory for Rome is similar to the message of eternal defeat and subjugation created through work in the round on the much earlier Trajanic Trophy at Adamklissi.[38]

It has been argued by a number of scholars that this sarcophagus may originally have been commissioned for a male member of the imperial family and that, for whatever reason, it was subsequently used for the burial of Helena. This interpretation assumes that such martial decoration was gender-specific and represented art made by men for men.[39] However, if Helena's power and position placed her 'beyond gender', then the iconography of the sarcophagus seems entirely appropriate to the commemoration of a female imperial figure, besides which narratives of the defeat of barbarian foes were as much about the very state of being a Roman as they were about being a Roman man. Battles with the barbarian enemies of Rome, and their defeat, signified Roman power and the historical legacy of a power that had been celebrated in scenes like these for hundreds of years.

In further support of the theory that this sarcophagus was not originally intended for Helena it has been argued that her Christianity was not represented by any explicit Christian symbolism on the casket, as might have been expected. However, overtly Christian symbolism was also absent on the Arch of Constantine. Here Trajanic and Antonine *spolia* recorded historic triumphs over barbarian opponents, and contemporary military victories by Constantine over enemies internal to the empire were celebrated by newly commissioned work. Taken together they represented the triumph and celebration of legitimate imperial authority. That this authority now also happened to be Christian was something that could equally be taken 'as read' in the case of the sculptural programme of Helena's sarcophagus.

IN THE EYE OF THE BEHOLDER

The tradition of the production of court cameos and gems, a particularly noteworthy characteristic of the Augustan and Julio-Claudian courts, was also employed by some of the fourth-century emperors, in the same way that a more general tradition of the production of court luxury goods, also including silverware and ivory diptychs, was revived or recreated.

Identification of the individual emperors is not always possible on these later gems, the iconography now having become much less individualised, as was also the case in other art forms. The first example, possibly of the emperor Licinius of the early fourth century, shows a triumphal progress by the emperor in a *quadriga* or four-horse chariot.[40] Attended by Victories, he guides his chariot over the top of a sprawling mass of his enemies lying on the ground. A second gem again carries a depiction of a chariot, with an unidentifiable imperial family group riding in it, accompanied by both Victories and centaurs, crushing or riding down two barbarians.[41] The appearance of the family here provides another interesting example of female imperial power being represented alongside the more usual and virtually exclusive male preserve of victory symbolism of one kind or another. A third gem relevant to this discussion, again of a fourth-century date, shows a mounted emperor holding a spear aloft in his right hand and riding down two male barbarians, one seemingly sprawled dead on the ground beneath the back hooves of the emperor's horse and the other holding up his shield to protect himself from the furious assault.[42]

As for silver plate, a number of outstanding examples survive, each of which gives a particularly vivid and clear message to its viewer. Most of these are what are known as *largitio* dishes, commissioned and distributed to celebrate particular imperial anniversaries.[43] The most significant of these is a silver *missorium* of the emperor Theodosius, found near Merida in Spain.[44] The scene on the plate depicts the emperor and his two regents, Arcadius and Valentinian II, seated before, or within, the imperial palace, while in attendance are Germanic troops, identifiable by their dress and weaponry which are rendered in great detail. Of especial note are their traditional weapons, their spears and oval decorated shields that place them at once outside the Roman empire and at the same time within, through the buying of their service and loyalty. Their presence both hints at the dangers lurking beyond the frontiers of the empire and at the success of the Roman state in harnessing such latent destructive power to its own ends, into the service of an empire that other barbarian groups threatened with their migrations and raids across the frontiers.

A less accomplished, and less detailed, silver plate, dated possibly to AD 364–75 and found near Geneva,[45] depicts the emperor Valentinian I or Valentinian II – the plate is very worn and identification is uncertain – standing in the very centre of the design, holding a *labarum* in his left hand and a small globe in his right hand, on which is perched a small figure of Victory who holds out a wreath towards him. Standing behind the emperor, three to either side of him, are six spear-carrying barbarian guards holding large oval shields in front of themselves. They wear crested helmets, unlike the guards on the Theodosian plate. Nevertheless, the identification of the insignia on two of their shields as having a parallel with designs on shields of barbarian units depicted in the *Notitia Dignitatum* confirms that they are non-Roman troops. In a narrow register of design, below the ground-line on which the figures stand, are strewn a shield, a sword and a helmet, discarded by a vanquished enemy.

One of the most striking aspects of this plate is the fact that while the viewer's eye is initially drawn to the figure of Valentinian – he is at the forefront of the design, in a central position and depicted at a larger scale than the other figures – it is nevertheless the massed rank of guards which dominates the design. They bring a sense of claustrophobia to the scene that appears almost overwhelming in its implications for the imperial authorities, a sense of endless numbers of barbarian troops who may be paid and relied on at one time but who may not always be reliable in intent. There is no better illustration of how barbarian mercenary support underpinned imperial power at this time. It is interesting to note how seldom art historians and archaeologists, when discussing these vessels, have even mentioned the barbarian guards.[46]

On a silver *largitio* dish of the mid-fourth century, now in the collection of the Hermitage museum in St Petersburg, the emperor Constantius II is depicted on horseback, holding a spear or lance in an attitude of ceremonial parade rather than combat, though Victory precedes him with a wreath raised up in her right hand and a shield lies at the horse's feet, as if recently discarded by a defeated or fleeing enemy.[47] Perhaps here allusion was as much to the defeat of enemies within the empire as it was to the defeat of barbarians without. Interestingly, following behind the emperor's mount is a barbarian bodyguard who also carries a spear or lance and a round shield on which is painted a *Chi Rho* Christian motif. This man is both a soldier in the service of Rome and, by implication if not necessarily in reality, of Christ.

While not directly connected to the present study, it is interesting to compare the stance, position and particularly the hairstyles of the barbarian guards on these three silver plates with those of the two guards who stand in attendance at the meeting of David and Saul, as shown on one of a series of early seventh-century silver plates, known as the 'David Plates' and coming from the 'Second Cyprus Treasure'.[48] Despite the fact that these figures are meant to be in a Middle Eastern setting at a much earlier time, nevertheless the overall setting for the meeting is unmistakably late antique and in a Roman imperial milieu. The guards are barbarians, used simply for their iconographic value rather than for any specific motive relating to their origins or ethnicity. It is thought that the 'David Plates' were commissioned for the imperial court of Heraclius, and that the iconographic themes linked to David were particularly apposite, given that Heraclius, like David, defeated his enemies the Persians and slew and beheaded their leader in combat in AD 627.

One of the most singular and evocative images of the later Roman world appears on an ivory and gilt diptych, now housed in the Cathedral Treasury at Monza, on the outskirts of Milan. These intimate and luxurious objects were made as gifts to be given by those Roman officials of consular rank to provinces, Senators, magistrates, and high-ranking individuals. The Monza diptych depicts the Roman general Stilicho, who was at the time arguably the most powerful and influential figure in the Roman world; yet, though his mother was Roman, his father was a Vandal, which made Stilicho a barbarian by descent.[49] His marriage in *c.* AD 384 to Serena, the emperor Theodosius' niece and adopted daughter, brought Stilicho into the imperial family and symbolised what had become by this time a necessary and pragmatic relationship between Roman civil power and the military power of certain barbarian groups. His dealings with the Visigoth leader Alaric were seen by some at Rome as deeply suspicious, yet by then his power within the Roman administration had grown so great that the questioning of his actions had become merely academic, so deeply entrenched were his power and influence.

The diptych consists of a pair of ivory panels folded together. Inside the diptych there were depicted both a portait and an idealised image whose construction would have been most carefully controlled and approved by the commissioning consul. On one leaf of the diptych Stilicho stands on his own, upright, stiff and formal, holding a spear in his right hand and a shield in his left, in a pose very similar to that of the barbarian bodyguards on the late fourth-century silver *missorium* of Theodosius discussed above. He is dressed in military uniform. Stilicho looks straight ahead, his bearded face expressionless. Such a transcendent pose is a typical signifier of latent or absolute power in the often theatrical official ceremonies and imperial displays of Late Antiquity. Here a sense of power was conveyed by a lack of movement in the work, and in the static, framed and enclosed nature of its composition.

The general appears against an elaborate architectural background, whether a facade or an interior is not clear. He is framed and contained within the architectural space which is itself cropped and framed by the border of the leaf of the diptych. This frame within a frame produced something of a sense of claustrophobia in the work, which is only slightly eased by the artist's introduction of a hint of depth into the scene, by posing Stilicho's feet to project out from, and break the bounds of, the frame. On the opposite leaf appear his wife Serena and their son Eucharius, also posed very formally and stiffly, facing the viewer. Again, both are shown devoid of facial expression. Serena holds a flower and Eucharius holds a book or tablet of some kind. The architectural background is also repeated.

Considered together, these images represent idealised portraits of Stilicho and his family. The very fact that he is shown with his family is most probably of great significance in itself. Such a grouping does not occur on other surviving consular diptychs, and here stresses the stability of their marriage alliance and its probable future continuance through the line of Eucharius. This, in turn, both acted as a message of stability within the Roman state and stressed the prime role that certain 'outsider' figures such as Stilicho would inevitably play in guaranteeing the future of the Roman administration.

Despite the fact that Stilicho was a military as well as a political figure, it is nevertheless significant that he appeared on the diptych in military dress and with weapons, albeit as symbolic attributes. On other diptychs, consuls were usually shown overseeing public games and ceremonies, demonstrating their largesse to the people, in terms of fulfilling social obligation rather than through providing physical protection. It is perhaps ironic that Stilicho's shield is a type which, though in wide use at this period, nevertheless is of a non-Roman, Germanic origin. Such shields by this time played an active role as props in official imperial ceremonies, with the emperor being raised on one to receive acclamation.[50] Thus the emphasising here of the 'otherness' of Stilicho's weaponry was almost an exercise in nostalgia, on the one hand evoking the primitive strength of the barbarian, while on the other stressing the incorporation of his power within the constraining and civilising framework of Roman power.[51]

Another diptych which makes an explicit and unusual link between the Roman state, the power and dominion of Christ, and the position of the barbarian, non-Roman peoples in relation to both, is the so-called Barberini Diptych. It probably portrays the emperor Anastasius and dates to the late fifth or early sixth century, but the emperor has also been identified as the later emperor Justinian.[52] The three differently sized registers of design, with the central, largest register being divided into three separate panels, included motifs which were a strange mixture of the sacred and the profane, of pagan and Christian symbolism, and of classical and Late Antique art styles.

The central register shows Anastasius or Justinian on horseback, holding a spear or lance in his right hand, though not in the kind of classic pose that has been seen so many times before when an emperor engages in symbolic combat with a barbarian opponent. Yet behind the emperor's horse stands an eastern barbarian or Persian who appears to be unarmed and gesticulating behind the emperor's back, while gripping his downturned spear shaft. The barbarian is obviously not an active combatant or one who is present to meet his symbolic and inevitable fate, to be skewered on the end of the emperor's lance. A Victory hovers in the air nearby, while seated on the ground at the horse's feet is a female deity or personification, probably Roma or Tellus, a device that seems to hark back to the iconography of the Augustan era and to the tiered gemstone designs of that time in particular.

In the upper register, in the heavens, appears the figure of Christ holding a sceptre, topped by a cross, and making a 'gesture of power' with his right hand. In attendance on either side of him are winged angels – these figures perhaps being Christianised and gender-changed Victories. In the bottommost register are depicted small-scale figures of eastern barbarian males, variously identified as Persians or Indians, bearing gifts, one of the figures entering from the left being shown carrying an ivory tusk. This is quite an intertextual reference, given that the diptych is a luxury item fashioned from just such material. These figures are almost intertwined with the figures of a lion, tiger and elephant that would have both helped the viewer geographically to locate and identify the origins of the barbarians and, perhaps, to stress their wild and uncivilised state. These peoples are not only non-Romans but they are also non-Christians.

The diptych therefore may be seen as utilising the images of barbarians in a most original way. They were still depicted as outsiders, here literally relegated to the realms below and to a world of uncivilised and untamed nature. They pay homage both to the Roman emperor here on earth and to Christ in the heavens. The relationship of the emperor to Christ is also one of shared, but exclusive, realms of power.[53] The emperor still appears here with the rather old-fashioned attributes of Victory and Roma/Tellus and perhaps the barbarians again formed another such stock accompanying motif, though one with a slightly new twist.

Another diptych, the so-called Halberstadt Diptych, has recently been reinterpreted as an eastern empire work, rather than, as previously thought, one from the workshops of the western empire.[54] The panels of the diptych are each divided into three registers of design, the uppermost registers and the large central registers portraying imperial figures.

If the reinterpretation is indeed correct, then this would be the earliest example of a diptych from the court of the eastern empire, dating to around AD 414. As on a number of other examples, the bottom registers of both leaves are filled with figures of seated or crouching barbarians, in this case including men, women and children. On the right panel, two bound males appear on either side of the scene, one depicted sideways-on to the viewer, the other facing outwards. This latter figure is being comforted by a female barbarian who touches him on the shoulder with both her hands. Next to her another woman leans down to pick up a small child. Some discarded or trophy weaponry fills in the background of the scene.

On the other leaf, a male barbarian offers up a shield, in tribute or in surrender. Another male sits slumped in dejection, his head resting on his knees. Between them are two women, one sleeping or cradling her head in despair, and the other attending to two animated small children, one at her knees and the other leaning over towards her from behind, as if trying to seek attention.

Certainly, while the general theme of the imagery employed here has been seen on numerous works of art from the early imperial period up to this time, this diptych is unusual in its conscious selection of images of women and children to inhabit the lower world, to which these barbarian peoples have been consigned through their defeat, rather than the more usual depiction of barbarian men.

The work may not, then, have been linked to the celebration of victories by a successful general, as might be expected from the presence of captives and spoils. Some clue to the motive behind the gendered approach detected here may lie in the representation of the figure of a woman in the upper register, above the three large, male imperial figures in the central register. She stands behind the seated imperial male figures at the circus games and was therefore perhaps intended to be literally 'the power behind the throne'.[55] Alan Cameron has suggested that she could be identified as Aelia Pulcheria, elder sister of Theodosius.[56]

A consular diptych of Constantius,[57] before he became the emperor Constantius III in AD 421, includes a lower register of the design on one leaf that is occupied by the small figures of cowed and defeated barbarians, including women and children, crammed in here in a claustrophobic manner that both emphasises their wretched lot and at the same time harks back to a similarly composed group on the Grand Camée de France. A similar reference to earlier compositional schemes has already been noted in the case of the Barberini Diptych. The evident suffering of these small figures was given little emphasis or importance in the overall scheme of imperial affairs as may be inferred from their minor scale and positioning.

AN EASTERN EYE

Though it is intended that this study not stray much beyond AD 410, and certainly that it should not consider Byzantine art in any detail, nevertheless some brief discussion of one or two major monuments set up in Constantinople, the new capital of the eastern empire, is apposite.

In AD 390 the Obelisk of Theodosius was erected in the hippodrome in Constantinople, according to historical sources.[58] It commemorated principally his victory over the usurper Maximus in that year. Its siting in the hippodrome, and the themes of many of the carved relief scenes on its base, alluded to new ways of portraying Victory and of linking the emperor with her, and are particularly relevant to this study. In Constantinople, triumphal processions ended here in the hippodrome, thus making the iconography of the column base perhaps of additional significance. On the highly decorated base on which the Egyptian obelisk stood were images of barbarians, but in a relatively minor role, as will be seen, though the reading of their role differs slightly and subtly from previous western imperial discourses on Roman–barbarian relations.

The emperor Theodosius, or Theodosius the Great as he came to be styled, reigned between AD 379–95 and founded a new dynasty, the House of Theodosius. As well as the erection of the obelisk, he had built a relief column which, with another set up by his son Arcadius, harked back to the columnal form of Trajan and Marcus Aurelius' still-standing monuments in Rome, and formed part of an allusive classicism that underpinned the dynastic art of the Theodosian house. The desire of Theodosius actively to promote his dynastic aspirations was reflected in the content of the art as well as in its form. Just as barbarian peoples figured heavily on the columns of both Trajan and Marcus Aurelius, so they did too on the Theodosian obelisk base and apparently on the now-destroyed columns.

Theodosius himself had perhaps contributed to the creation of a period of military and political stability in the eastern empire, at least by his decision to accept substantial and powerful groups of German barbarians into the empire in the role of *foederati* or allied troops. Their power underpinned his dynastic aspirations which, in turn, underpinned at least the promise of prosperity and safety in the future for Byzantium and the east.

The trend towards the use of the urban hippodrome or circus as an imperial ceremonial venue had started in Rome earlier in the fourth century, while the race or spectacle had become linked with imperial patronage and power in a way that was to evolve into an almost institutionalised artistic motif in the latter part of the century and into the fifth century, as on the Theodosian obelisk base and on the so-called ivory consular diptychs, given as diplomatic gifts in this later period. That the Theodosian obelisk was sited in the hippodrome of the eastern capital of the empire further emphasised this link, as did the particularly staged and almost theatrical nature of imperial appearance and display in the late antique period. It echoed the relationship of the Circus Maximus to the Palatine in Rome.

On the four decorated sides of the Theodosian obelisk base are, on the lower part of the pediment, scenes of chariot racing and building work connected to the erection of the obelisk, and inscriptional panels at front and rear, surmounted by four larger scenes involving the emperor and his entourage. Depicted frontally, and in the disengaged style of Late Antiquity that denoted the transcendent otherness of the emperor and of the court, the scenes individually are of the court watching the race in the hippodrome – though watching is perhaps not the correct word to describe their forward stares into the distance – and of the emperor about to present, or having himself just been presented with, a victory laurel wreath, as musicians play at the foot of the tiered rostrum.

In these scenes, the idea of victory is of a triumph in a race, of imperial prestige being linked to the very idea of triumph, and victory being both for, and by, the emperor. Imperial largesse, through the sponsorship and support of such spectacles, staged both to satisfy and motivate the general populace, was now a potent symbol of power, and the majority of the surviving consular diptychs, with the significant exception of that of the general Stilicho, again made this explicit link between power and largesse, between imperial authority and victory as represented by the image and idea of the race. It is thus interesting to see the emergence of a depiction of imperial authority that did not rely simply on the deployment of the defeated or subservient barbarian.

However, on one of the other faces of the obelisk base was a more traditional depiction and exposition of imperial authority, where power, achieved and held through an association with Victory, is represented by the defeat and obeisance of barbarian peoples. As the emperor, his court and retinue sit impassively in the hippodrome tiers, the emperor and his juniors under a protective canopy and attended on either side by spear-carrying Germanic barbarian guards like those on the silver *missorium* of Theodosius,[59] below them barbarian captives or vassals seek clemency or audience. The dynastic aspirations of Theodosius were reflected in the presence here not only of his fellow-emperor Valentinian II, but also of their allotted successors.

Two groups of five male figures each, one having come into the presence of the emperor from the right and the other from the left, kneel on one leg before the rostrum, holding gifts. Their caps identify some of them, arriving from the right, as eastern barbarians, probably Persians, and those on the left as western ones, though among this group may be an African. The whole scene was not a submission scene as such, but rather a demonstration of the geographical dominion of

Theodosius' reign. Theodosius was here being represented as the ruler of the barbarians, as both able to curb their threatening power through military might and, if needs be, to divert their power to the service and maintenance of Rome and Byzantium by their employment as imperial bodyguards. This may be seen as being a particularly potent message when so many threats to the stability of the empire could be deemed to come from the actions of enemies within, such as Maximus, whose defeat was commemorated by the monuments. The obelisk base scene involving figures of barbarians was both a traditional scene of barbarian submission and a motif that was to become Christianised in the context of the three magi submitting to the infant Jesus, as has already been discussed above in relation to the art of the age of Constantine and later emperors.

Some of the twenty or so surviving pieces from the spiral frieze from the Column of Arcadius depict Roman troops, members of the forces of the usurper Maximus, laying down their arms in surrender, two soldiers at the head of the line of surrendering soldiers being posed in a similar way to the figures of submissive barbarians so familiar from the repertoire of imperial art and authority. A sixteenth-century drawing made of the column before its destruction[60] shows that the main theme of the frieze was the expulsion of the Goths from Constantinople, though familiar compositional elements, including trophy piles of arms and armour and seated, mourning female barbarian captives, were also present. The barbarians had reached the eastern capital, as some years before they had come to the gates of Rome.

ENDGAME

The third and fourth centuries saw an increasing level of interaction between the Roman and barbarian worlds, with a redefinition of the relationships between the two, particularly as Roman society sought to redefine its own values and needs. This process was reflected in the art and imagery of the period, as would be expected. Examples such as the mid-third-century Ludovisi sarcophagus, with its dense decoration of battle scenes, demonstrate that the fear of war with the barbarians now lay at the very core of the Roman psyche.[61] Previous moral certainties were giving way to a feeling that struggle rather than virtue was the guarantor of the continuation of the present order. At the same time, the execution of imperial power was becoming inextricably linked to an increasingly elaborate ritual of display and ceremony, with the person of the emperor, and other members of the imperial court, becoming distanced from those around them, both in actuality and in artistic styles of imperial representation.

The trend towards the dehumanisation of the barbarians continued in both monumental art and on coins. Through the use of *spolia*, sometimes of fragments depicting barbarians, connections were made with earlier, more stable times. Perhaps the viewer was expected to take comfort from the portrayal of enemies whose attested defeat might give hope of a similar outcome to contemporary struggles against new barbarian enemies.

The appearance of barbarian bodyguards on a number of items of fourth-century court silver and on the Theodosian obelisk in Constantinople testified to changing power relationships between the Roman and barbarian worlds. The ivory diptych of Stilicho perhaps marked a point of no return. For Rome, the military incursions of barbarian peoples into Italy culminated in the sacking of the city itself in AD 410 by the Goths under the leadership of Alaric. Further assaults on the city and the surrounding countryside were made by the Vandals in AD 455 and other barbarian forces in AD 472, with the final symbolically laden event in this succession of barbarian triumphs being the abdication of the boy-emperor Romulus Augustulus in favour of the Ostrogothic leader Odovacar in AD 476.

SIX

IMAGE AND REALITY

The preceding three chapters have examined the use of images of barbarians in Roman art from the time of Augustus up to the early fifth century, and have been structured in a broadly chronological way. It is now intended to pursue a more thematic approach and to consider the contexts in which such images appeared.

In Rome, citizens would not only have been familiar with images of barbarians from the monumental art of the city but would also probably have encountered real barbarians themselves, while in the crowd at an imperial triumph or at gladiatorial spectaculars, and in the streets and better-off homes of the city where foreign slaves were ubiquitous. Those who had served in the Roman army would also have been familiar with a culture of military life where images of defeated barbarian peoples were commonplace, and where imperial agendas impinged on everyday life as nowhere else. Away from the public institutions and spaces, images of barbarians also appeared widely on coinage, and in private contexts. Brief consideration will be given to this latter, less easily understood occurrence.

Such a constant bombardment of its citizens with images of subject peoples might perhaps be expected to have resulted in the creation of a culture of xenophobia within the empire, or simply to have been a reflection of the incipient prejudices of the people themselves. This difficult issue will also be discussed in this chapter, and will lead on to a consideration of Roman self-definition through the portrayal of barbarian peoples.

IMAGE AND REALITY

TRIUMPH AND TROPHY

The triumph was an occasion when, in Rome, reactions towards newly conquered peoples and countries, and the defeat of long-time or traditional enemies, would have become crystallised by public participation in the drama.[1] Real, flesh-and-blood barbarians were usually forced to play a role in the ceremony of the triumph. For many in Rome, their perceptions of barbarian peoples would have been forged at such events, rather than through the viewing of state-sponsored works of art.

At a triumph the spectator would expect to see the parading of captured booty and enemy prisoners, sometimes women and children as well as defeated male warriors. On occasion, particularly famed or notorious individual opponents of Rome would be present in their humiliation, the most gruesome and grotesque example of this last being the parading of the severed and probably decomposed head of the Dacian king Decebalus.[2]

The victorious general, and later exclusively the emperor, would ride in the triumph in a *quadriga* or four-horse chariot, wearing the victor's laurels and a golden crown, and with his face painted or coloured red to symbolise his otherness from mere mortals on this occasion. A triumph at which both real barbarians and images of barbarians were paraded would have created in the viewers' minds a perception of the world in which the power of Rome held sway over the bodies of other peoples. A number of depictions of barbarians being forced to take part in triumphal processions has been considered in earlier chapters, the most striking being that from the Temple of Apollo Sosianus in Rome, with two captives seated on a bier and chained to a trophy.[3]

But the pomp and splendour of the imperial triumph would have been so much dead wood and dry straw without the concept that there was 'no triumph without equality', and that 'without the equal opponent there could be no valour'.[4] Thus the defeated barbarian would not have been viewed in an entirely negative way, though any admiration may have been well disguised and subsumed by mockery and invective on these occasions.

A similar processing with images of conquered peoples, whether in the form of bronze statuary or of more temporary maquettes, took place at the funeral of Augustus, and may have happened at other imperial funerals.[5] Given the Roman tradition of parading the *imagines*, images of ancestors, at certain times of the year, it is interesting to see that similar powers may have been attributed to images of what may be called ancestral barbarian foes. The discussion of battle sarcophagi in Chapter Four included consideration of one example from Rome on which Romans battled with Gauls. By the time this particular sarcophagus was commissioned in the mid-second century it was many years since these two groups had been at war. Indeed, Gauls were by then citizens of the empire and their representatives sat in the Roman senate. The Gauls had now become a historic enemy, almost a mythological enemy in some respects, and it is in this context that their appearance on this sarcophagus should perhaps be interpreted. Barbarians on the *spolia* reused in the Arcus Novus and the Arch of Constantine were similarly redefined by the passage of time.

From the time of Republican Rome up to the fourth century AD, the image of the trophy was an important and well-defined motif in the Roman state artistic vocabulary. The erection of a trophy on a battlefield had its origins in the Greek world, where it was an impermanent structure and not, as it became in late Republican and Roman imperial times, a monumental structure.

The transformation of the trophy from what was really a stage-set or prop for a battlefield ceremony to a static motif, where action and event became fossilised in marble or stone, is particularly interesting within the overall rhetoric of Roman imperial ideology. The trend towards this transformation would appear to have begun in the Republican period under the aegis of individual generals wishing to commemorate their own achievements and victories. There is something quite haunting and unsettling about the vision of the trophy on many works of art, the empty helmet hung above the empty cuirass giving the impression of the presence of a body, and yet not of a body. The defeated body was represented in its absence by the paraphernalia of war. Without an armoured outer skin the defeated body was naked, probably dead and mouldering.[6]

SLAVES AND GLADIATORS

Consideration of class, status and gender might at times have influenced Roman attitudes to foreigners and barbarians. For many Romans their only encounters with foreigners would have been with those who were brought to Rome as slaves, or as hostages paraded in triumphs. Attitudes towards such subservient individuals could be readily transferred to larger groupings or nations by association, or could be subsequently confused, rather than wiped out, by the extension of citizenship to previously subservient groups or the granting of freedom to former slaves.

How many barbarians came to Rome as slaves, following the defeat in war of a particular people? How many came there as hostages, and what was the fate of the majority of these hostages? How many came or were brought to Rome to fight as gladiators? These are all questions that need to be briefly addressed.

Estimates of the numbers of slaves brought to Rome, initially as captives following successful military campaigns, suggest that there was an indissoluble link between the military power of Rome and the economics of the Roman system. For example, 44,000 prisoners were possibly sold into slavery following the Roman victory over the Alpine tribe of the Salassi in 25 BC, and later an estimated 100,000 prisoners met a similar fate after the victory of the emperor Septimius Severus over the Parthians at the siege of the city of Ctesiphon in AD 198.[7] Such figures suggest that conquest by Rome would have turned millions of prisoners of war into slaves over the years, which would, in turn, have contributed towards the creation of a false perception of foreign peoples among the population of Rome. Such a perception would have been distorted not only by a hierarchy of difference or otherness, based on military power, but also by a realisation of economic difference and dependency.

The inevitability of slavery following defeat might help to explain the prevalence of barbarian suicide scenes in Roman imperial art, including, for example, the copied statue of the 'Suicidal Gauls' and the self-inflicted deaths of Decebalus and other Dacian chieftains depicted on Trajan's Column. These could, perhaps, be explained as being as much to do with avoiding a life of wretched slavery as they were valiant statements or expected responses to defeat among certain barbarian peoples.[8]

There are numerous scenes on Roman imperial monuments of groups of barbarian prisoners being rounded up for transportation into slavery, as for example on the Column of Marcus Aurelius where a group of Dacian women is herded on board a ship, doubtless for transport overseas. There may often have been a sexual undercurrent to master–female slave relationships, as well as an imbalance of power between master and male slave. In a passage from the *Meditations* of Marcus Aurelius, the emperor proudly claimed that he was able to refrain from taking sexual advantage of his slaves. This suggests that the practice of sexual misconduct and rape in these situations was so common and accepted that this denial of his taking part in such practices was expected to be read as evidence of Marcus' spiritual superiority, reflected in sexual abstention.[9]

The link between the captive barbarian and the gladitorial system has been discussed by Carlin Barton in her book *The Sorrows of the Ancient Romans*.[10] There, she quotes the assertion by Cicero, the first-century BC Roman writer, that in his time the gladiators were 'either debased men or foreigners', foreigners who in most cases would have been brought to Rome for this express purpose – 'Gauls, Spaniards, Arabs, Thracians, Germans, Asians, Syrians, Greeks'.[11] Gladiatorial combats even became part of the celebration of conquests and formal triumphs in Rome, and Barton notes that, for instance, on the occasion of the celebration of his Dacian victory, the emperor Trajan sponsored an extended series of gladiatorial contests, involving 10,000 combatants engaged in the arena over a period of four months.[12]

Even allowing for literary licence in the reporting of the numbers involved, the scale of such organised and ritualised slaughter was probably considerable. That it was linked not to the formalised slaughter of war but rather to peace in the aftermath of war seems both contradictory and confusing to the modern mind. The gladiatorial events and the events of war were here conflated to become metaphorical signifiers of the potential power inherent in the Roman state's control over the process even of death itself. Yet in order for them to be rationalised within the Roman psyche as being an integral part of the same cultural matrix that found space for the writings of Cicero and the wall paintings of Pompeii, both events again relied on the concept that 'without the equal opponent there could be no valour'.[13]

It would also seem to be the case that the imagery of victory in general, incorporating the barbarian captive, was appropriated in the context of the ritual and celebration of gladiatorial games. This was perhaps in the same way that in the later empire the iconography of imperial victory, particularly on the so-called consular diptychs, was extended by the adoption of depictions of victory in the arena or the circus as being more widely symbolic in political and military terms.

A highly decorated bronze gladiator's helmet, found at Pompeii, demonstrates this process.[14] A symmetrical scene of inscribed decoration includes, at its centre, the restoration or dedication of military standards, perhaps the standards lost in battle in Parthia and returned to Augustus. Certainly one of the two kneeling men holding a standard is wearing a Phrygian cap and may be a Parthian. The other standard bearer is bearded and dressed like a Celt, the two together implying the symbolic conquering of both east and west by Rome, another popular theme in Augustan political art. This central scene is flanked on either side by a trophy, on which a winged figure of Victory is depicted hanging a captured shield. Next to each trophy stands a bound barbarian, their hands tied behind their backs, a man to the right and a woman to the left. The male barbarian's long, flowing hair, bare torso, cloak and leggings identify him as a northern barbarian, probably a Gaul. The boar's head trumpets hung on the trophies again support this interpretation.

Also from Pompeii comes a tall bronze bowl, largely plain but with a continuous frieze of Celtic shields around the vessel, some motifs of crossed spears and shields beneath the handles, and handles on either side of the vessel in the form of two fighting barbarian men, their trousers or leggings suggesting that they are probably Celts or Gauls.[15] Dated to the second or first century BC, this could be some kind of gladiatorial or ceremonial trophy, with the Gauls being either combatants in the arena or simply rendered as symbolic of bravery in combat, a Hellenistic trope which has been seen displayed in its purest form in the sculptures of the Attalid Gauls. Roman historians often commented on how inter-tribal conflict within Gaulish and barbarian societies in general was endemic, so that Gaul-on-Gaul combat, such as is depicted here, may not necessarily have related to the formalised gladiatorial games in Italy.

A SOLDIER'S STORY

The Roman army, like most armies or state institutions, could be said to have possessed its own internal, and inevitably insular, culture. This was reflected in the art produced by, and on behalf of, the officers and soldiers serving across the empire. Almost inevitably, the image of the defeated barbarian foe was a common motif in military art, and a number of instances of its appearance will be discussed here. The army, though, should not necessarily be thought of as a monolithic organisation, so that differences can be expected in the way that senior officers commemorated their achievements in art in comparison with junior officers, legionaries in comparison with auxiliaries, serving soldiers with veterans, and so on.

Images of barbarians appear on a number of Roman legionary monuments, including the Antonine Wall distance slabs discussed in detail in Chapter Four and on an earlier monument set up at Mainz in Germany, probably in the *principia* or headquarters building of the Flavian legionary fortress. The form of the monument at Mainz, from which numerous sculptural fragments survive in the collection of the Landesmuseum, is uncertain.[16] Its precise date is also open to question, though it is assumed that its martial imagery would be appropriate to the celebration of victories during Domitian's campaigns against the Chatti. On the numerous column bases from the probably arcaded monument can be found portrayals of both the Roman victors and the barbarian vanquished, along with Victories and the spoils of war piled up as trophies.

Particularly evocative is one column base face carved with the figures of two virtually naked, bound barbarian men.[17] Not only are the men's hands tied behind their backs but they are also chained together at the neck, each seemingly pulling away from the other as the chain becomes taut between them. These men, their bodies twisted round to face the viewer, have their genitals fully depicted by the artist, as if further to emphasise both their vulnerability and their impotence. A similar message comes from another of the column bases, on which is depicted a seated, weeping female barbarian who, though fully clothed, is nevertheless a vulnerable, dejected and isolated figure.[18] These barbarian figures contrast with the column bases on which the armed and determined figures of Roman legionary soldiers appear.[19]

Military funerary memorials, principally tombstones and sarcophagi, depicting barbarians also form an important and coherent body of evidence. Sometimes more elaborate monuments were created to commemorate individuals who had served in the Roman army, the Tomb of the Julii at Saint-Rémy[20] being the best-known and best-preserved of this type.

Two other examples of this type may be considered. Fragments of reliefs from an elaborate second-century mausoleum at Nijmegen in Holland depict bound male barbarians seated on the ground amidst captured arms and armour and a weeping or mourning female barbarian, again seated amidst a pile of shields.[21] From Nickenich, on the Rhine in Germany, associated with a monumental cenotaph of Claudian date, comes a two-tier relief panel depicting in the upper tier a male figure, probably the deceased, brandishing a club in the manner of Hercules and holding a slave chain in his other hand. In the lower register are a male and female barbarian, the chain wound around their necks, in the same way that the barbarian captives on the Mainz monument were constrained. This is a unique piece, and the linking of the power of the deceased to that of the god Hercules is a conceit perhaps to be expected in a military context. However, an alternative reading might suggest that the deceased could have been a rich citizen or magistrate here depicted providing captives for games and combat in the arena.[22]

Auxiliary cavalry tombstones of the first and second centuries AD have been the subject of a great deal of academic study though this has tended to concentrate on epigraphic and military issues until relatively recently, when the iconography of the artistic motifs on these tombstones has also been considered.[23]

It was indeed the viewing of one such tombstone, that of the first-century Thracian cavalryman Rufus Sita, now displayed in Gloucester City Museum, that sparked my own interest in the portrayal of barbarians. Sita's tombstone provides a good example of one of the three main types of auxiliary cavalry tombstone of this period, known either by the German name of *Reitertyp* or, more awkwardly, as 'horseman and fallen foe' stones.[24] The other subtypes are a horseman on his own (that is, shown without an opponent), or a horseman with a soldier-servant present in the background (again without a barbarian enemy), and finally a type on which horseman, servant and trampled barbarian all appear together, the latter type obviously being potentially far more complex in terms of the interrelationships and power differences between the three protagonists.

Sita's tombstone was discovered in the area of Wotton, the location of the military cemetery associated with the fort at Gloucester.[25] Its inscription records that he was an *eques* in the Sixth Cohort of Thracian Cavalry – Thrace being located in present-day Bulgaria – and that he died at the age of forty, after twenty-two years of service. The tombstone stands almost 1.5 metres high and is surmounted by a sphinx flanked by two lions, both the sphinx and the lion being common classical funerary motifs. The bottom register of the stone is taken up by a panel bearing the dedicatory inscription, while the central and largest portion of the tombstone is reserved for a relief carving.

In this carved scene, a cavalryman is depicted charging towards the right, holding a lance or spear in his right hand, the tip of the spear being aimed downwards towards a foe lying on the ground. In his left hand the horseman holds a shield. A certain amount of care has been taken to provide the horseman, and indeed his horse, with well-carved and detailed armour and accoutrements, something that may have been further emphasised by the use of paint on the tombstone when first erected. Sita's tombstone is not the most detailed example in this respect, but nevertheless his helmet, spear, shield and sword are authentically portrayed, while reins and trappings can be seen on the horse. The fallen foe, a naked male barbarian, lies on the ground looking up towards the looming cavalryman, as his horse rears up in anticipation of the fatal spearthrust. The barbarian holds up his sword in self-defence, but there is an inevitability about the outcome that is only seconds away.

There are slight variations on the Sita subtype, but generally the final blow is about to be struck, or is shown being struck, with the fallen foe either lying prostrate and looking up at the rider, as here, or curled up in a protective huddle under the trampling hooves of the charging horse.[26] In one instance, on a tombstone from Halton Chesters in Northumbria, the barbarian is shown trying to pull out the shaft of a spear lodged in his chest.[27]

These 'rider and foe' tombstones are found mainly in Britain and on the Rhineland, and must be interpreted in terms both of what they can tell us about military matters and about iconographic significance. It is not simply that we are seeing a Roman slaying a barbarian on these stones, rather we are seeing an auxiliary soldier of non-Roman origins, most of those commemorated coming from either Thracian or Gallic units, slaying a barbarian on Rome's behalf, a somewhat more complicated scenario than it might at first seem.[28] It is generally accepted that this military tombstone type originally appeared in the Rhineland in the first half of the first century AD, though later, similar types appeared in the third century in the Danubian region and on memorials to the *Equites Singulares Augusti* in Rome.[29]

Some authorities have looked for a classical prototype for these tombstones, and indeed the Hellenic stele of Dexileos, who was killed in the Battle of Corinth in 394 BC, could have been a forerunner of the type, though given the considerable length of time between the manufacture of the Dexileos stele and the creation of the cavalry tombstone types, this seems unlikely.[30] Some possible sources of the motif could be in late Etruscan art, in figures of mounted huntsmen on early Roman sarcophagi, or in charging cavalrymen in early imperial battle pictures, but it does seem more likely that the type originated from outside the classical world, in Thrace itself, and that somehow it was connected to a local rider-god cult there. A tombstone dating to the first century BC from Abdera in southern Thrace depicts a horseman and his servant, though no defeated enemy or scene of combat is here present.[31]

Though the tombstone motif of the horseman and fallen enemy may then have had its origins outside the Roman tradition, nevertheless it was easily recontextualised and assimilated within the iconography of war and victory celebrated by the Roman army. This in its own way was similar to the process of religious syncretism that went on throughout the multifarious provinces of the empire. Here, what was originally a religious or cultic motif had now become almost purely martial in its new context, though to Thracian soldiers in the Roman army the original significance of the motif would probably not have been lost.

These tombstones represented records of individual soldiers' lives and achievements within both their ethnic auxiliary units and the Roman army as a whole. Legionary tombstones did not show martial scenes, and therefore the combat scenes on the auxiliary tombstones may have been highly significant. These scenes did not portray the barbarian foes as anything other than worthy opponents, overcome by skill and guile in single combat. It would certainly not have been apposite to have shown the defeated foe as pathetic or easily overcome, as this would have almost denigrated the now-dead soldier's military pride.

The artists' concentration on the detailing of the cavalryman's equipment and arms, and on horse trappings and accoutrements, was probably itself significant, in that this seemed to signify pride in the uniform and the status that it gave the soldiers, both individually and collectively. In these depictions, the fellow-cavalrymen of the deceased would have been able to recognise their own story: their ethnic or racial origins through the record of the inscription; their professional role as soldiers in the service of Rome through the Latin and form of the inscription as well as more obviously through the scene depicted; and pride in their adopted personae through the detailed recreation of their arms and armour and horse trappings. The literalness of these commemorative monuments was their very strength, in that for the auxiliary soldiers their life in the army, their duties, uniform and equipment would have defined their very existence, and were crucial to their experiences and memories of whatever combat and action they had seen.[32]

Examples of the more complex soldier–servant–barbarian tombstones include memorials to Gaius Romanius Capito[33] and to Titus Flavius Bassus,[34] from Zahlbach and Cologne in Germany respectively. Both cavalrymen belonged to the *Ala Noricorum*, Noricum being one of the eastern, Danubian provinces. The tombstone of Romanius shows him riding down a barbarian foe in much the same manner as appears on the majority of the auxiliary tombstones, though here the barbarian is fully clothed and less evidently of a Celtic ethnic type. Behind Romanius' horse stands his servant holding a number of spears, in case his master should require rearming during the engagement. On the Bassus tombstone, only certain details are different. For instance, the falling barbarian here carries a shield, as does Bassus' servant. Otherwise the tombstones' depictions can be viewed as being standard motifs with a very specific meaning within a military context. It must remain uncertain why the servant type of auxiliary cavalry tombstone was unknown in Britain, and how, if at all, the two main types differed in terms of status or achievements of the commemorated deceased, or if the choice of tombstone type was simply a cultural one.

Battle itself, though, could be a purely symbolic artistic motif, as it had been in the Greek world, symbolising victory over death, and particularly when related to private or funerary contexts may need to be read in a more detached manner. Its occasional use as a motif employed on gemstones, that most personal of commissioned items, should also perhaps be seen in this light.[35]

While no exhaustive search has been made for instances of depictions of Roman–barbarian battles on items of Roman military equipment and armour, a number of easily accessed examples suggest that such martial iconography was commonplace in the Roman army, principally on decorated breastplates, cuirasses and helmets, or on horse armour and trappings. This is something that should hardly occasion surprise, though perhaps a difference between such battle scenes in the professional milieu of the army and those deployed in the context of imperial art may be detectable. Indeed, it has been argued by some authorities that it was the 'debased' art of the military that had a detrimental influence and effect on the development of the state art of Late Antiquity, as if that art was not in fact an index of its own time.[36]

A large number of *baltei*, literally belts, but in this case referring to highly decorated items of military uniform, depict either battles between Romans and barbarians or defeated barbarians on their own. One of the best examples comes from Brescia[37] and depicts a centrally and prominently displayed Roman cavalryman trampling and putting to flight a group of seven barbarian footsoldiers and riders. All the individual figures are three-dimensional and are affixed to the *balteus*, and it is quite likely that once detached these could be mistakenly interpreted as single genre figures. Given the elaborate nature of this piece, and its sheer weight, it is likely to have been a parade-ground item rather than a standard piece of day-to-day equipment. The bronze figure of the dead or fallen Gaul, dressed in trousers but with a bare torso, lying face-downwards on the ground with one arm under his body and the other under his head, from the forum at Alesia in Gaul[38] may be derived from a similar horse trapping or item of armour. The same is true of numerous other examples, including a fleeing horseman from Bologna, a dead or wounded horseman lying prone in the saddle and being borne by his crumpling mount from Mogilovo, and both mounted and infantry figures from Herculaneum.[39]

Parade or sports helmets decorated with battle scenes are also known, as are decorated scabbards and standards, including a small item of Tiberian metalwork, the silver

Niederbieber *signum*,[40] that bears the image of the standing, cuirassed emperor, holding a spear in his right hand as if on guard duty, with a bound Germanic barbarian captive and a mass of captured weapons and armour strewn on the ground around the emperor's feet. Decorated cuirasses, like those that appear on statuary, may also have been used for ceremonial purposes.

PREJUDICE AND PRIDE

A key question must be whether the Roman attitude to barbarians at any time reflected a xenophobic or even racially prejudiced bias towards any of the barbarian peoples routinely portrayed in Roman art or brought into the empire by incorporation.[41] It could be argued that prejudice was aimed only at those outside the Roman cultural norm, and that the political mechanism to transform non-citizens into citizens was a mechanism of equalisation, and not one of irreversible division.

There would nevertheless appear to be some element of overt distinction in the fact that even when citizens were involved in legal or other disputes at Rome, if they were non-Romans their case would be handled by the *Praetor Peregrini* – that is, the *praetor* 'of the foreigners'.[42]

A certain amount of snobbishness about the appearance and manners of senators from Gaul, who came to Rome to take their seats and play their province's part in the decision-making process there, can be discerned from historical sources.[43] Dislike and distrust, though not necessarily hatred, can be read into many Roman literary and artistic narratives. So, however, can fear, admiration and nostalgia, in the form of the idealisation of the uncorrupted barbarian.

Moving away from the major literary and historical sources, where irrational prejudice might not in any case be expected to have had an obvious voice, some hints of a prejudiced stance may be found in a number of more intimate texts of which two examples can be given here. The first of these is the text of a birch-bark letter written home by a soldier stationed at the frontier fort of Vindolanda in northern Britain in the first century AD. In it he refers to 'Brittunculi' – perhaps to be translated as 'little Brits' or 'wretched little Brits' – and it is clear from the context that he is referring to barbarians beyond the nearby frontier.[44] Perhaps such a dismissive attitude might naturally be expected from someone serving in the Roman army, where an obviously institutionalised contempt for others may have been officially fostered.

The second example also probably derived from a military context, though it was found at a *villa rustica* at Vettweip-Froitzheim in Germany.[45] It takes the form of a dice shaker used in Roman gaming, formed out of a metal sheet pierced by decorative cut-outs and with a cut-out inscription formed by four words placed one above the other on the front of the shaker. The inscription reads: PICTOS VICTOS HOSTIS DELETA LUDITE SECURI – the Picts are beaten, the enemy annihilated, let us play without a care.

Roman xenophobia can also be traced in their earlier dealings and relationships with the Sabine population close to Rome, and with other non-Roman Italian peoples.[46] It may be that such attitudes were so ingrained within certain sections of Roman society and in the Roman psyche that there is a more elaborate narrative of fear and loathing that could be written than one solely involving barbarian peoples.

Whether xenophobia turned into racism is uncertain. Black Africans became regular subjects in Roman genre art, as has been well demonstrated in a number of extensive studies by Frank Snowden.[47] Snowden has described how the Blacks – he uses the generic Graeco-Roman term 'Ethiopian' – who came in contact with, or were part of, the cultures of Egypt, Greece and Rome first became popular subjects for artists in the sixth century BC and that this trend continued to the end of the fourth century AD. He dismisses the idea that these artistic studies were somehow intended to be degrading of their black subjects, and argues that purported instances of deliberate caricature or comic appearance have often been interpreted out of context.[48] Depictions of individuals as amusing or absurd figures were, he argues, as common among 'white' subjects as they are among black. He deduced from a reading of literary and historical sources that there was little deliberate attempt to barbarise black peoples any more than there was with other barbarian groups, and that there can be traced similar trends of idealisation in the descriptions of Blacks as can be found for the northern barbarians at certain times, particularly up to the second century AD.[49]

Snowden's thesis is that black peoples were commonly portrayed in ancient art for aesthetic reasons only, and that while there may also have been a certain element of anthropological fascination with their physical appearance and skin colour, these were no more or less than questing traits inherent in Graeco-Roman culture, both visual and literary. Blacks appeared in a variety of guises in Roman art, as individual studies, as musicians, gladiators, grooms and so on. These were not all slaves or in subservient roles. The variety of artistic media in which they were represented is also worthy of comment, including as it did mosaics, wall paintings, stone and bronze statuary, pottery, terracotta and glass.[50] In contrast, northern and eastern barbarians were almost exclusively portrayed as defeated in battle or as captives. It is difficult to think of an ethnically distinct figure from these regions who is depicted otherwise.

There are only a few depictions of the defeated black adversaries of Rome, the most noteworthy being two bronze statuettes of seated, bound, youthful male prisoners which may date to the late first century BC and be connected with Augustan-era retaliatory raids from Roman Egypt.[51] A black man's head on a herm from the baths of Antoninus Pius at Carthage may be of a defeated enemy.[52] Small terracottas of armed and armoured Blacks produced at Alexandria need not necessarily be of enemies of Rome and could equally represent gladiators, actors or mimes. This absence could simply reflect the fact that though historical sources record numbers of barbarian incursions into both Roman Egypt and Roman North Africa, and the inevitable military responses to these threats, these were only ever on a small scale and thus not the kind of military engagement to have been worthy of triumphal celebration or commemoration in state art, either in the provinces or at Rome.

The general opinion holding sway in academic circles at the present time is that there was certainly no specific colour prejudice within the Roman empire at any period, following Snowden's thesis.[53] As discussed above, studies of the representation of black people in Roman art suggest that, though Blacks became popular subjects in genre art, this was not through any strategy to degrade or control the black subjects but rather it was an aesthetic choice, tempered with an anthropological fascination that transcended skin pigmentation.

THE COLONIAL GAZE

There were undoubtedly significant variations in the uses and meanings of the image of the male barbarian and of the female barbarian in Roman art, and to perhaps a lesser extent of the barbarian child. The female barbarian was the most common mortal woman, as opposed to goddesses or personifications, in Roman state art.[54] This must have reflected not only a distinct historical role for the female barbarian in the visual narrative of Roman history but also a very distinct perception of her in the minds of the viewers of these artworks, though, of course, such a perception would not have remained constant throughout the period under consideration.

The image of the female captive, either represented explicitly by the image of a 'real' barbarian woman and her fate, or implicitly by the use of female personifications in a way that was at odds with the original Greek conception of such figures, is a tellingly common motif. Its use related to the gendered nature of Roman imperial power, and almost certainly also testified to a fear of female transgression and unsuitable behaviour, both by barbarian women and by the women of Rome and the empire.

Part of a strategy of defining 'acceptable' female roles and behaviour was played by the employment of mythological exemplars in Roman art for didactic purposes.[55] Mention has been made of the particular Augustan use of imagery for didactic and moralising purposes when directed at the women of Rome, and of how the appearance of depictions of the rape of the Sabine women and the punishment of Tarpeia in the Basilica Aemilia would have sent a very clear message to its viewers about Roman and non-Roman relationships, and about male–female relationships in Augustan Rome. These particular works, or rather the messages they conveyed, should certainly be read alongside the more transparent power/gender imagery of the reign.

A detailed study by Eve D'Ambra of the sculptural frieze of Domitian's Forum, the so-called Forum Transitorium in Rome, concerned itself with mythological imagery used in an imperial context, images that were almost exclusively of women, something that was itself unusual.[56] Though there were no mortal or barbarian women depicted here, nevertheless D'Ambra's reading of the friezes and their use of the myth of Arachne, punished for so openly and defiantly challenging the goddess Minerva to a weaving contest, as a signifier for wider social policies and controls in contemporary Domitianic society is incisive. Encapsulated within the act of weaving itself were ideas relating to the value and dignity of female creative pursuits – in this context a dignity and moral value defined and assigned by male imperial ideology – while Arachne was present as a warning of the potential fate of those (women) who transgressed.[57]

There may also have been some significance not only in the number of instances in which barbarian women appeared in Roman art, but also in the matter of whether they appeared on their own, as mothers accompanied by young children, with a male companion or husband, or with a male companion and children as an emblematic family unit. Personifications of barbarian lands were, of course, always female, though it is recognised that these were not intended to be images of real women, even if the possibility must have existed for such confusion to arise in the eyes of some viewers. The interpretation of female personifications as non-gendered images has already been questioned in Chapter Two, and need not be reiterated here.[58]

The Roman use of ethnic personifications, an artistic strategy adopted from Greek art, could be both positive and negative in intent. Personifications could be shown in submissive postures or roles, or they could be depicted in scenes that, while not suggesting full equality with Rome, at least did not stress inequality and subservience.[59] The use of personifications became particularly commonplace in the reign of the emperor Hadrian, the conflation of a woman's body and a geographical location or physical feature being particularly indicative of gendered thinking in an imperial Roman context. Of course, this was equally applied to Rome – such as the Roma or Tellus figures on the Augustan Ara Pacis and Gemma Augustea – or to Italy and the provinces of the empire. However, it did not require a great deal of imagination to understand the implications inherent in the regular equation of a woman's body with conquered or subject territory, and it did not necessarily require that this equation be made as over-explicitly as in the case of the Claudius/Britannia and Nero/Armenia sculptures from the Sebasteion at Aphrodisias.

Some discussion has already taken place in the preceding chapters concerning the sometimes quite jarring imagery depicting Roman violence against non-Roman women, whether real or mythological women or those in the guise of personifications. That there is always sexual tension and sexual violence between the men of an invading or victorious force and the women of a conquered area is unfortunately and sadly true for all conflicts, ancient and modern.[60]

While the hair-pulling scenes on the Gemma Augustea and the Column of Marcus Aurelius are isolated examples in Roman art, they may have derived from the hair-pulling motif in a mythological battle on the Altar of Zeus at Pergamon and could thus be construed as being stock Graeco-Roman images.[61] Nevertheless, they were used in contexts which, in the case of the Augustan example, denoted a generalised state of mistreatment of a captive and, in that of the Antonine image, a more focused use in the context of the fate of female victims in the German campaigns of the time. The Aphrodisian Julio-Claudian depiction of Claudius physically overcoming and conquering Britannia is an altogether different kind of image, but one which nevertheless denoted one version of the nature of the relationship of the male conquerors with the female conquered, between whom sexual and social boundaries were perhaps deemed not to exist.

In the context of gendered power relationships, it is perhaps worth briefly considering here the way in which specifically male power was depicted in other ancient arts. Certainly, in Mesopotamian art and texts there is an inherent connection

between 'maleness' and the holding of power. The strong, virile
and almost-perfect bodies of eastern rulers, such as the
'muscles and the body of a lion' attributed to king Isme-Dagan
of Isin or the statuesque figure of Naram-Sin of Agade on his
victory *stelae*, conveyed similar, unequivocal messages to their
respective reader and viewer.[62] It was not the case that Roman
emperors used a similar strategy of having their own bodies
depicted in this exaggerated manner. Indeed, only a few
examples of such occurrences can be cited, such as the figures
of Augustus, Claudius and Nero in heroic nudity or semi-
nudity at the Sebasteion in Aphrodisias.[63] Other, less overt
strategies to emphasise strength or physical power were
pursued through the constant militarisation of the emperor's
garb and the defying of the ageing-process seen in the later
portraits of emperors such as Augustus and particularly
Trajan.[64] A number of scholars have pointed out the
generalised connection attributed to male appearance in some
societies whereby power equals potency, and power thus
becomes aesthetically alluring and a potent aphrodisiac. In this
respect, it has been argued that 'the rhetorical power of images
that combine an erotic charge with violence, as represented in
military battles, derives precisely from an engagement with the
sensual body'.[65]

In the earlier part of the period under consideration, before
what could be called the 'Aurelian watershed', that time
around which attitudes to barbarian peoples seem to have
hardened, there may have been more of an emphasis, in terms
of numbers of appearances, on the use of more mixed-gender
images of barbarian groups and peoples. It has been surmised
that in some depictions of barbarian couples, the fact that the
man was bound or in chains and that the woman remained
untied, in a mournful or dejected pose, indicates a definite
strategy of suggesting barbarian male aggression and female
passivity, for the woman evidently posed no threat and was
therefore not constrained.[66] All the more extraordinary, then,
was the depiction of the Dacian women torturing Roman
prisoners on Trajan's Column.

When barbarian couples were depicted, this would seem to
have been a way of staking out some element of common

ground, of a common humanity between the Romans and the barbarian peoples portrayed. An absence of such pairings could be construed as the opposite – a declaration of a state of complete otherness.

As well as sharing common humanity with the Roman couple, the barbarian couple, though defeated and often shown dejected and distraught, could then be transformed by the incorporation of their land into the empire and subject territory of Rome. While they themselves may not have become citizens, their children and their children's children may have achieved such a status, perhaps through the service of a son in the auxiliary units of the Roman army. A people defeated by Rome was not necessarily a despised people.

IN PRIVATE AS IN PUBLIC

Though images of barbarians were not exclusively employed in imperial contexts, such contexts nevertheless were the most numerous and significant. These images, however, also appeared in other public spheres, on privately financed monuments and buildings, in temples and theatres, and in private contexts such as in the home.

The Arch of the Argentarii in the Forum Boarium in Rome, described and discussed in Chapter Five, though a 'private' monument, nevertheless utilised various artistic motifs more usually associated with state art. Another unusual appearance of the barbarian image in a private context was at the Sebasteion at Aphrodisias where such images were part and parcel of the visual vocabulary for the presentation and artistic articulation of the imperial cult of the Julio-Claudian dynasty.

There are also examples in state art, such as the group of triumphal arches in Gallia Narbonensis, at Saint-Rémy, Carpentras and Orange, which, though undoubtedly to be classed as imperial monuments, nevertheless did not bear the image of the emperor himself, but yet carried the evolved repertoire of triumphal imagery, including that of the defeated or captured barbarian, which had emerged in the late-Republican period.

Written sources suggest that in some theatres in Rome the stage curtains were on occasions adorned with perhaps surprisingly untheatrical motifs, including, according to a line in Vergil's poem the *Georgics*, images of 'Britons rising woven in crimson curtains'.[67] While no actual examples of such textiles have survived, it is probably safe to assume that these Britons would have taken the form of dejected or bound captives.

Images of barbarians also appeared on mass-produced, mould-made terracotta plaques, used as decorative revetting on house roofs. Known today as Campana reliefs – named after the nineteenth-century collector, the Marchese Campana – these were produced for buildings in Rome from the Augustan period until the second century AD.[68] The designs on these plaques include one that showed Gallic captives standing on either side of a temporary, battlefield trophy, and, most interestingly, another that depicted a triumph in progress, with barbarian captives being paraded through the streets on the back of a cart or waggon, or carried on a litter. A plaque in the collection of the British Museum depicts two male barbarian captives standing on a cart moving forwards in a triumphal procession, with Roman officials walking beside the cart and holding on to the ends of ropes which are noosed around the necks of the prisoners. Unusually, the captives' hands are not bound and they are both portrayed in the act of gesturing with their outstretched arms either towards their captors or towards a perhaps cheering or baying crowd watching the triumphal parade. Each of these straggly-haired and bearded men has a markedly pained expression on his face, which, with the rest of their body language, leaves the viewer in no doubt that they are in great distress.

Another terracotta plaque or relief panel, again in the British Museum collection, was made in Rome itself in the first quarter of the first century AD by, or in the workshop of, the artisan M[arcus] Anton[inus] Epaphra[s], and depicts a Roman soldier guarding a barbarian captive, once more probably a Gaul, naked apart from a cloak draped over his shoulders. The soldier holds one end of a rope that binds the prisoner. To the left of the figures stands a battlefield trophy, in this case a tree-trunk on which is draped a cloak and some weapons, including a circular shield.

Inset ivory panels from the door of the Augustan Temple of Apollo on the Palatine Hill in Rome were described by the writer

Propertius as being decorated with pendant scenes of the sacking of the Temple of Apollo at Delphi by the Gauls in 279 BC – an attack thwarted by the intervention of the god himself, as has been detailed earlier in Chapter One – and the mythological killing of the children of Niobe by Diana and Apollo.[69] Given that this temple was also known as the Temple of Actian Apollo, linking the god to Augustus' strategic and decisive victory over Anthony and Cleopatra, it could be considered to be a public, rather than private, building, and thus one where allusive, but nevertheless politicised art such as this would not have been considered out of place. The Egyptian provenance for another ivory inlay panel from Oxyrhynchus (now in the British Museum), perhaps showing the same momentous events at Delphi, may again link this piece allusively to the victory of Augustus, and to a date in the late first century BC. The figure on the panel is unmistakably a Gaul, depicted in front of a large and elaborate public building that is probably the temple at Delphi.[70] The Oxyrhynhus panel may also have been a decorative setting in a temple door.

There is only a single instance of the representation of barbarians in mosaic art, that of Berber prisoners to be seen on the mid-second-century AD pavement in the public basilica at Tipasa, described in Chapter Four. In the amphitheatre at Zliten in Libya there has been found a mosaic depicting celebratory games held there in which a number of human victims are being fed to wild beasts in the arena, as can also be seen on a mosaic from El Djem.[71] It has been suggested that they could be prisoners taken in AD 70, after the defeat of infiltrating barbarians from the Garamantes tribe. This interpretation is open to doubt, and even were it to be accepted, it would nevertheless still be true to say that mosaic was not a generally accepted medium in the Roman world for political or ideological art.

A wall painting from a private house in Pompeii, probably dating to the first century BC, includes the depiction of two trophies, obviously set up on battlefields, one apparently composed of a stack of Gaulish weapory around the foot of the trophy's trunk, and the other depicting a similar pile of eastern arms and armour. While these could be alluding to contemporary historical events, they could also be scenes of mythological triumph, though utilising the accoutrements of contemporary defeated enemies.[72]

Whether barbarians were widely depicted in private contexts, particularly as genre figures in Roman art, in terms of their being commonly represented as the subject of small-scale bronze statuary, or statuary in other media such as terracotta, will be considered here briefly. Discussion of this question will be subjective, given that no extended survey or quantification of such material in museum and private collections has been undertaken. There may indeed be rather more such representations in museum collections throughout the world than is immediately apparent from a perusal of published sources.[73]

Some years ago, a few examples were listed by the late Professor Jocelyn Toynbee as part of a larger survey of the art of Roman Britain, though this list is probably no longer definitive, even for this single province.[74] Britain is one of the few provinces for which we have a synthesis of such material, and it must therefore remain uncertain whether the British collection is in any way typical of any broader trends.

The bronzes listed by Toynbee included the small figures of two barbarian riders, one from London being heavily bearded and with distinct straggly, limed hair, holding a circular shield and in his other now-missing hand perhaps holding a weapon of some sort. He is dressed in a heavy cloak and leggings.[75] A third British bronze, again from London, is a naked, bearded barbarian man caught in a curious pose that suggests he may be depicted in flight.[76] Two bronzes of barbarian male prisoners or slaves come from London[77] and Brougham in northern Britain.[78] Both figures sit or crouch and are bound by ropes that on the more complete London bronze can be seen to be tied around the man's neck, around his hands, which are held out in front of him, and then around his feet. Rather than being free-standing statuettes, all these figures probably formed part of the decoration for a military *balteus* or ceremonial horse trapping.

Toynbee also discussed a steelyard weight from Leicester in the form of a bust of a black youth.[79] To Toynbee's list can be added a more recent find of a small bronze of a bound, bearded barbarian male figure from somewhere in northern

Britain which again would appear to be a decorative mount of some kind, probably for attachment to a piece of ceremonial military equipment such as a *biga* or waggon.[80]

A very useful corpus of appearances of barbarians in the art of the western provinces that encompassed present-day France, Belgium and Germany has been compiled by Hélène Walter.[81] The study allowed her to make a number of detailed analyses of the distribution of such representations, to examine their contexts and to quantify the number of their appearances in different media. The corpus describes 173 depictions, though if one discounts the artwork of the monumental arches at Orange (listed as seventy individual depictions), Saint-Rémy, Carpentras and Besançon, of the Augustan Trophy monument at Saint-Bertrand-de-Comminges, auxiliary cavalry tombstones in the Rhineland, a military monument at Mainz and a number of other frieze fragments from triumphal or funerary monuments, then only twenty-six other, smaller-scale representations of barbarians so far have been recorded from these areas. Given that a number of these are appliqués, probably from military equipment, then read in tandem with the British evidence it would suggest that genre figures of barbarians were not, perhaps unsurprisingly, common or popular in the western provinces of the empire.

Leaving Britain and the western empire, a number of other examples of genre art can also briefly be discussed. A bronze statuette of a male captive, found in Brescia in northern Italy, may derive from some kind of small monument or have adorned a triumphal chariot or bier.[82] It was perhaps one of two figures of captives – one male and one female would be most usual – standing or placed to either side of a trophy. This male figure is unusual, though, in that his appearance and dress do not instantly place him as any particular barbarian ethnic type. He is young, clean shaven, with short, neat, closely cropped hair and is completely naked, save for a cloak or cape-like garment which leaves most of his lower body, his genitalia and legs exposed. His hands are bound behind his back, as is usually the case with male barbarian prisoners, and he stands upright and proud. This man is not the normally bedraggled and pitiful barbarian captive figure that is most often seen in Roman triumphal art, and it might therefore be surmised that either he was intended to represent a deliberately sympathetic portrayal or he was a particularly important or significant individual, a barbarian 'prince'. The date of the statuette is uncertain, but it could belong to the second century AD. Similar pieces are known from Herculaneum and Milan.[83]

The Egyptian city of Alexandria had a long tradition of producing genre figures of both people and animals in terracotta, and in the Hellenistic and Roman periods some figures of Celts or Gauls and of African mercenary soldiers were produced. Among the British Museum collections is a squat figurine of a Gaul, easily identified by his nakedness – he wears only a cloak – his distinctive weapons and his thick, limed hair.[84] Comment has been made on the exaggerated size and modelling of the genitalia of this figure, and indeed it may be that the depiction of overt 'primitive' manliness in this manner was part of the overall conception of the nature of the male barbarian.[85] A similar observation has been made above with reference to the genitalia of the Attalid statue of the Dying Gaul. Given that the Alexandrian terracotta would appear to date to c. 220–180 BC, it is probably correct to identify the Gaul as a mercenary soldier, fighting in the pay of the kingdom of Ptolemaic Egypt, and not as a barbarian enemy. He is certainly not depicted in any way that suggests inferiority or which compromises his dignity.

It is interesting to contrast this terracotta with a much later Egyptian, probably Alexandrian, product of the second century AD, again in the British Museum. This is of a bearded Roman soldier, his short sword gripped in his right hand and being thrust towards the rather indistinct figure of a barbarian at his side, perhaps kneeling on the ground in submission and perhaps being held by the hair by the Roman victor, a relatively common pose for such figures, as already noted.

The victorious Roman, rather than simply being an ordinary serving soldier, could be an emperor: Hadrian, one of the Antonines, or Septimius Severus perhaps. While the fanciful conceit of an emperor himself subduing a symbolic barbarian is common, it is certainly not common in the minor arts, and indeed would be most unusual in terms of the imperial image being debased in this way. In terms of statuary representations, one has only to think of Trajan riding down a Dacian foe on the Great Trajanic Frieze, of a cuirass-clad Hadrian stepping on a prostrate barbarian in the Hierapytna statue group, or of the equestrian figure of a serene Marcus Aurelius riding over a dead or defeated German.

It is difficult closely to date the majority of statuettes of barbarians as many of them are unprovenanced. The fact that so many are of obviously Gaulish warriors or captives probably places these examples in the period of the first century BC to first century AD. It cannot statistically be proven in any way, but there is an impression that the Gallic Wars held some particularly important place in the Roman psyche. This might have been reflected in a trend for 'souvenir' art, a trend that does not seem to have been continued in later periods to anywhere near the same extent in terms of the representation of other barbarian peoples. Many of the figures of Goths or Germans in museum collections, rather than being genre art as such, are actually more likely to have been fixtures or fittings from items of military equipment or are ceremonial items perhaps for use in triumphal processions.

Imperial art in the form of luxury gifts, principally gems, silverware and, in Late Antiquity, ivory diptychs, was sometimes highly politicised in its content, and reference has been made throughout the preceding chapters to individual significant examples involving images of barbarians. Barbarians were also commonly portrayed on Roman coinage.[86] It was, though, relatively uncommon for silverware to be decorated with explicitly historical or political imagery. Allusion, mainly through the utilisation of mythological themes, was employed to put political messages across in some instances. A number of notable exceptions, probably given as imperial and official gifts, include the two cups or *skyphoi* from the Boscoreale Treasure known as the Augustus and Tiberius cups, and the much later *largitio* plates of Theodosius, Valentinian and Constantius II.

In the private sphere, political imagery was also largely absent from pottery decoration, and what appears may be considered to have been derived from those few silver prototypes available. Certainly, in the decorative repertoire of the Italian Arretine ware potters, and subsequently that of the Samian or *terra sigillata* potters of Gaul, can be found only a few examples, with the image of the captive barbarian chained to a trophy, the most ubiquitous symbol of Roman imperial power and authority, being the most common.[87] On ceramic lamps, while figures of winged Victories were relatively common, on the whole political imagery was again quite unusual.[88] In the collection of the British Museum is a lamp, possibly from Corfu and dating to the period AD 70–100, on which appears a standard scene of a trophy hung with captured arms and armour, with a male and female barbarian seated on the ground to either side. The probably Germanic male has his hands tied behind his back and the woman sits in the common pose of the 'mourning captive' and is dressed in a heavy hooded garment pulled up to cover her head.

A BORROWED VISION

We have few records of how the barbarians interpreted their own dealings with the Roman world. However, in the first half of the third century, the Sassanian dynasty in Persia, in its attempts to revive the glories of the past regimes of Darius and Xerxes in the area by its own desires for territorial expansion, almost inevitably came into conflict with Rome. This was to prove initially disastrous for Rome, in that Shapur I successively defeated three Roman emperors, Gordian III, Philip the Arab and Valerian, the latter emperor actually being taken prisoner by the Sassanians following the defeat of his forces in AD 260. These great victories were commemorated both by a trilingual inscription at Naqsh-i Rustam and on five carved relief panels, one at Darabgerd, three at Bishapur and one at Naqsh-i Rustam.[89]

The most striking of these reliefs is carved on to a rock face above a pool at Darabgird, near Shiraz, in Shapur's home province of Fars. Here are depicted Shapur on horseback, laying his hand on the head of the emperor Philip, while Valerian moves towards him, perhaps also seeking clemency, and Gordian lies on the ground behind the horse. This particular relief, along with all the others with the exception of one of the Bishapur carvings, represented a composite, conflated version of the victories of Shapur and certainly did not reflect real time in its depiction of the three emperors together in a single representation of their individual defeats.

The exceptional, partially damaged relief at Bishapur depicts a kneeling figure of a Roman emperor, either Valerian or Philip, between two horses, on which were probably mounted Shapur and his father Ardashir, perhaps in a scene of investiture, one in which the figure of the emperor is somewhat superfluous – he certainly would not have been present in person at such an event – and indeed in which he appears to be little more than an imagistic attribute of the Sassanian rulers. Following this tradition, at Taq-i-Bastan a later rock-cut relief shows the standing figures of Shapur II and his successor Ardashir II, attended by the third figure of a Roman officer, lying sprawled on the ground beneath their feet, either dead or in submission. This Roman is most likely the emperor Julian, whose ill-fated expedition of AD 362–3 led to his death in battle against the Persians.

It has been suggested that the design of these Persian reliefs, with the exception of the Bishapur investiture scene which is considered to have a local origin, was heavily influenced by Roman imperial prototypes, but whether such detailed knowledge of the grammar and structure of imperial triumphal imagery could possibly have been employed in designing the victory monuments of Shapur I is open to question.[90] Certainly, the artistic strategy of the programme of commemorative artworks created for Shapur I was one in which he laid claim to be the successor to the empires of Darius and Xerxes and to have power over the Roman usurpers and expansionists.

It can be conclusively demonstrated that Roman imperial imagery had a resonance that extended beyond the immediate context of its celebration or ritualised commemoration. A small metal plaque, which would once have adorned a helmet, dates to the early seventh century AD and in all probability comes from Turin, in northern Italy,[91] and provides a good example of this phenomenon. The helmet seems to have belonged to King

Agilulf of the Lombards, and he is depicted seated on a throne in the centre of the plaque, staring forwards and with a fixed expression on his face, almost in the manner of the depiction of a late Roman emperor, with his own spear-carrying bodyguards in attendance on either side of him. Everyone looks forward and into the distance, as two winged Victories hover to left and right. Entering into the presence of the king from both sides come fellow-barbarian supplicants, some carrying gifts, these supplicants in their attitude, bearing and evident subservience being equivalent to the barbarians of Roman art seeking clemency from the emperor.

All the elements of this scene were taken directly from late Roman imperial art. Artistic narratives of power and political relationships have here been annexed wholesale, with little or no regard or understanding, unless an element of parody was intended, which is not necessarily totally out of the question. The adoption of such imagery, and of elements of imperial ceremony, was part of a process of legitimising the position of the Lombardic rulers. A Lombardic, barbarian king formalising his dealings with fellow-barbarians in this way was perhaps suggesting that power and the imagery of power were not always necessarily the same thing.

SEVEN

WAITING FOR THE BARBARIANS

The isolating of images of barbarians on Roman works of art can provide numerous insights into the social, political and cultural contexts in which these images were created and consumed, and the study of such images over an extended timescale does allow significant trends to be observed. Not only do some of the images allude directly to the history and fortunes of the empire, but they also at times hold up a mirror to the attitudes, values, hopes and fears of the ruling echelons of Roman society.

It has been shown how abstract ideas were sometimes conveyed through images of barbarians, and how these images contributed towards the creation of an aesthetic of power. The construction of an artistic identity for the various barbarian peoples who were, at different times, the enemies of Rome, was really an extended act of Roman self-identification. However, it will also be apparent that no single, overarching theory can unite the interpretation of this material. There are as many contradictions in the evidence as there are consistencies, and consideration will now be given to assessing both the context of strategies of representation, and of allegory and metaphor in the service of political rhetoric.

Some of the images of barbarians discussed in the preceding chapters could be described as elements of an art of reportage, based on the authority of historical fact, or of an art of fable and parable, whose authority was the imagination and whose goal was the bodying forth of accumulated memories amassed in

Roman society's past.[1] Each of these strains of art had its own aesthetic and narrative. The grammar of an art reliant on memory was part of the overall structure of social memory and cultural identity that translated experiences of the world into buildings, objects, music, literature, art and human behaviour. In times of social or political upheaval, culture became the stage on which the drama of change was played out, and here the manipulation of memory became a central concern. Memory admitted to neither the primacy of the past nor the promise of the future, and denied the uniqueness of the present. Therein lay its latent power.

Major questions that have been considered in this study have been whether the bodying forth of the image of the barbarian as a necessary part of the repertoire of imperial artistic strategies had its roots in the art of the Roman Republic, and whether attitudinal stances to those who were defined as 'other', which included the barbarian, were adopted whole, or in part, from the Greek world. It has been demonstrated that a watershed in the official Roman attitude towards the barbarian can be identified, centred around the reign of the emperor Marcus Aurelius. The later Roman use of images of barbarians was not as part of an art of ambiguity, but rather of an art of uncertainty, which in some instances was part and parcel of a pornography of state-sanctioned violence.

Another issue that has been considered is how images of barbarians were often simply 'stock images', repeated motifs whose symbolic value actually lay in their repeated use and power of allusion rather than in their content. This is certainly true of the extended tradition of so-called 'battle paintings' in Graeco-Roman art,[2] and many of the instances of the portrayal of combat with barbarians from the first to the fourth centuries AD must be viewed in this context. Almost without exception, in early Greek art, battle scenes, even if commemorating historical events attested by inscription or dedication, were mythological in content, that is they were battles between gods and giants or Lapiths and centaurs, with a later trend being towards battles between Greeks and Amazons and, later still, between Greeks and Gauls.

While the depiction of opponents thus varied with both time

and context, some of the so-called battle topoi remained remarkably resistant to change, and were retained in the canon of Graeco-Roman art unchanged for hundreds of years, their use being almost *de rigueur* in Roman imperial art. The most common of these topoi included: a rider lancing his opponent; an enemy soldier attempting to fend off the killing blow; the suicide of a defeated foe; a soldier about to deliver the killer blow, having grabbed his opponent by the hair, and the cavalryman falling wounded from his stricken horse.[3] To these could be added other motifs from classical art, such as the mourning captive, and even motifs from other, non-Graeco-Roman sources, such as the rider and fallen foe motif.[4]

There is, of course, a chronological pattern of change in the dominance of images of one barbarian ethnic group over another that reflected geo-political changes. Gauls or Celts, Dacians, Parthians, Germans and Goths all had their time of dominance, in terms of the number of their portrayals as a perceived reflection of a particular enemy's importance in the Roman psyche. An extended discussion in Chapter Four on the art of the Antonine battle sarcophagus considered one example of the genre on which the battling barbarian opponents of the Romans were Gauls, at a time considerably removed from that when the Gallic people were at war with the empire. These historical opponents had by then evidently become little more than symbolic, mythological or generic barbarian enemies, and their particular appearance, their ethnic personality and their material cultural attributes were no longer themselves anything other than a mirage, no matter how accurately they might have been rendered on this particular sarcophagus.

It is interesting to consider the possible linearity of Edward Said's concept of Orientalism[5] as having its origins in the Greek world, with Roman attitudes towards the eastern barbarians again being part of the same rhetoric of power relations, mediated through the creation and manipulation of cultural, national and regional stereotypes. The negative qualities attributed to the Persians by the Greeks – their love of luxury, their effeminacy and so on[6] – were subsequently redeployed by the Republican Romans to describe and denigrate the Samnites.[7] Colonial desire – the tendency to make the 'other' erotic – and the quasi-mythologising role played by the strategy of rendering the 'other' exotic within imperial ideology and colonial relations must have been an important factor in Roman–barbarian relationships, even if covertly rather than overtly.[8]

A striving after veracity in the representation of barbarian peoples could be interpreted as evidence of a general Roman ethnographic interest in barbarian peoples, and in differences between barbarian peoples. This is something that the historical sources also pursued through their detailed descriptions of barbarian customs, traditions, beliefs and social practices. Nevertheless, there would appear to have been a sharply defined word–image opposition, in that the visual bodying forth of barbarians, no matter how much attention to detail was lavished on the individual barbarian depictions, was always in the context of their defeat and subjugation and never in the context of the 'scientific' observation of their societies, as occurred in many of the written sources, however artfully constructed.

Of course, as has already been discussed in Chapter One in relation to the reading of Julius Caesar's descriptions of the supposedly first-hand observation of blood-curdling Gaulish customs and inhumanities, many of these texts constituted discourses of primitivism and should be read as such, as indeed should much of Tacitus' *Germania*.[9] However, it is interesting to note that it was text alone that was used by the Romans as the most appropriate medium and forum for pursuing this political and ideological agenda. In state art, no such strategy was adopted, nor can it be seen reflected in genre art.

The great detail inherent in so many representations of barbarians in Roman art implies that some level of interaction took place between artist and subject on some, if not all, occasions.[10] It must remain a possibility, for instance, that war artists accompanied the Roman forces on their campaigns in Dacia, allowing them to sketch and record the physiognomy of the Dacian on the ground, either through observation of them in battle or, more likely, by the drawing of prisoners brought into the Roman encampments. There is also the possibility that artists engaged in the post-mortem drawing of the dead bodies or severed heads of slaughtered Dacians. Of course, the opportunity would also have been afforded the artist, on occasions when prisoners were transported to Rome to take their reluctant part in a victory triumph and thence to become slaves, to study them there as living exhibits. It is difficult to believe that such interaction or observation did not lie behind the barbarian images on many Roman monuments.

This cultural, rather than strictly political or military, contact would have been equally a contact of inequality, and one in which the capturing of an ethnic type through drawing, thence to be recreated in stone in seeming perpetuity, mirrored the physical capture of the barbarian body and the barbarian land, in a way that united image, flesh and soil together in the rhetoric of imperial ideology. Subject became object, and the humanity of the people depicted became compromised rather than extinguished.

If, as is likely, first-century depictions of Britons did appear on the probably late third-century Arcus Novus, and that these Claudian *spolia* were included in an attempt to link the Britannic exploits of Claudius to those of the Tetrarch Constantius Chlorus, then these images would have been imbued with an altogether new significance, a significance that was not dissimilar from one of the links established by the *spolia* on the later Arch of Constantine. While Claudius had obviously celebrated his victory over barbarian opponents, the Britons of the third century over whom Constantius Chlorus triumphed were citizens of the Roman empire, 'enemies within' in terms of the political and economic threat posed by the breakaway regimes of Carausius and Allectus to the legitimate imperial authorities in the west.[11] To have linked opponents in a civil war with historic barbarians in this way was quite extraordinary.

On the so-called Arras Medallion,[12] a gold ten-*aureus* piece forming part of the large Arras Treasure, the reverse consists of a series of conflated scenes connected to Constantius Chlorus' British victory, including one of his ships assaulting London via the River Thames, and, in the background, an equestrian portrayal of the emperor himself riding towards, or into, the surrendering city. The city is represented by its battlemented walls and by the letters LON beneath, and by a kneeling female figure, a *tyche* – a personification of the city – who holds out both her arms in greeting or submission to the approaching emperor. Thus the medallion design avoided the direct depiction of the civil strife, yet in its depiction of the equestrian emperor and the submissive, kneeling female figure alluded to the well-established motif, probably going back to the time of Domitian, that more usually used the figure of the defeated barbarian in submission.

Who created and who viewed these images of barbarians has also been discussed, as has the issue of how the creation of both stock and stereotypical images of barbarians was part of a complex imperial strategy for coming to terms with changes and crises within the empire. The majority of the major state monuments that have been considered in this study were in Rome itself, and the expectations and experiences of the viewers there, at the very heart of the empire, must be assumed to have been somewhat different to those of viewers of state art in the provinces. The employment of images of barbarians on major imperial monuments in the provinces would appear to have been most widespread in the first and second centuries AD, certainly in terms of the number of such monuments in Gaul in particular. In the later Roman period, while numbers of individual monuments on which barbarians appeared were commissioned and erected in various provinces, these tended to be single monuments rather than multiple programmes.

It will already be relatively obvious that images of barbarians are not only readable in terms of their iconography, but also in terms of the context in which they occurred and, to a lesser extent, in terms of the artistic media in which they were executed. There would certainly seem to be a particular significance in the way that monuments on which images of defeated barbarians appeared, along with other signs and symbols of imperial victory and power, were quite narrowly defined in terms of their form and their location.

The most obvious, and not altogether surprising, observation that can be made with regard to location is that most of the monuments of this type were erected in Rome itself, though even there the imagery was most usually confined to triumphal or commemorative arches. Mention has already been made in

Chapter Two of the significance of the siting of the Augustan trophy monuments at La Turbie and at Saint-Bertrand-de-Comminges, and of the clustering of victory arches in the province of Gallia Narbonensis in particular. That images of defeated or captive barbarians also appeared on town or city gates principally at an early imperial date in Italy and Gallia Narbonensis suggests that the monuments were also being used to delineate both real and conceptual boundaries between civilisation and barbarism, between the tamed and the wild, between Roman urbanism, with its inherent order, and barbarian chaos, and of course between inside (safety) and outside (unfettered and potential danger).

The same sort of binary opposition can also be seen in the representation of barbarian figures or personifications exclusively on the so-called 'country facade' of the Arch of Trajan at Benevento. In common with some of the other monuments just listed, this arch was positioned at an important part of the Roman road network in Italy. In many of these cases, the monuments could be said to have been sited at points where real (geographical) and imagined (cultural and social) boundaries existed together in an uneasy juxtaposition, mediated through art, image and epigraphic text.

The location of a Claudian victory monument at the coastal site of Richborough, thought to be the gateway for the Roman invasion of Britain in AD 43, was perhaps chosen equally for its symbolic 'boundary' function as for the site's actual role in the conquest. However, nothing is known of the form of the Richborough monument above foundation level, or of its decorative scheme which may have included figures of Britons in battle against Romans or enslaved in their defeat. But almost at the other end of the island, over one hundred years later, the decorated legionary distance slabs adorning the inner face of the Antonine Wall in Scotland most certainly helped mark out, in no uncertain terms, the very frontier of the empire at that time, and the stark boundary between Roman and barbarian worlds and minds.

Only a few distance slabs were decorated with imagery which included barbarians. Nevertheless, so powerful and unequivocal were the 'barbarian slabs' that their message was clear. Indeed, most of the other slabs could be viewed as being somewhat innocuous and anodyne in comparison, including as they did only epigraphic records of military building work. There may have been a further geographical significance in the fact that the most elaborately decorated of the distance slabs, and indeed the largest, was positioned at Bridgeness, possibly marking the very eastern end of the Antonine frontier in Scotland.[13]

There is no doubt that the common appearance of images of barbarians in Roman art cannot simply be explained away as having been part of a strategy of 'aesthetic choice'. Such a conclusion would not seem to consider the possibility that the artist or viewer's gaze could have been at the same time both admiring and proprietorial, that representation could have formed part of a system of 'colonial desire', an exoticising of the barbarian body in a way that created a dependency in both the subject and the object of the gaze. It has been suggested in interpreting some instances of the portrayal of female northern barbarians that such a voyeuristic tendency can at times be fleetingly detected when trying to define the relationship between conqueror and conquered, as displayed in an image of the desired body.[14]

The process by which Rome was to become the dominant state in Italy was itself a complex series of negotiations and constant renegotiations of self-identity, through changing power and political relationships between Rome and the other Italian cities and regions. A detailed study of this aspect of the creation of the Roman identity has been undertaken by Emma Dench in her book *From Barbarians to New Men*,[15] and there she comments that 'Rome's practice of incorporating other peoples into her citizen body was accompanied by a distinct ideological development which drew on Athenian images of barbarians, country-people and Spartans, but which resulted in a figure peculiar to Rome: the incorporated outsider who embodied Rome's morally upright past.'[16] A tantalising representation of conflict and treaty between Rome and Samnium is provided by the very fragmentary wall painting from a tomb on the Esquiline Hill in Rome, described in detail above in Chapter One, and in the compositional strategies employed there to depict unequally the main Roman and Samnite protagonists, that is to contrast the civilised victorious Roman and the defeated 'barbarian' Samnite.

The changes in terms of governance, and political experiences and expediency, embodied in the succession from Republican to imperial Rome, and those changes in the imperial system itself between the first century BC and the fifth century AD, required the creation of a new version of political and historical ideologies that defined Roman and barbarian relationships in a more fluid, and yet less adaptable, way. At times, there would appear to have been a need for Rome to construct and confront a generic rather than a specific barbarian opponent, an opposite of Rome's civilisation and achievement, a fictive figure and idea on which military and political ideologies could focus through opposition.

Chronological patterns have been identified, though these are somewhat fluid in definition. The watershed around the time of Marcus Aurelius, where feeling seems to have become subjugated to thought, probably marked a point at which in public affairs at least there was an abandonment, or perhaps more properly a rejection, of those virtues of character and behaviour which previously had been accepted as defining the proper conduct of a public figure. This is not to suggest that there was a deliberate and conscious move towards the elimination of these virtues from public life, or the rooting-out of individuals for whom conduct driven by adherence to the virtues was as much the motor of their behaviour in private as it was of their operations in the public sphere of politics or military life. Rather, expediency became more important than propriety, action more valued than gesture or charade. If the rawness of the scenes on the Column of Marcus Aurelius and on other examples of post-Aurelian state monuments represented a change of perception of the conduct of public life and military life, then perhaps it would be expected that such a fundamental change in attitude would also be reflected in other kinds of ways in Roman life and society. This change represented, in art, almost a pornography of political violence.

It is perhaps of significance that there were only a few instances in which power over the barbarian, in terms of their appearance as an attribute or contrastive image, was linked to female, as opposed to male, imperial power. The portrayal of Livia, wife of the emperor Augustus and mother of Tiberius, on the Grand Camée de France was intended to enhance the gem's message of dynastic strength and future continuance, and to be contrasted with the opposite fate of the defeated and dejected barbarian opponents of Rome, crowded and compressed into the narrow, lower register of design beneath the imperial figures.[17] A similar message comes from the Julio-Claudian Marriage Cameo, though here the barbarian defeated were represented *in absentia* by the disembodied spoils of their arms and armour.[18] The Berlin cameo vase, again of Julio-Claudian date, placed a defeated barbarian in the guise of a future conquest for the dynasty whose continuation was celebrated here by the attendance of Venus at the birth of an imperial child.[19] While it has been suggested that the actual child whose birth was being celebrated by the commissioning of the vase was female, this remains doubtful. These images certainly at least linked the barbarian to dynastic imperial power, though perhaps not directly to that of the imperial women specifically.

The most convincing evocation of female imperial power in art is the sarcophagus of the empress Helena, on which martial imagery and victory over barbarian opponents acted as a symbol of her power and influence within the imperial court of Constantine. However, this juxtaposition has been explained away by some writers as a case of 'mistaken identity', arising from the reuse of a man's coffin for Helena's burial and entombment.[20]

A similar, though less clear-cut, instance of female power is provided by the depiction of Julia Domna on the Severan arch at Leptis Magna, on a relief panel in which barbarians also appear, though she may be portrayed here as part of the Severan family and dynasty, rather than as a figure of authority in her own right.[21] The same is probably true of a relief on which Julia Domna appears in the guise of a Victory, crowning her son Caracalla as he celebrates victory over northern barbarians, representative images of whom appear on the relief tied to a trophy. Though a recent reinterpretation of the Halberstadt ivory diptych must await scholarly response, if the female, probably imperial, figure who appears in the upper register of the design on one of the leaves is accepted as being Aelia Pulcheria, depicted here quite literally as the power behind the throne, then a further example of the linking of female imperial power to images of barbarians can be added to this albeit short list.[22]

The Stilicho consular diptych is again unusual when viewed in the overall context of such objects, not only for the reasons outlined above in detail in Chapter Five but also because it stressed the idea of family harmony and a consequent promise of a secure future, by the depiction also of his wife Serena and his son Eucharius.[23] This implied once more some guarantee of peace through the exercise of female power, in this case not by being involved in the defeat of a barbarian but rather by 'conquering' him through marriage and thus annexing and harnessing his latent power.

A stereotype is as much a hollow form as it is a hologram, for it consists of a mass of sometimes incoherent, and often contradictory, data whose questioning and ordering are mediated through the image of the stereotype or stored there in readiness, perhaps for ever, if there is no will within an individual, a group or a society to engage in the creative understanding of the world in which they operate. If there is that will, the stereotype, like the generality or the definition of trends and patterns, satisfies a need and may be redefined, maybe more positively, maybe less positively, in the very process of questioning.[24]

The barbarian in Roman art, whether male or female, whether a Gaul, a German, a Dacian, a Parthian or a Goth, was simply an image, cast from its creator's mind and formed from human clay that had no life and no breath. The image, in whatever form, existed because it was needed by the Romans to define their position in the world, as is suggested in the Cavafy poem 'Waiting for the Barbarians': 'Now what's going to happen to us without barbarians?/ They were, those people, a kind of solution.' The image of the barbarian was situated in a political landscape that formed a background for this otherwise hollow torso.[25]

NOTES

These notes are not intended to provide full bibliographies on each of the many monuments and other works of art discussed in the text. Much of this discussion is in any case based either on personal inspection of the actual artworks or on analysis of published catalogues and photographs. Only where direct reference has been made to other authors' interpretations and arguments are these works cited. However, the single most invaluable reference book for this study has been Diana Kleiner's *Roman Sculpture* (Yale University Press, 1992), and the notes below will in many cases direct the reader to both Kleiner's presentation and discussion of a particular monument or other artwork and to her bibliography for that monument, statue or object.

The majority of works I have cited are inevitably in English, but a number of the most significant French, German and Italian sources have also been included here and in the bibliography.

PREFACE

1. In particular see Hannestad, N. 1988.
2. See Zanker, P. 1988a, from whose title the quote comes, on Augustan political art in particular. On how Augustan political symbolism extended into the private sphere see also Zanker, P. 1988b.
3. On propaganda and 'the creation of belief' see Charlesworth, M.P. 1937. On Augustan art and propaganda see both Zanker, P. 1988a and Ramage, E.S. 1997 for up-to-date surveys. On propaganda in Late Antiquity see, for example, Bruun, P. 1976 and Peirce, P. 1989. The interrelationship between imperial art and propaganda underwrites the whole study by Hannestad, N. 1988. For wide-ranging review articles on the political use of images, and Roman art and imperial policy, see respectively Gregory, A.P. 1994 and Brilliant, R. 1988. On a broader chronological front see the papers on political uses of art collected in Castriota, D. (ed.) 1986.
4. In particular see Elsner, J. 1995 and Zanker, P. 1997.
5. In a way, the gauntlet was thrown down for this book by Kampen, N.B. 1991a, p. 247 n. 31, where she laments that 'no work has addressed the gender or family issues in the representation of barbarians'. It is hoped that I have gone some way towards giving this topic, and other issues relating to images of barbarians, the

ENEMIES OF ROME

attention it deserved. This is not, though, the first large-scale study of the relationship between Romans and barbarians, and reference should also be made in particular to Chauvot, A. 1998, Christ, K. 1959, Cunliffe, B. 1988a, Dauge, Y.A. 1981, Heather, P. 1999, Saddington, D.B. 1961, Schneider, R.M. 1986, and Wells, P.S. 1999. On Roman ethnic stereotypes and frontiers see Miller, D.H. 1977. On Roman attitudes towards, and interaction with, nomadic peoples see Shaw, B.D. 1982a and 1982b. On barbarians in the writings of Polybius see Schmitt, H.H. 1958, and of Strabo see Thollard, P. 1987, and in those of the later Roman historian Ammianus Marcellinus see Wiedemann, T.E.J. 1986. On Byzantine concepts of the foreigner see Ahrweiler, H. 1998. For an anthropological perspective on the idea of barbarians see Berndt, C.H. and Berndt, R.M. 1971. On violent relationships between Romans and barbarians see Zanker, P. 1998 and 2000.

6. On British imperial attitudes to Roman imperialism see Hingley, R. 1993, 1994 and 1996, and Freeman, P. 1996, 1997a and 1997b. Together these papers provide the fullest possible bibliography on the subject.

7. On post-colonial perspectives see the papers in Webster, J. and Cooper, N.J. (eds) 1996 and Mattingly, D. (ed.) 1997, the latter collection directly addressing the idea of discrepant experiences of Roman imperialism. For a different perspective on imperialism in the ancient world see the earlier collection of papers in Garnsey, P.D.A. and Whittaker, C.R. (eds) 1978.

8. See the review article by Brilliant, R. 1998, centred on Jaś Elsner's 'Art and Text in Roman Culture' of 1996.

ONE: A FEAR OF DIFFERENCE

1. See Kleiner, D.E.E. 1992, pp. 301–2 in particular, and Chapter Four of this present study.

2. On medallions replacing cameos as *donativa* see Marsden, A.B. 1999.

3. On 'bar, bar, bar' see Coleman, J.E. 1997, pp. 178, 207 nn. 9 and 10, and p. 208 n. 12, and Hall, E. 1989, pp. 3–5.

4. On the complexities of Roman relationships with '*peregrini*' – 'aliens' – see in particular Balsdon, J.P.V.D. 1979, pp. 30–71, and Veyne, P. 1993.

5. Principally see Hall, E. 1989. Barbarians in Greek literature and historical writing have also been considered by Bacon, H.H. 1961, Hartog, F. 1992, and Long, T. 1986. The issue of Greek ethnocentrism is dealt with by Coleman, J.E. 1997, while for an in-depth study of ethnic identity in the Greek world see Hall, J. 1997. On the relationship between Greeks and others in the age of Alexander the Great see Rotroff, S.I. 1997. See also Bovon, A. 1963 on the notion of the barbarian during and after the Persian Wars. On Greek art as a reflection of a changed worldview in the Hellenistic

190

NOTES

period see Onians, J. 1979. On Greek and non-Greek interaction as reflected in art and architecture see Colledge, M. 1987. For a short study influenced by Hall's work, looking at identity in Roman Cyrenaica see Marshall, E. 1998.

6. Cartledge, P. 1993, pp. 38–9.
7. On Greek battle paintings as source material for Roman art see, for instance, Hamberg, P.G. 1945, pp. 174f., Hannestad, N. 1988, pp. 36–7 and p. 361 n. 144, Ling, R. 1991, pp. 10–11 and Leander Touati, A-M. 1987, pp. 27–8 and n. 81. On the Alexander sarcophagus see Pollitt, J.J. 1986, pp. 43–5 and Cohen, A. 1997. For a more general collection of papers on iconography and urban society in ancient Greece see Berard, C. et al. (eds) 1989.
8. See Pollitt, J.J. 1986, pp. 45–6 and p. 306 n. 42.
9. For a photograph of this krater, now in the Museo Nazionale, Naples, see Richter, G.M.A. 1960, pp. 360–1 Plate 480.
10. Sparkes, B. 1997.
11. On the contacts between the Greeks and Celts in general see Momigliano, A. 1975, pp. 50–73 and see Chevallier, R. 1961, Juthner, J. 1923, and Mosley, D. 1971 on Greeks and barbarians in general. The best single short account of the Attalid sculptures can be found in Pollitt, J.J. 1986, pp. 83–97, with the Altar of Zeus being discussed on pp. 97–110. Stewart, A. 1997, pp. 216–19 also discusses the altar. On the Attalid Gauls see Polito, E. 1999.
12. On the historical and political setting of Pergamene art see Pollitt, J.J. 1986, pp. 79–83 and Hansen, E.V. (ed.) 1971b. See Hansen, E.V. 1971a for a bibliography on the Attalid Gauls up to 1971.
13. In addition to Pollitt, J.J. 1986, and Stewart, A. 1997, pp. 219–20, on the 'dying Gaul' see also Howard, S. 1983, and on the 'suicidal Gauls' see also Ferris, I.M. 1997. These are also fully discussed in Polito, E. 1999.
14. On the idea of these works as 'essays in nostalgia' see Ferris, I.M. 1997. On what he has dubbed 'negative ethnocentrism', an over-compensatory respect displayed by the Greeks to certain other peoples, see Coleman, J.E. 1997, pp. 194–9. Stewart, A. 1997, p. 220 notes that 'whereas the beauty of dying warriors on classical monuments is both homoerotically and tragically appealing, these evoke more of a sadomasochistic response'.
15. On the subject of Greek heroic nudity and clothed 'others' see Osborne, R. 1998. On Celts and nakedness see Bonfante, L. 1989, pp. 562–3. On the interconnection between nakedness and the captive state in Mesopotamian art see Asher-Greve, J.M. 1998, p. 20. There she notes that 'in the context of war and captivity the bodies of enemies convey the message of victory and subjugation. Whereas enemies can be portrayed as fierce soldiers in order to emphasize the heroic victor, the gender of women and possibly male civilians seems irrelevant and they are represented as a mass of conquered bodies.' The former was certainly also the case in the Greek and Roman

191

worlds, though cases of the latter de-gendering are more or less
absent. The clear delineation of the fate of non-combatant female
enemy barbarians was evidently of significance in itself.

16. On this woman's death as metaphor see Ferris, I.M. 1995, pp. 26–7
and 1997, p. 23. On the curtailment of fertility as 'death' for
barbarian women see Kampen, N.B. 1991a, p. 245.
17. On suicide in Roman art see Leander Touati, A.M. 1987, p. 19 n. 41,
and Marszal, J. 1994. On the trope of suicide in general see Bronfen,
E. 1992.
18. Bronfen, E. 1992, p. 142. I have discussed ideas derived from Bronfen
more fully in Ferris, I.M. 1997, pp. 23–4. On suicide as a cultural
choice in an otherwise colonial situation, see Spivak, G.C. 1988 and
1999 on suttee, Donaldson, L.E. 1992 on the suicide of the colonised
'object' and Young, R. 1995 and Chiang-Liang Low, G. 1989 on the
power of the predatory and proprietorial so-called 'colonial gaze'. On
the psychological aspects of colonial relationships as reflected in the
writings of Franz Fanon see Bulhan, H.A. 1985.
19. Hall, E. 1989, p. 149.
20. On the idea of the dual colonial discourse see Webster, J. 1995 and
1996 and accompanying bibliographies. On colonial discourse theory in
general and on its use of the stereotype see Bhabha, H.K. 1983 and
1984, and Brigham, J.C. 1971. The quotation comes from Barton, C.
1992, p. 132. On ideas associated with primitivism in the ancient world
see Lovejoy, A.O. and Boas, G. 1935, and Romm, J.S. 1992.
21. Pollitt, J.J. 1986, pp. 93–5.
22. For more recent examples of the portrayal of 'primitive' peoples see
Bell, L. 1982 on Victorian painters of subject peoples, and Smith, B.
1984 on the work of the artists who accompanied Captain Cook to
the Pacific. The idea of the artist as cultural voyeur comes from
Smith's fascinating and provocative study.
23. On the Civitalba frieze see Andreae, B. 1991, pp. 61–2, Momigliano,
A. 1975, p. 62, and Rankin, D. 1987, p. 211.
24. The suggestion was apparently made first by Mario Segre, according
to Momigliano, A. 1975, p. 62.
25. For a broader discussion of the Celts at Delphi see Momigliano, A. 1975,
pp. 61–2 and Rankin, D. 1987, pp. 83–102.
26. Momigliano, A. 1975, p. 61 for this observation.
27. Ibid., p. 62.
28. On Etruscan funerary urns with battle scenes, and particularly those
involving Celts, see Ducati, P. 1910, Nielsen, M. 1975, Holliday, P.J. 1982
and Mackintosh, M. 1986, pp. 5–8 and pp. 20–1nn. 30–46. One of the
best sources of illustrative material is still Bienkowski, P. 1908.
29. Momigliano, A. 1975, p. 63.
30. Andreae, B. 1991, p. 61.
31. Rankin, D. 1987, p. 212.
32. Examples from Canosa can be seen in the collections of the British
Museum. On Cales, see Momigliano, A. 1975, p. 63.

NOTES

33. The best single source on this subject is Dench, E. 1995.

34. Just as the Romans did not generally depict their Italian enemies, so the reverse was true. The sixth-century BC stone statue of the Capestrano Warrior (in the National Museum, Chieti) from the Picene territory stands stiff and alone. If Romans were his enemies, and his alertness a coda of opposition to Roman Republican expansionism, then it would have been taken as read as such.

35. On the Esquiline painting see Hannestad, N. 1988, pp. 36–7 and p. 361 nn. 148–50, on which this discussion is based.

36. See Kuttner, A.L. 1995, pp. 78–80 and p. 250 n. 60. On pre-Augustan trophies see also Picard, G.C. 1957, pp. 101–231. On Roman generals' victory monuments in the time of the Punic Wars see Pietela-Castren, L. 1987. On culture and the Roman identity under the Republic see Gruen, E.S. 1992.

37. On the Piazza della Consolazione reliefs see Kleiner, D.E.E. 1992, pp. 51–2 and the bibliography p. 57.

38. On the monument of Aemilius Paullus see Kleiner, D.E.E. 1992, pp. 26–7 and bibliography p. 56.

39. On the Lecce frieze see Andreae, B. 1973, Plate 190, and Strong, D. 1961, p. 88 n. 14.

40. See the various descriptions of individual triumphs given in Versnel, H.S. 1970. On triumphal and monumental arches in general see Curtis, C.D. 1908, Kleiner, F.S. 1989, and Wallace-Hadrill, A. 1990. On 'lost' monuments in Rome, including triumphal arches, depicted on coins see Hill, P.V. 1989.

41. Pliny's description is discussed in the context of competition among Republican generals in Kuttner, A.L. 1995, p. 79 and p. 250 n. 60.

42. Ibid., p. 79.

43. For the most recent discussion on this topic see Webster, J. 1995 and 1996, and Welch, K. and Powell, A. (eds) 1998, particularly the papers by Barlow, J. and Rawlings, L. On the idea of 'the just war' in Roman society see Drexler, H. 1959. For an interesting study on the recent manipulation of the image of the ancient Gaul, particularly in the context of French nationalism, see Champion, T. 1997.

44. The point, though, has been made by Momigliano, A. 1975, pp. 59–60 that the Roman desire to know more about the Celtic peoples through historical and anthropological studies was more driven than the attitude of the Greeks to these peoples. On the subject of classical ethnographies of Celts see also Rankin, D. 1987, Tierney, J.J. 1960 and 1964, and Dobesch, G. 1991.

45. On the Caesarian coin issues relating to Gaul see Foss, C. 1990, p. 13 Nos 1–7.

46. This and other Caesarian coin issues are also discussed in Hannestad, N. 1988, pp. 22–3.

47. Hannestad, N. 1988, and on coins and barbarians in general see Levi, A.C. 1952, Belloni, G. 1976, Foss, C. 1990 and Overbeck, B.H. 1993. See also Burns, T.S. and Overbeck, B.H. 1987 on Germans on

Roman coins. The topic of portrayals of barbarians on Roman coins would make a book-length study in itself, and has therefore been relatively under-presented in this present book in relation to sculpture and genre art.

48. See Walter, H. 1993, pp. 104–5 and Plate LVII, and Museum of Fine Arts, Boston 1976, p. 65 No. 87 for a description, photograph and bibliography on the Alesia statuette.

49. On the Caesarian link with these statues see Soprintendenza Archeologica di Roma 1998, pp. 44–5 and Polito, E. 1999.

50. On Caesar and the city of Rome see Favro, D. 1996, pp. 60–78.

51. For a line illustration of this relief and a discussion of its content see ibid., pp. 65–6 and Figure 35. Note though that Hafner, G. (1969, p. 244) identifies the emperor as Aurelian, overseeing the building of city walls in the later third century.

52. On the linking of the Marseilles fragments and the arches at Arles, Narbonne and Beziers with Caesar's campaigns see Silberberg-Peirce, S. 1986, p. 322 n. 36.

53. It was Marcus Agrippa who turned down the triumphs voted for him and perhaps set the precedent on which Augustus acted. On the triumph in general, discussed more fully in Chapter Six below, see Payne, R. 1962, Versnel, H.S. 1970 and Brilliant 1999. On the triumph as urban theatre see Favro, D. 1994 and, again, Brilliant 1999.

TWO: AUGUSTAN IMAGES OF WAR AND PEACE

1. Zanker, P. 1988a. For an alternative view of Augustan culture see Galinsky, K. 1996.

2. On the *Ara Pacis* see Kleiner, D.E.E. 1992, pp. 90–9 and the bibliography, p. 119, and Hannestad, N. 1988, pp. 62–74.

3. For various contributions to this debate see principally Simon, E. 1968, Rose, C.B. 1990 and Kuttner, A. 1995. Torelli, M. 1982, p. 60 n. 72 calls the identification of these children as barbarians 'perfect nonsense'. He favoured the 'Trojan games' theory to account for their incongruous garb, though his comment obviously pre-dates the studies of Rose and Kuttner. On Rome and its client kingdoms see Braund, D. 1984.

4. The phrase was coined by Rose, C.B. 1990.

5. On the identity of the western child see Kuttner, A. 1995, pp. 117–23 and pp. 271–3 nn. 80–102 and of the eastern child pp. 103–4 and p. 266 nn. 41–50.

6. On the identification of this woman see Kuttner, A. 1995, pp. 102–4 and p. 266 n. 50.

7. Suetonius *Life of Augustus* 21.2.

8. On Augustan social policies targeted at women and families see, in particular, Corbier, M. 1991, Kleiner, D.E.E. 1978, and Raditsa, L.F. 1980. On this civic morality as it even impacted on women's dress codes in Rome see Sebesta, J.L. 1998.

NOTES

9. Favro, D. 1996, p. 174 and p. 317 n. 73.
10. On the caryatids and 'rituals of masculinity' in the Augustan Forum see Kellum, B. 1996, for the former in particular pp. 171–2.
11. Ibid., p. 171.
12. On the Portico of Nations see Favro, D. 1996, p. 174, p. 232 and p. 317 n. 73 and Kuttner, A. 1995, pp. 81–4 and pp. 251–4 nn. 68–92. On the statues of barbarians in the *Basilica Aemilia* see Schneider, R.M. 1986, p. 117.
13. On the *Sebasteion*, see in particular Erim, K.T. 1982 and 1990, Smith, R.R.R. 1987, 1988 and 1990, and Rose, C.B. 1997.
14. On masculine imagery in the very form of the Augustan city see Kellum, B. 1996.
15. On the *Basilica Aemilia* see Kampen, N.B. 1991b and Kleiner, D.E.E. 1992, pp. 88–9 and bibliography p. 119. On rape in the visual arts see Cohen, A. 1996 and Bryson, N. 1986. On the rape of Lucretia in Livy see Joplin, K. 1986. See also the discussion of the Claudius and Britannia relief on pp. 55–8 and Chapter Two, n. 78 below.
16. On Roman attitudes to other Italian peoples see Dench, E. 1995.
17. On the location and reconstruction of this tripod monument see Schneider, R.M. 1986, especially Tafel 9.
18. On the subtle balancing of ideologies of war and peace in Augustan art see, in particular, Zanker, P. 1988a and Gruen, E.S. 1985 and 1990. See also Ferris, I.M. 2001.
19. On the Mantova frieze see Kleiner, D.E.E. 1992, p. 86 and the bibliography, p. 119.
20. See Chapter One, pp. 6–13 and Chapter One, nn. 11–19.
21. On the 'Pasquino group' statue of Menalaos and Patroklos see, for instance, Pollitt, J.J. 1986, pp. 117–18.
22. On the Temple of Apollo Sosianus see Kleiner, D.E.E. 1992, pp. 84–6 and bibliography, pp. 118–19.
23. On the Turin frieze see Zanker, P. 1988a, p. 311 and p. 313 Fig. 244. On the fragmentary frieze with arms and captives from Bologna see Picard, G.C. 1957 Plates XXVIII–XXIX. It is probably part of a contemporary or slightly later monument.
24. On the Prima Porta Augustus see Kleiner, D.E.E. 1992, pp. 63–7 and bibliography, p. 117, Hannestad, N. 1988, pp. 50–6, and Zanker, P. 1988a, pp. 188–92. On cuirassed statues in general, with discussion of the Prima Porta Augustus see Vermeule, C.C. 1960 and 1980, and Gergel, R.A. 1994.
25. On the *Gemma Augustea* see Kleiner, D.E.E. 1992, pp. 69–72, and bibliography, p. 117, Hannestad, N. 1988, pp. 78–82, and Zanker, P. 1988a, pp. 230–3. On the dynastic ideology on the *Gemma* see Pollini, J. 1993. On the more general issue of the use of imperial imagery on gemstones see Zadoks-Josephus Jitta, A.N. 1964.
26. Zanker, P. 1988a, p. 230–1.
27. Jeppesen, K.K. 1994, p.340.
28. Ibid., p.345.

ENEMIES OF ROME

29. On Augustan moral policies in relation to art see Zanker, P. 1988a, pp. 156–66, Kellum, B. 1986 and 1990, Kleiner, D.E.E. 1978 and Kampen, N.B. 1991b. On the social policies themselves as they affected women see Corbier, M. 1991, Pomeroy, S.B. 1975, pp. 150–63 and n. 13, and Kampen, N.B. 1994, pp. 121–3.

30. See above, n. 18.

31. On Augustan marriage legislation see Corbier, M. 1991.

32. On Trajan's *alimenta* scheme as represented and celebrated on the Benevento arch see Chapter Three, pp. 73–6 and Chapter Three, nn. 16–20.

33. This observation was made by Eirrann Marshall in a paper on children in Roman art, at a dayschool 'Childhood in Antiquity' at the School of Continuing Studies, University of Birmingham 1998.

34. This claim was, of course, made by Suetonius in his *Life of Augustus* 28.3.30.2. 'Since the city was not adorned as befitted the majesty of the empire and was exposed to flood and fire, he so beautified it that he could justly boast that he had found it a city of brick and left it a city of marble.'

35. On the Tropaeum at La Turbie see Formigé, J. 1949, Lamboglia, N. 1983, Prieur, J. 1982, and Silberberg-Peirce, S. 1986, pp. 311–13.

36. On the Saint-Bertrand Tropaeum monument see Boube, E. 1996 and Silberberg-Peirce, S. 1986, pp. 313–14.

37. On the Italian arches see Jouffroy, H. 1986.

38. See Gros, P. 1979, Kleiner, F. 1998, and Silberberg-Peirce, S. 1986 who deal principally with the triumphal monuments of Gallia Narbonensis. See Frothingham, A.L. 1915, and Mierse, W. 1990 for more general discussions of the political background to the erection of territorial arches and the Augustan building programme in the western provinces.

39. Silberberg-Peirce, S. 1986, p. 319.

40. On this perhaps decapitated head at Arles see Silberberg-Peirce, S. 1986, Plate 17 and on the arch in general pp. 314–15.

41. On the images associated with the capture of Greek Marseilles see Silberberg-Peirce, S. 1986, pp. 314–15.

42. For the fullest publication of this mausoleum see Rolland, H. 1969. See also Kleiner, D.E.E. 1992, pp. 112–13 and bibliography, p. 120.

43. For the fullest publication on the arch see Rolland, H. 1977.

44. See Chapter One, n. 51 above.

45. On the arch at Carpentras see Silberberg-Peirce, S. 1986, p. 318 and D'Ambra, E. 1998, pp. 35–7.

46. On the Vienne arch see Silberberg-Peirce, S. 1986, pp. 318–19.

47. Given the centrality of images of Augustus and the imperial family in art at Rome, this apparently deliberate exclusion in art elsewhere could repay further consideration.

48. On the Besançon arch see Chapter Four below, p. 100, Woolf, G. 1998, pp. 75–6 and Walter, H. 1986.

49. On the provision of city and town gates as symbols of Augustan political promotion see Zanker, P. 1988a, pp. 328–30, Richmond, I.A.

NOTES

1933, and Whittaker, C.R. 1997, pp. 144–5. In addition, on the Saepinum gate see Coarelli, F. and Regina, A. 1984. On imperialism and the cities of Italy see also Lomas, K. 1998 and Whittaker, C.R. 1994.

50. On the arch at Pola see Kleiner, D.E.E. 1992, pp. 111–12, and bibliography p. 120.

51. On Petronius' campaign see Snowden, F.M. Jnr 1970, pp. 132–4 and 1983, p. 30 and pp. 52–3.

52. On these statuettes see ibid., 1970 p. 134 and Plate 84, and ibid., 1983, p. 30 and Plate 29.

53. On the Julio-Claudian dynasty's strategy of dynastic commemoration see Rose, B. 1997.

54. On the Grand Camée de France see Kleiner, D.E.E. 1992, pp. 149–51, and bibliography p. 164.

55. On the Marriage Cameo see ibid., pp. 151–2, and bibliography p. 164.

56. On the Berlin cameo vase see Kuttner, A. 1995, pp. 130–1 and pp. 227–8 nn. 86 and 87.

57. On the birth cameo see ibid., p. 32 and p. 227 n. 86.

58. The point was made apparently by F. Ghedini 1987 'L'Alabastron di Berlino: Un Dono di Caligola a Cesonia?', but is refuted by Kuttner, A. 1995, p. 227 n. 86. I have not been able to obtain the Ghedini article and here rely solely on Kuttner's note.

59. On the Boscoreale cups see in particular the extraordinarily detailed and complexly argued volume by Kuttner, A. 1995. In addition, see Kleiner, D.E.E. 1992, pp. 152–4, and bibliography p. 164.

60. On the prototype monument on which Kuttner believes the Augustus and Tiberius cup designs were based see Kuttner, A. 1995, pp. 193–8 and pp. 298–300 nn. 61–75.

61. Ibid., p. 164 and p. 288 n. 14.

62. This connection between events depicted on the Boscoreale cups and the Ara Pacis forms one of the main themes in Kuttner, A. 1995. See also Rose, C.B. 1990, p. 60.

63. On the taking away of barbarian children see Ferris, I.M. 1994, pp. 28–9 and on child hostages and imperial wards see Kuttner, A. 1995, pp. 94–123 and pp. 261–74 nn. 1–102.

64. On the identification of these personified provinces see Kuttner, A. 1995, pp. 69–93 and pp. 243–61 nn. 1–140.

65. Henig, M. 1983, p. 142.

66. On Archaic and classical references in Augustan art see Zanker, P. 1988a, pp. 239–63.

67. On the arch at Orange see Kleiner, D.E.E. 1992, p. 154, and bibliography p.164, and especially Amy, R. et al. 1962 (two volume supplement to *Gallia*).

68. On the Britannic Arch of Claudius see Kleiner, D.E.E. 1992, pp. 154–6, and bibliography p. 165. See also Koeppel, G. 1983 and Barrett, A.A. 1991. At Richborough, given that only the foundations of this monument survive, the absence of attempts at reconstruction is not surprising. Perhaps it was a pendant to the Claudian arch in Rome.

ENEMIES OF ROME

69. On the Fiesole relief see Picard, G.C. 1957, p. 334 Figure 8.
70. Kleiner, D.E.E. 1992, p. 154 gives the earlier date.
71. On the naval spoils see Amy, R. et al. 1962, pp. 94–106.
72. Kleiner, D.E.E. 1992, p. 154 seems to favour the Pergamene sources for the battle scenes but not Hellenistic battle paintings or drawings for the 'outlining' techniques used on the arch friezes.
73. On the Claudian arch in Rome see ibid., p. 154 and Barrett, A.A. 1991. See *Riflessi di Roma. Impero Romano e Barbari del Baltico*, 1997 Exhibition Catalogue, Milan, No. 41, for the head of a barbarian that is attributed here to the arch.
74. See Chapter Five, pp. 128–31.
75. Kuttner, A. 1995 p. 166, pl. 84.
76. On the imperial figures represented in the Sebasteion see Erim, K.T. 1990, Smith, R.R.R. 1987, 1988 and 1990, and Rose, C.B. 1997, pp. 164–9 and Plates 199–209. On the imperial cult in Asia Minor in general see Price, S.R.F. 1984.
77. Erim, K.T. 1982, p. 280. On the symbolism of the Amazon in Graeco-Roman art in general see duBois, P. 1982, von Bothmer, D. 1957, Henderson, J. 1994, Shapiro, H.A. 1983, and Tyrell, W.B. 1984. On the later mythologising of the woman as warrior see Nochlin, L. 1989, pp. 22–5, and 1999.
78. On Claudius and Britannia see Erim, K.T. 1982, Ferris, I.M. 1994, pp. 26–7, and Rose, B. 1997, p. 166 and Plate 206.
79. Warner, M. 1985, pp. 280–1.
80. On the Amazonomachy relief panel see Erim, K.T. 1990, pp. 18–20 and Fig. 12.
81. On Nero and Armenia see Rose, C.B. 1997, p. 166 and Plate 209.
82. On Augustus and Nike see ibid. and Plate 200.
83. On the other Augustus and barbarian relief see ibid. and Plate 201.
84. On the Tiberius relief see ibid. and Plate 202.
85. On the Germanicus relief see ibid. and Plate 203.
86. On the *ethne* see Smith, R.R.R. 1990, pp. 93–5 with examples in Figures 3–5.
87. On the difference between Greek and Roman personifications see ibid., p. 95. See also Bienkowski, P. 1900.
88. On the concept of the fragment of the body as a metaphor, though in this case for modernity, see the lecture reproduced as Nochlin, L. 1994. My own, as yet unpublished, conference paper 'Entformung. Fragmentation, Association and Disassociation', delivered at the 1996 Theoretical Archaeology Group (TAG) meeting, looked at the theoretical concepts surrounding the manipulation of fragmentary remains and objects in the past, based on the theories of collage developed by Kurt Schwitters and on those of Nochlin. There is quite clearly a great deal of scope for an extended study of the Roman trophy from such standpoints. Pacteau, F. 1994, pp. 57–72 has considered the duality of various past systems for representing the human body as (divided) dissected parts and (unified) anatomical

drawings, as being a reflection of the 'tension between the belief in the body as an ideal form, and the body as dehumanized parts' (Pacteau, F. 1994, p. 61), and again these ideas seem worthy of development in the context of Roman art historical studies.

89. A point made by Smith, R.R.R. 1990, p. 95, for example.
90. On personifications in the Hadrianeum see Chapter Three, pp. 86–8, and Kleiner, D.E.E. 1992, pp. 283–5, and bibliography p. 314.

THREE: THE TRAJANIC BARBARIAN

1. The bibliography on the column is enormous, and no attempt will be made here to detail all the available sources. Principally see Kleiner, D.E.E. 1992, pp. 212–20, and bibliography pp. 263–4, Richmond, I.A. 1935, Rossi, L. 1971, Hannestad, N. 1988, pp. 154–67, Lepper, F. and Frere, S.S. 1988, and Claridge, A. 1993. On the suicide of Decebalus see Speidel, M.P. 1971. While Claridge's paper quite rightly views the column as a Hadrianic funerary monument, it will nevertheless be discussed here as a Trajanic symbol.
2. On the construction/destruction contrast see Davies, P.J.E. 1997, pp. 62–4 and Ferris, I.M. 2003.
3. The various scholarly debates on these matters are fully discussed in Lepper, F. and Frere, S.S. 1988.
4. The suggestion was made by B. Fehr and is quoted and extended by Davies, P.J.E. 1997, p. 63 n. 123.
5. The fullest treatment available on the history and significance of the trophy in Greek and Roman art is Picard, G.C. 1957.
6. On 'nostalgia' for the primitive see Chapter One, nn. 14 and 20.
7. The plates in Lepper, F. and Frere, S.S. 1988 follow Cichorius' system and have been used here.
8. See Kampen, N.B. 1991a, pp. 219–20.
9. This argument is quoted in Lepper, F. and Frere, S.S. 1988, p. 90. They themselves favour the most obvious interpretation of the women as being Dacians. The scene otherwise is largely undiscussed.
10. On this scene and other headhunting scenes see Lepper, F. and Frere, S.S. 1988, pp. 70–1, and Rossi, L. 1981, pp. 187ff.
11. On the Tropaeum Traiani see Kleiner, D.E.E. 1992, pp. 230–2 and bibliography p. 264, Rossi, L. 1971, pp. 55–65, and 1972, Richmond, I.A. 1967, Hannestad, N. 1988, pp. 171–3, and Mackendrick, P. 1975, pp. 95–105. See also Vulpe, R. 1963 on Germans on the trophy.
12. This point is made in Richmond, I.A. 1967, pp. 43–6.
13. I make these points in Ferris, I.M. 2003.
14. Kleiner, D.E.E. 1992, p. 230.
15. See Chapter Three, n. 12.
16. On the Benevento arch see Kleiner, D.E.E. 1992, pp. 224–9 and bibliography p. 264, Hannestad, N. 1988, pp. 177–86, and Torelli, M. 1997. On the Pozzuoli monument see Gialanella, C. 1997, pp. 89–90 and Figure 49. The monument could alternatively date to

the time of Domitian. Gialanella gives it a date range of the second half of the first century to the earlier second century.

17. These points are made by Currie, S. 1996, p. 167.
18. On this seemingly cynical point of view see Torelli, M. 1997, pp. 150–2. Pliny's quote comes from Panegyricus 28.5.
19. On the representation of children on the arch see Currie, S. 1996 and Ferris, I.M. 2003.
20. On Trajan, 'the father of the country', see in particular Currie, S. 1996, pp. 167–73.
21. This striking phrase comes from Fears, J.R. 1981.
22. On the Great Trajanic Frieze see Kleiner, D.E.E. 1992, pp. 220–2 and bibliography p. 264, Hannestad, N. 1988, pp. 168–70, and particularly the in-depth monograph of Touati, A.M.L. 1987.
23. On *spolia* see Chapter Five, pp. 128–32.
24. On the order/disorder dichotomy on the frieze see Leander-Touati, A.M. 1987, pp. 27–9 in particular.
25. See ibid., pp. 38–9 in particular.
26. On Trajan in combat see ibid., pp. 21–2.
27. On imperial rider reliefs in general see Schleiermacher, M. 1984. On the Domitianic equestrian statue see Hannestad, N. 1988, pp. 139–42. The literary source is Statius *Silvae* I, 1, 1–107.
28. On the overall issue of the Trajanic barbarian see Ferris, I.M. 2003.
29. On the Ephesos ivory see Kuttner, A. 1995, p. 245 n. 16.
30. On the subject of the Athens cuirassed statue being identified as Trajan see Kleiner, D.E.E. 1992, p. 241.
31. On Trajanic coinage depicting barbarians see Levi, A.C. 1952, pp. 14–20 and Foss, C. 1990, pp. 100–2 and 105–6. On the barbarian as an attribute see Levi, A.C. 1952, pp. 25–40.
32. On the provenance of the stone for the massive statues of Dacians from the Trajanic Forum see Waelkens, M. 1985. On the Villa Borghese Dacian see Campitelli, A. 1997.
33. On the reconstruction of this tripod monument see Schneider, R.M. 1986, Tafel 8.
34. On the ever-youthful portrait types of Trajan see Kleiner, D.E.E. 1992, p. 208 who calls him 'the ageless adult'. The same also applied to the ever-youthful portraits of Augustus.
35. On the tombstone of Tiberius Claudius Maximus see Speidel, M.P. 1970.
36. On the original sources referring to the post-mortem mistreatment of the remains of Decebalus see Cassius Dio 68.14.3. and *Fasti Ostienses* AD 106.
37. On the Ranuleh statue see Abbaye of Daoulas 1993. Vermeule, C.C. 1968, p. 88 suggests that this work may be later.
38. On issues connected with the Parthian victories see Foss, C. 1990, pp. 105–6 Nos 74–7.
39. On Hadrianic personifications see Toynbee, J.M.C. 1934 and Hannestad, N. 1988, pp. 194–200.

NOTES

40. On hunting in Hadrianic art see, for instance, Kleiner, D.E.E. 1992, pp. 251–3.
41. On the Hierapytna Hadrian see Kleiner, D.E.E. 1992, p. 241 and Hannestad, N. 1988, pp. 200–1.
42. See Chapter Three, n. 31.
43. On 'the theology of victory' see Fears, J.R. 1981.
44. See Chapter Two, pp. 55–62 and Chapter Two, n. 87.
45. On the Hadrianeum (an Antonine commission) see Kleiner, D.E.E. 1992, pp. 283–5 and bibliography p. 314.
46. On the subject of 'gendered geography' in the Roman world see in particular Moynihan, R. 1985 and Nicolet, C. 1991. For studies of a similar process of linking landscape and geography with women's bodies, occurring in British poetry and literature of the 1930s, see Bergonzi, B. 1978, and Montefiore, J. 1994 and 1996, pp. 104–12. The 1930s material would make fascinating comparative data for re-examining the theoretical motives behind the Roman gendered geography.

FOUR: THE TIDE TURNS

1. On the column see Kleiner, D.E.E. 1992, pp. 295–301 and bibliography p. 314, Hannestad, N. 1988, pp. 236–44, Caprino, C. et al. 1955, Becatti, G. 1957 and Scheid, J. and Huet, V. 2000.
2. For a scene-by-scene presentation of photographs of the column, reproductions of the drawings of the base and a descriptive narrative see Caprino, C. et al. 1955. Individual descriptive entries of the scenes discussed in this chapter will not be cited.
3. This point was made more explicitly in the Julio-Claudian reliefs in the Aphrodisias Sebasteion discussed in Chapter Two, pp. 55–62.
4. On the torture scene on Trajan's Column see Chapter Three, pp. 68–9 and Chapter Three, n. 9.
5. On the flight into exile on the Tropaeum Traiani see Chapter Three, pp. 70–3.
6. On the fragment as signifier or metaphor see Chapter One, n. 88. These remind me of Arthur Graeme West's 'archipelago of corrupt fragments' in his 1916 war poem 'Night Patrol'.
7. On these reused Aurelian panels see Kleiner, D.E.E. 1992, pp. 288–95 and bibliography p. 314, and Hannestad, N. 1988, pp. 226–36.
8. This is a more or less unique motif.
9. The composition of this scene may be linked to the surviving equestrian statue of Marcus.
10. On the Torlonia Relief see Kleiner, D.E.E. 1992, pp. 254–6 and Kuttner, A. 1995, pp. 165–6 and Plate 89.
11. On the equestrian statue of Marcus see Kleiner, D.E.E. 1992, p. 271 and Hannestad, N. 1988, pp. 219–23.
12. On Domitianic and Trajanic equestrian statues see Chapter Three, pp. 78–9 and n. 27.

13. On the missing barbarian figures see Kleiner, D.E.E. 1992, p. 271 where she notes that the presence of the figure was recorded in the twelfth century *Mirabilia Urbis Romae*. The fact that the Marcus barbarian is missing perhaps gives the work a serenity and gravitas more appealing to modern tastes than the original might have been.

14. On the Aquincum mould see Kleiner, F.S. 1989, pp. 203–4 and Figure 2.

15. On the Besançon arch see Woolf, G. 1998, pp. 75–6, Walter, H. 1986 and 1993, pp. 46–8. On the Parma reliefs see Picard, G.C. 1957, pp. 449–51 and Plate XXVI.

16. On trophies and arches as geographical markers see Silberberg-Peirce, S. 1986 and Chapter Two, pp. 42–9 and pp. 54–5.

17. On the Ephesos altar see Kleiner, D.E.E. 1992, pp. 309–12 and bibliography p. 315.

18. On the origins of the motif of barbarian suicide see Leander-Touati, A.M. 1987, p. 19 n. 41.

19. On the Tripoli arch see Kleiner, D.E.E. 1992, pp. 308–9 and bibliography p. 315.

20. On the Carthage herms see Snowden, F.M. Jnr. 1970, p. 142 and Plate 85.

21. On the Tipasa mosaic see Dunbabin, K.M.D. 1978, p. 24.

22. On battle sarcophagi see Kleiner, D.E.E. 1992, pp. 301–3 and bibliography pp. 314–15, Leander-Touati, A.M. 1987, p. 35, Andreae, B. 1956, pp. 14–16, and Hamberg, P.G. 1945, pp. 172–89.

23. On the Portonaccio sarcophagus see Kleiner, D.E.E. 1992, pp. 301–2, and Strong, D.E. 1961, p. 54 and p. 99.

24. On the evidence for and against Pompilius see Kleiner, D.E.E. 1992, p. 301.

25. Kampen, N.B. 1981.

26. The phrase belongs to ibid., p. 49. On *pietas* and victory see Charlesworth, M.P. 1943. For a reference to an as yet unpublished paper on *clementia* scenes on both public and private monuments see Dowling, M.B. 1994.

27. On the Clementia sarcophagus see Kleiner, D.E.E. 1992, p. 302.

28. On the Via Appia sarcophagus see Strong, D.E. 1961, p. 99 and Plate 96 and Reinach, S. 1888.

29. On the Attalid Gauls see Chapter One, pp. 8–15 and nn. 11–22.

30. On the Mantova sarcophagus see Strong, D.E. 1961, pp. 98–9 and Plate 95.

31. On the Etruscan/Italian-Roman tradition see Chapter One, pp. 17–18 and n. 28.

32. On the Vatican Achilles and Penthesilea sarcophagus see ibid., pp. 350–1.

33. On hunt sarcophagi see ibid., pp. 390–2.

34. On the Septimus tombstone see Bianchi Bandinelli, R. 1970, p. 342 and Plate 381.

NOTES

35. On the Antonine Wall distance slabs see Keppie, L.J.F. 1975 and 1979, Keppie, L.J.F. and Arnold, B.J. 1984, pp. 28–58 and Ferris, I.M. 1994. More specifically on the significance of the images of winged Victories on a number of the slabs see Hassall, M.W.C. 1977.
36. On the Bridgeness slab see Keppie, L.J.F. and Arnold, B.J. 1984, pp. 27–8 No. 68.
37. On this unusual composition see Phillips, E.J. 1975.
38. On this motif see Chapter Six, pp. 154–60 and n. 24.
39. On the Hag Knowe slab see Keppie, L.J.F. and Arnold, B.J. 1984, p. 32 No. 84.
40. On the Summerston Farm slab see ibid., pp. 49–50 No. 137.
41. On the Hutcheson Hill slab see ibid., pp. 53–4 No. 149.
42. For a comparative reading of the Antonine Wall slabs and the earlier auxiliary cavalry tombstones see Ferris, I.M. 1994.
43. The phrase 'resigned and contemplative' comes from Keppie, L.J.F. 1979, p. 9.
44. This point is made at greater length in Ferris, I.M. 1994.
45. On the disposal of the slabs and their burial see Keppie, L.J.F. 1975.
46. On this changing value system see Kampen, N.B. 1981.
47. These views come from Phillips, E.J. 1975.

FIVE: THE ENEMY WITHIN

1. On the Arch of Septimius Severus see Kleiner, D.E.E. 1992, pp. 329–32 and bibliography p. 354, Brilliant, R. 1967, and Hannestad, N. 1988, pp. 262–7.
2. References to Hellenistic battle paintings can be found at various points throughout this book, but see in particular Chapter One, pp. 5–6 and n. 7.
3. This is an interesting twist on the miniaturisation of the barbarian noted as a trend in Roman art and on coinage from the second century onwards by Levi, A.C. 1952.
4. On the Trajanic alimentary programme, as reflected in the artwork of the Benevento Arch, see Chapter Three, pp. 73–6 and nn. 16–20.
5. This notably extended inscription refers to the dynasty's successes both 'at home and abroad' and would have helped the viewer to understand the context of the artistic scheme of the monument.
6. On the Arch of the Argentarii see Kleiner, D.E.E. 1992, pp. 334–7 and bibliography, p. 354. See also Pallotino, M. 1946.
7. On the Trajanic linking of conquest and commerce see Chapter Three, p. 64 and n. 2. On an earlier, possibly Caesarian, artwork which also makes this link see Chapter One, pp. 26–7 and n. 51.
8. On the Regisole see Brilliant, R. 1974, p. 114.
9. On the Domitianic prototype see Chapter Three, pp. 78–9 and n. 27.
10. On the Arch of Severus at Leptis Magna see Kleiner, D.E.E. 1992, pp. 340–3 and bibliography, p. 354, and Hannestad, N. 1988, pp. 270–7.

ENEMIES OF ROME

11. In many respects these portrayals of vulnerable children hark back to Augustan art.
12. It should be noted, however, that this was never as pronounced as in the case of the barbarian as attribute of the emperor, as particularly appeared regularly on coinage.
13. On the coffin of Helena discussed in this context see Chapter Five, pp. 133–5 and n. 37.
14. On the Cyrene frieze see Vermeule, C.C. 1968, pp. 79–80. On the Corinth facade see ibid., pp. 83–8 and Figures 27–30.
15. On the Caracalla/Julia Domna relief see Hassall, M.W.C. 1977, p. 337 Figure 13.4.c. and p. 338.
16. On the Achilles and Penthesilea sarcophagus see Kleiner, D.E.E. 1992, pp. 350–1.
17. On the Ludovisi sarcophagus see ibid., pp. 389–90 and bibliography pp. 396–7, and Hannestad, N. 1988, pp. 290–3.
18. Kleiner, D.E.E. 1992, p. 389.
19. On the sarcophagus lid see Kuttner, A. 1995, Plate 88.
20. On the Boscoreale cups and their possible influence on later artworks see Kuttner, A. 1995, pp. 155–72 and pp. 287–91 nn. 1–30.
21. On the Arcus Novus see Kleiner, D.E.E. 1992, pp. 409–13 and bibliography p. 428. See also Laubscher, H.P. 1976.
22. On the Claudian arch see Chapter Two, pp. 54–5 and n. 68.
23. Kleiner, D.E.E. 1992, p. 413.
24. On the Decennalia relief see Kleiner, D.E.E. 1992, pp. 413–17 and bibliography p. 428, MacCormack, S.G. 1981, pp. 170–1, and Hannestad, N. 1988, pp. 309–11.
25. On the Arch of Galerius see Kleiner, D.E.E. 1992, pp. 418–25 and bibliography p. 428, Pond-Rothman, M.S. 1977, MacCormack, S.G. 1981, pp. 174–7, and Hannestad, N. 1988, pp. 313–18.
26. On the Domitianic prototype equestrian statue see Chapter Three, pp. 78-9 and n. 27.
27. On the Trajanic equestrian triumph on the Great Trajanic Frieze see Chapter Three, pp. 77–9 and n. 26.
28. See Chapter Six, pp. 175–6 and nn. 89–90.
29. The portrayal of the Rape of the Sabine Women and the related punishment of Tarpeia in the Basilica Aemilia was part of the Augustan programme of moralising art, as detailed in Chapter Two, pp. 33–5 and n. 15.
30. On the Arch of Constantine see Kleiner, D.E.E. 1992, pp. 444–55 and bibliography p. 464, Hannestad, N. 1988, pp. 319–26, and Peirce, P. 1989.
31. On the significance of the *spolia* incorporated in this monument see in particular Holloway, R. 1985 and Peirce, P. 1989.
32. On these giant figures of Dacians see Chapter Three, pp. 81–2 and n. 32.
33. On the Aurelian pieces in their original context see Chapter Four, pp. 97–8 and n. 7.

NOTES

34. On the earlier pedestal designs see Chapter Four pp. 118 and 125 respectively.
35. On Sant' Appolinare see, for instance, Elsner, J. 1995, pp. 222–39.
36. On Julia Domna on the Leptis arch see Chapter Five, pp. 120–1.
37. On the sarcophagus of Helena see Kleiner, D.E.E. 1992, pp. 455–7 and bibliography, p. 464. On the more general issue of the power of the imperial women at various times see Fischler, S. 1994 and Lefkowitz, M. 1993, and for Late Antiquity see Holum, K.G. 1977 on Pulcheria and Holum, K.G. 1982 on Theodosian empresses.
38. The suggestion that the form of the Adamklissi monument is a kind of eternal return is made in Chapter Three, p. 72.
39. This stance was most recently taken by Elsner, J. 1998, p. 148.
40. On the Licinius gem see Calza, R. 1972 Tav. LXVII No. 124.
41. On the 'chariot' gem see ibid., Tav. LXXXIV No. 154.
42. On this equestrian gem see Bianchi Bandinelli, R. 1971 Plate 329.
43. On *largitio* dishes in general see Toynbee, J.M.C. and Painter, K.S. 1986, pp. 15–16 (where they are termed 'political plates'), and Strong, D.E. 1966, pp. 199–201.
44. On the *missorium* of Theodosius see Strong, D.E. 1966, p. 200 and Plate 64, MacCormack, S.G. 1981, pp. 214–20, Reece, R. 1983, pp. 241–2, and particularly Toynbee, J.M.C. and Painter, K.S. 1986, pp. 27–8.
45. On the Geneva plate of Valentinian see MacCormack, S.G. 1981, pp. 204–5 and Plate 51, and Toynbee, J.M.C. and Painter, K.S. 1986, p. 27.
46. The catalogue description of the Theodosius plate given in Toynbee, J.M.C. and Painter, K.S. 1986, pp. 27–8 makes no mention at all of the four barbarian guards.
47. On the Constantius dish see Beckwith, J. 1968, p. 10, Kent, J.P.C. and Painter, K.S. 1977, p. 11, MacCormack, S.G. 1981, pp. 43–4, and Toynbee, J.M.C. and Painter, K.S. 1986, p. 27.
48. On the 'David Plates' see Kent, J.P.C. and Painter, K.S. 1977, pp. 102–12, in particular p. 106 No. 181, and Toynbee, J.M.C. and Painter, K.S. 1986, pp. 50–7.
49. I have used the Stilicho diptych as a case study in Ferris, I.M. 1997.
50. On the ceremony of raising the emperor on a shield see Wallace-Hadrill, J.M. 1977, and MacCormack, S.G. 1981, p. 217. On Germanic influences on other imperial celebrations see McCormick, M. 1986, pp. 114–15.
51. On the dual significance of stressing/denying Stilicho's otherness see Ferris, I.M. 1997, pp. 25–7.
52. On the Barberini Diptych see Beckwith, J. 1968, pp. 38–40, and MacCormack, S.G. 1981, pp. 71–2 and Plate 22. See Cameron, A. 1983 on the link between elites and icons in Byzantine society.
53. This is depicted in a similar manner to the relegation of the barbarians to a lower realm on the Grand Camée de France, with the Julio-Claudian dynasty reigning supreme on earth and Augustus ascending into the heavens. See Chapter Two, p. 49–50.

54. The discussion on the Halberstadt Diptych here is based on Cameron, A. 1998.

55. The phrase comes from ibid., p. 389.

56. The argument behind this identification is given in ibid., pp. 387–9.

57. On the Constantius Diptych see MacCormack, S.G. 1981, p. 210 and Plate 56.

58. On the Obelisk of Theodosius see Hannestad, N. 1988, pp. 332–8, Beckwith, J. 1968, pp. 15–16, MacCormack, S.G. 1981, pp. 56–7 and Plates 17–18, and Hannestad, N. 1988, pp. 332–8.

59. See Chapter Five, n. 44.

60. On the Obelisk of Arcadius see MacCormack, S.G. 1981, pp. 57–9 and Plates 19–21.

61. It is not implied here that this 'fear' was actually crippling the functioning of late Roman society. The confident architecture and art associated with the Christian Church suggests otherwise, as is evident from a perusal of Brown, P. 1992 and Onians, J. 1999, pp. 279–89. I am grateful to Martin Henig for raising this point.

SIX: IMAGE AND REALITY

1. Versnel, H.S. 1970.

2. On Decebalus' head see Chapter Three, n. 36.

3. On this image from the Temple of Apollo Sosianus see Chapter Two, pp. 36–7 and n. 22.

4. Barton, C.A. 1993, p. 28.

5. On this occurring at the funeral of Augustus see Kuttner, A.L. 1995, p. 52.

6. See Chapter Two, n. 88.

7. On the relationship between conquest and slavery see Bradley, K. 1994, pp. 10–56. The figures quoted here come from Bradley, p. 33. On the Greek attitude to foreigners being tainted by the ubiquity of foreign slaves see Coleman, J.E. 1997, pp. 180–1. On the origins and place of the foreign slave in the Greek and Roman worlds see Wiedemann, T.E.J. (ed.) 1988. On the Roman view of the extra-degraded state of the prisoner of war as slave see Bradley, K. 1994, pp. 27–8.

8. Suicide as an escape from being sold into slavery is discussed by Bradley, K. 1994, pp. 44–5.

9. On the sexual exploitation of slaves, and on Marcus Aurelius' boast, see ibid., p. 28. The fantasy of erotic domination in master–slave relationships is dealt with in Benjamin, J. 1983.

10. Barton, C.A. 1993.

11. Ibid., p. 13.

12. Ibid., p. 13.

13. Ibid., p. 28.

14. On the Pompeii helmet see von Petrikovits, H. 1983, p. 183 Plate V.

15. On the Pompeii bowl see Ward-Perkins, J. and Claridge, A. 1976, Catalogue No. 124.

NOTES

16. On the sculpture from the monument at Mainz see Selzer, W. 1988, pp. 239–43.
17. Ibid., p. 241 No. 263.
18. Ibid., p. 260 No. 239.
19. Ibid., p. 239 No. 259, p. 241 No. 264 and p. 243 No. 266.
20. On the Tomb of the Julii see Chapter One, p. 27 and n. 42.
21. On the Nijmegen mausoleum see Walter, H. 1993, pp. 60–5 and Plates XXXVII–XXXIX.
22. On the Nickenich cenotaph see ibid., pp. 80–5 and Plate LI.
23. On military tombstones in general see Anderson, A.S. 1984.
24. On the horseman and fallen foe tombstones see Anderson, A.S. 1984, pp. 17–19, Mackintosh, M. 1986, and Ferris, I.M. 1995.
25. On military equestrian tombstones from the Cotswold region in Britain see Webster, G. 1993, pp. 44–8. Rufus Sita's tombstone is described there, pp. 47–8, and illustrated in Plate 36.
26. See Ferris, I.M. 1995.
27. On the Halton Chesters tombstone see Phillips, E.J. 1977, pp. 95–6 No. 259 and Plate 70.
28. On this complex interplay of roles see Ferris, I.M. 1995, p. 25. D'Ambra, E. 1998, pp. 56–7 makes the Longinus tombstone from Colchester even more complex than it is, by misidentifying the cavalryman Longinus himself as a Briton rather than a Thracian.
29. On the later types see Coulston, J.N.C. 1987, p. 145 and Bishop, M.C. and Coulston, J.N.C. 1993, p. 26.
30. On the link with the Dexileos stele see Toynbee, J.M.C. 1962, p. 158 and Richter, G.M.A. 1960, p. 162 and Figure 217.
31. On the imagery associated with the idea of the divine rider in Roman art and on its origins see Mackintosh, M. 1986 and 1995.
32. See Ferris, I.M. 1995, p. 29 for a comparison of these 'literal' representations with similarly direct images of infantry soldiers on the First World War monuments of Charles Sargeant Jagger. Jagger was himself an ex-soldier who strived to present the war veterans with images in which they could see themselves.
33. On the Romanius tombstone see Selzer, W. 1988, p. 156 No. 87 and Walter, H. 1993, pp. 73–4 and Plates XLVI–XLVII.
34. On the Bassus tombstone see Walter, H. 1993, pp. 87–8 and Plate LII.
35. On gemstones and funerary symbolism see, for example, Henig, M. 1977.
36. This point is, for example, made in Phillips, E.J. 1975, p. 180 where he notes that the battle scene on the Bridgeness distance slab 'has a brutality which is contrary to the spirit of classical art and which appears to have originated in popular military art'.
37. On the Brescia *balteus* or fixture from an equestrian statue see Stella, C. 1987, pp. 68–9. For another good example from Piemonte in Italy see Bianchi Bandinelli, R. 1970, Plate 111.
38. On the Alesia figure see Walter, H. 1993, pp. 104–5 and Plate LVII, and Museum of Fine Arts Boston 1975 No. 87.

39. On the Bologna example see Bianchi Bandinelli, R. 1970, Plate 109, and on the Mogilovo one see Plate 110. On the Herculaneum examples see Stella, C. 1987, p. 68 where she also cites other examples from Velia, Rimini and Este.

40. On the Niederbeiber *signum* see Kuttner, A.L. 1995, p. 187, p. 233 n. 41, p. 297 nn. 52–3 and Plate 120.

41. On the issue of prejudice in the Roman world see Sherwin-White, A.N. 1967, Ruggini, L.C. 1968, Snowden, F.M. Jnr 1970, pp. 169–95 in particular, Snowden, F.M. Jnr 1983, pp. 35–60, Balsdon, J.P.V.D. 1979, Walbank, F.W. 1972, and Momigliano, A. 1975.

42. Balsdon, J.P.V.D. 1979.

43. As discussed by Balsdon, J.P.V.D. 1979, p. 65, Cicero being the most shocked and outraged of those at Rome.

44. On the Vindolanda letter see Bowman, K. 1994, p. 106 Tablet II.164. I have not discussed here the theory that the *Britannia* coin issues of AD 153–5 had a deliberately restricted circulation to Britain only. It has been argued that the figure identified as *Britannia capta* on the coins was intended to be provocative and humiliating to the people of the province, following the crushing of a revolt in northern Britain. However, Walker, D.R. 1988, pp. 295–7 has put forward a convincing contrary case that argues against this scenario.

45. On the Mainz dice shaker see Hellenkemper, H. et al. 1990, pp. 261–3. I am grateful to Roger White for drawing my attention to this object.

46. On Roman–Italian relationships see Dench, E. 1995.

47. Snowden, F.M. Jnr 1970, 1983 and 1997, Thompson, L. 1989 and Vercoutter, J. et al. 1976.

48. Even as late as 1997, the same stance was taken by Snowden on Greek and Roman attitudes to Blacks. On this see Snowden, F.M. Jnr 1997, pp. 119–21.

49. Snowden, F.M. Jnr 1983, pp. 55–9.

50. For numerous examples see, for instance, Snowden, F.M. Jnr 1970, Plates 40–77, 82–5 and 101–17. On Pompeii mosaics depicting hyper-sexual black males, and a reading of these that identifies no overt racial prejudice in the pictures see Clarke, J. 1996.

51. Snowden, F.M. Jnr 1983, Plate 29. See Chapter Two, pp. 48–9.

52. Snowden, F.M. Jnr 1983, Plate 32. See Chapter Four, p. 102.

53. Snowden's 1983 book indeed was called *Before Color Prejudice*.

54. This observation was made by Kampen, N.B. 1991a, p. 233.

55. On the fear of women transgressing and for examples of mythological exemplars in earlier imperial art see D'Ambra, E. 1993a, pp. 78–103. On the subject of 'transgressing women' more generally see Stallybrass, P. and White, A. 1986, and Stonebridge, L. 1997. For a consideration of the use of mythology in the service of Romanisation in the western provinces see Picard, G.C. 1979.

56. D'Ambra, E. 1993a.

NOTES

57. Ibid., pp. 78–108.
58. See Chapter Two, pp. 60–1.
59. On the ambiguity of Roman personifications see Smith, R.R.R. 1990, p. 95.
60. On the equation of military conquest with sexual conquest see D'Ambra, E. 1993a, pp. 84–6 and Kellum, B. 1996, p. 171. On the strain of Roman humour that linked sexuality with aggression see Richlin, A. 1983.
61. On the hair-pulling scene on the Great Altar see Pollitt, J.J. 1986, p. 102. On the hair-pulling motif in general see Touati, A.M.L. 1989, p. 23 n. 59, and Zanker, P. 2000 on Roman violence against women and children.
62. On the sexualising of images of rulers see Winter, I.J. 1996 on Naram-Sin of Agade.
63. On the Sebasteion reliefs see Chapter Two, pp. 55–61 and nn. 76–87.
64. On the ever-youthful Augustus and Trajan, 'the ageless adult', see Chapter Three, n. 35.
65. Winter, I.J. 1996, p. 19.
66. On the chained/unchained, threatening/ unthreatening opposition see Kampen, N.B. 1996, p. 20.
67. Virgil, *Georgics*, 3. l. 25. On the importance of the theatre as an arena for political art see Zanker, P. 1988a, pp. 324–6.
68. On Campana plaques see Bailey, D. 1983, pp. 191–2.
69. See Chapter One, pp. 16–17 and nn. 23–35.
70. The reference for this object comes from Bailey, D. 1995, p. 2.
71. On the Tipasa mosaic see Dunbabin, K.M.D. 1978, pp. 24, 275–6 and Plate 7. On Zliten, see Dunbabin, pp. 66, 278 and Plates 46–9. On the El Djem mosaic see Dunbabin, pp. 66, 259 and Plates 50–1.
72. On the Pompeii paintings of trophies see Picard, G.C. 1957, pp. 220–4 and Plate VII.
73. No attempt has been made as part of the present study to produce a catalogue of these objects. For Britain, Toynbee's study brings the list up to 1964, while for Gaul Walter's work brings it up to 1993. For examples of other small bronzes see Museum of Fine Arts, Boston 1975 (Catalogue of *Romans and Barbarians* exhibition), Nos 4 (a Gaulish prisoner), 6 (a mounted figure), and 7 (a falling Gaulish warrior about to be slain by Roman soldier who pulls his hair and knees him in the back). See also Bienkowski, P. 1928, and the Abbeye of Daoulas 1993 and Riflessi di Roma 1997 catalogues. On a chalcedony figure of a barbarian see Bailey, D.M. 1999.
74. Toynbee, J.M.C. 1964.
75. Ibid., p. 119 and Plate XXXIIa.
76. Ibid., p. 120 and Plate XXXIIb.
77. Ibid., and Plate XXXIId.
78. Ibid., and Plate XXXIIc.
79. Ibid., and Plate XXXIIe.
80. Unpublished. This item was brought into the Bowes Museum,

Barnard Castle, County Durham in 1980 for identification by a metal-detectorist. Its exact provenance is unknown.

81. Walter, H. 1993.
82. On the Brescia statuette see Stella, C. 1987, pp. 68–9.
83. According to Stella, C. 1987, p. 68.
84. On this terracotta figure see Bailey, D. 1995. See also Reinach, S. 1911 for further examples of Gauls in Alexandrian art.
85. Bailey, D. 1995, p. 1.
86. Still the most comprehensive study of barbarians on Roman coins is Levi, A.C. 1952. But see also Foss, C. 1990 on historical coins in general.
87. For some examples of barbarians on pottery vessels see, for example, Walter, H. 1993, Plate LXX Nos. 183–5, and Picard, G.C. 1957, p. 303 Figure 7.
88. Museum of Fine Arts, Boston 1976, p. 5 No. 8A.
89. On the identifications of the humiliated emperors on the Shapur I Taq-i-Bastan relief panels see Calza, R. 1972 Taf. CXXXII No.277. On the Bishapur reliefs see Herrmann, G. 1980. See also Hannestad, N. 1988, p. 445.
90. On the possible Roman influences on the victory reliefs of Shapur I see Mackintosh, M.C. 1974.
91. A photograph of this object appears in Brown, D. 1971, p. 128 No. 89. A similar emulation may also be discerned in the assemblage of artefacts in the Sutton Hoo ship burial, on which see Filmer-Sankey, W. 1996. Again, through possession of a Roman-style signet ring Childeric and other barbarian kings probably thought of themselves as Roman. On this ring see MacGregor, A. 1999.

SEVEN: WAITING FOR THE BARBARIANS

1. On the concept of fable and reportage see Hynes, S. 1976, p. 208. The terms derive from the writings of Stephen Spender. On memory in Roman society see Ferris, I.M. 1999.
2. See Chapter One, p. 6 and n. 7.
3. On these common topoi see Touati, A.M.L. 1987, p. 28 n. 81.
4. On the source of the mourning captive motif see Phillips, E.J. 1975, p. 179. On rider and fallen foe motifs see Chapter Six, n. 24.
5. Said, E.W. 1991, and more generally on culture and imperialism Said, E.W. 1993.
6. On supposed Persian vices see Hall, E. 1989 and 1993.
7. On the supposed barbarity of the Samnites see Dench, E. 1995.
8. On 'colonial desire' see Donaldson, L.E. 1992 and Young, R. 1995. I also raise the issue in Ferris, I.M. 1997, pp. 23–4. On the interrelationship between colonialism and culture in general see Dirks, N. 1992.
9. On the subtext of the Caesarian commentaries see, most recently, Webster, J. 1995, pp. 6–7, Webster, J. 1996, pp. 118–20, and Welch, K. and Powell, A. (eds) 1998.

NOTES

10. On the interaction between artist and subject, and the possibilities for control through representation in a colonial context, see Bell, L. 1982 and Smith, B. 1984.
11. On the Claudius/Constantius Chlorus connection see Kleiner, D.E.E. 1992, p. 413.
12. On the Arras Medallion see Hannestad, N. 1988, pp. 311–13 and MacCormack, S.G. 1981, pp. 29–31 and Plate 9.
13. On the significance of the location of the Bridgeness slab see Keppie, L.J.F. 1975.
14. On colonial desire see Young, R. 1995.
15. Dench, E. 1995.
16. Ibid., p.68.
17. On the Grand Camée de France see Chapter Two, pp. 49–50 and n. 54.
18. On the Marriage Cameo see Chapter Two, p. 50 and n. 55.
19. On the Berlin cameo vase see Chapter Two, pp. 50-1 and Chapter Two n. 56.
20. On the sarcophagus of Helena see Chapter Five, pp. 134–5 and n. 37.
21. On Julia Domna and the Leptis arch see Chapter Five, pp. 120–1.
22. On the Halberstadt diptych see Chapter Five, pp. 141–2 and nn. 54–6.
23. On the Stilicho diptych see Chapter Five, pp. 138–40 and n. 49.
24. On the theoretical consideration of stereotypes and their representation see Dyer, R. 1993.
25. To paraphrase W.H. Auden.

BIBLIOGRAPHY

Abbeye of Daoulas 1993. *Rome Faces the Barbarians*. Daoulas, Cultural Centre Abbeye of Daoulas with the National Library.

Ahrweiler, H. 1998. 'Byzantine Concepts of the Foreigner: Nomads', in Ahrweiler, H. and Laiou, A.E. (eds) 1998.

Ahrweiler, H. and Laiou, A.E. (eds) 1998. *Studies on the Internal Diaspora of the Byzantine Empire*. Harvard University Press, Cambridge, Mass.

Amy, R. et al. 1962. *L'Arc d'Orange*. Supplément à *Gallia* XV.

Anderson, A.S. 1984. *Roman Military Tombstones*. Shire Archaeology, Aylesbury.

Andreae, B. 1956. *Motivgeschichtliche Untersuchungen zu den Römischen Schlachtsarkophagen*. Berlin.

Andreae, B. 1973. *The Art of Rome*. Macmillan, London.

Andreae, B. 1991. 'The Image of the Celts in Etruscan, Greek and Roman Art', in Kruta,V. et al. (eds) 1991, 61–9.

Archer, L., Fischler, S. and Wyke, M. (eds) 1994. *Women in Ancient Societies: an Illusion of the Night*. Macmillan, Basingstoke.

Asher-Greve, J.M. 1998. 'The Essential Body: Mesopotamian Conceptions of the Gendered Body', in Wyke, W. (ed.) 1998, 8–37.

Bacon, H.H. 1961. *Barbarians in Greek Tragedy*. Yale University Press, New Haven.

Bailey, D.M. 1983. 'Terracotta Revetments, Figurines and Lamps', in Henig, M. (ed.) 1983, 191–204.

Bailey, D.M. 1995. 'A Gaul from Egypt', in Raftery, B. (ed.) 1995, 1–3.

Bailey, D.M. 1999. 'A Chalcedony Barbarian', in Henig, M. and Plantzos, D. (eds) 1999, 79–82.

Balsdon, J.P.V.D. 1979. *Romans and Aliens*. Duckworth, London.

Barlow, J. 1998. 'Noble Gauls and their Other in Caesar's Propaganda', in Welch, K. and Powell, A. (eds) 1998, 139–70.

Barrett, A.A. 1991. 'Claudius' British Victory Arch in Rome', *Britannia* XXII, 1–21.

Barton, C.A. 1993. *The Sorrows of the Ancient Romans. The Gladiator and the Monster*. Princeton University Press, Princeton.

Becatti, G. 1957. *La Colonna di Marco Aurelio*. Domus, Milan.

Beckwith, J. 1968. *The Art of Constantinople*. 2nd edn, Phaidon, Oxford.

Bell, L. 1982. 'Artists and Empire: Victorian Representations of Subject Peoples', *Art History* Vol. 5, No. 1, 73–86.

BIBLIOGRAPHY

Belloni, G. 1976. 'Aeternitas e Annientamento dei Barbari Sulle Monete'. In *T. Canali della Propaganda nel Mondo Antico*, 220–8, Milan.

Benjamin, J. 1983. 'Master and Slave: the Fantasy of Erotic Domination', in Snitow, A. et al. 1983, 280–305.

Berard, C. et al. 1989. *A City of Images. Iconography and Society in Ancient Greece*. Princeton University Press, Princeton.

Bergmann, B. and Kondoleon, C. (eds), 1999. *The Art of Ancient Spectacle. Studies in the History of Art. Center for Advance Study in the Visual Arts Symposium Papers XXXIV*. Yale University Press, New Haven.

Bergonzi, B. 1978. *Reading the Thirties: Text and Contexts*. Macmillan, London.

Berndt, C.H. and Berndt, R.M. 1971. *The Barbarians. An Anthropological View*. C.A. Watts, London.

Bhabha, H.K. 1983. 'The Other Question – the Stereotype and Colonial Discourse'. *Screen* 24/6, 18–36.

Bhabha, H.K. 1984. 'Of Mimicry and Man: the Ambivalence of Colonial Discourse', *October XXVIII*.

Bianchi Bandinelli, R. 1970. *Rome: the Centre of Power*. Thames & Hudson, London.

Bianchi Bandinelli, R. 1971. *Rome: the Late Empire*. Thames & Hudson, London.

Bienkowski, P. 1900. *De Simulacris Barbararum Gentium Apud Romanos. Corporis Barbarorum Prodomus*. Imprimerie de l'Université des Jagellons, Cracow.

Bienkowski, P. 1908. *Die Darstellungen der Gallier in der Hellenistichen Kunst*. Vienna.

Bienkowski, P. 1928. *Les Celts dans Les Arts Mineurs Gréco-Romains. Avec des Recherches Iconographiques sur Quelques Autres Peuples Barbares*. Imprimerie de l'Université des Jagellons, Cracow.

Bishop, M.C. and Coulston, J.C.N. 1993. *Roman Military Equipment*. Batsford, London.

Bois, P. du 1982. *Centaurs and Amazons: Women and the Prehistory of the Great Chain of Being*. University of Michigan Press, Ann Arbor.

Bonanno, A. 1976. 'Roman Relief Portraiture to Septimius Severus. Portraits and Other Heads on Roman Historical Reliefs up to the Age of Septimius Severus', *British Archaeological Reports*, International Series 6, Oxford.

Bonfante, L. 1989. 'Nudity as a Costume in Classical Art', *American Journal of Archaeology* 93, 543–70.

Bothmer, D. von 1957. *Amazons in Greek Art*. Clarendon Press, Oxford.

Boube, E. 1996. *Le Trophée Augustéen*. Collections du Musée Archéologique Départemental de Saint-Bertrand-de-Comminges No. 4. Musée de Saint-Bertrand-de-Comminges.

Bovon, A. 1963. 'La Representation des Guerriers Perses et la Notion de Barbare dans la Ire Moitié du Ve Siècle', *Bulletin de Correspondance Hellénique* 87, 579–602.

ENEMIES OF ROME

Bowman, K. 1994. *Life and Letters on the Roman Frontier: Vindolanda and its People*. British Museum Press, London.

Bradley, K. 1994. *Slavery and Society at Rome*. Cambridge University Press, Cambridge.

Braund, D. 1984. *Rome and the Friendly King: the Character of the Client Kingship*. Croom Helm, London.

Brigham, J.C. 1971. 'Ethnic Stereotypes', *Psychological Bulletin* LXXVI, 15–38.

Brilliant, R. 1967. 'The Arch of Septimius Severus in the Roman Forum', *Memoirs of the American Academy in Rome* 29.

Brilliant, R. 1974. *Roman Art from the Republic to Constantine*. Phaidon, Oxford.

Brilliant, R. 1988. 'Roman Art and Roman Imperial Policy', Review in *Journal of Roman Archaeology* 1, 110–14.

Brilliant, R. 1998. 'Some Reflections on the "New Roman Art History"', *Journal of Roman Archaeology* 11, 557–65.

Brilliant, R. 1999 '"Let the Trumpets Roar!" The Roman Triumph'. In Bergamnn, B. and Kondoleon, C. (eds) 1999, 221–30.

Bronfen, E. 1992. *Over Her Dead Body. Death, Femininity and the Aesthetic*. Manchester University Press, Manchester.

Brown, P. 1971. *The World of Late Antiquity*. Thames and Hudson, London.

Brown, P. 1992. *Power and Persuasion in Late Antiquity*. University of Wisconsin Press, Madison.

Bruun, P. 1976. 'Notes on the Transmission of Imperial Images in Late Antiquity', in *Studia Romana in Honorem Petri Krarup*, Odense, 121–31.

Bryson, N. 1986. 'Two Narratives of Rape in the Visual Arts, Lucretia and the Sabine Women', in Tomaselli, S. and Porter, R. (eds) 1986, 52–72.

Buitron-Oliver, D. (ed.) 1997. 'The Interpretation of Architectural Sculpture in Greece and Rome', *Studies in the History of Art* 49. National Gallery of Art, Washington.

Bulhan, H.A. 1985. *Franz Fanon and the Psychology of Oppression*. Plenum, London.

Burns, T.S. and Overbeck, B.H. 1987. *Rome and the Germans as Seen in Coinage*. Catalogue for the Exhibition. Emory University Museum, Atlanta.

Calza, R. 1972. *Iconographia Romana Imperiali*. L'Erma di Bretschneider, Rome.

Cameron, A. 1993 (revsd edn). 'Images of Authority: Elites and Icons in Late Sixth-Century Byzantium', *Past and Present* 84, 3–35.

Cameron, A. 1998. 'Consular Diptychs in their Social Context: New Eastern Evidence', *Journal of Roman Archaeology* 11, 385–403.

Cameron, A. and Kuhrt, A. (eds) 1993 (revsd edn). *Images of Women in Antiquity*. Croom Helm, London.

Campitelli, A. 1997. 'La Statua di Dace di Villa Borghese', in *Riflessi di Roma. Impero Romano e Barbari del Baltico*, 73–4.

BIBLIOGRAPHY

Caprino, C. et al. 1955. *La Colonna di Marco Aurelio*. Studi e Materiali del Museo dell'Impero Romano, Rome.

Cartledge, P. 1993. *The Greeks: a Portrait of Self and Others*. Oxford University Press, Oxford.

Castriota, D. (ed.) 1986. *Artistic Strategy and the Rhetoric of Power: Political Uses of Art from Antiquity to the Present*. Southern Illinois University Press, Carbondale.

Celik, Z., Favro, D. and Ingersoll, R. (eds) 1994. *Streets of the World: Critical Perspectives on Public Space*. University of California Press, Berkeley.

Champion, T. 1997. 'The Power of the Picture: the Image of the Ancient Gaul', in Molyneaux, B.L. (ed.) 1997, 213–29.

Charlesworth, M.P. 1937. 'The Virtues of a Roman Emperor. Propaganda and the Creation of Belief', *Proceedings of the British Academy* 23, 105–33.

Charlesworth, M.P. 1943. 'Pietas and Victoria. The Emperor and the Citizen', *Journal of Roman Studies* 33, 1–10.

Chauvot, A. 1998. 'Opinions Romaines Face aux Barbares au Ive Siècle AP. J.-C.', Collections de L'Université des Sciences Humaines de Strasbourg. Études d'Archéologie et d'Histoire Ancienne.

Chevallier, R. 1961. *Grecs et Barbares*. Fondation Hardt Entretiens VIII, Geneva.

Chiang-Liang Low, G. 1989. 'White Skins/Black Masks: the Pleasures and Politics of Imperialism', *New Formations* IX.

Christ, K. 1959. 'Römer und Barbaren in den Höhen Kaiserzeit', *Saeculum* 10, 261–98.

Claridge, A. 1993. 'Hadrian's Column of Trajan', *Journal of Roman Archaeology* 6, 6–22.

Clarke, J. 1996. 'Hypersexual Black Men in Augustan Baths: Ideal Somatypes and Apotropaic Magic', in Kampen, N.B. (ed.) 1996b, 184–98.

Coarelli, F. and Regina, A. La 1984. 'Abruzzo Milise', *Guida Archeologica Laterza* 9. Rome.

Cohen, A. 1996. 'Portrayals of Abduction in Greek Art: Rape or Metaphor?', in Kampen, N.B. (ed.) 1996, 117–35.

Cohen, A. 1997. *The Alexander Mosaic: Stories of Victory and Defeat*. Cambridge University Press, Cambridge.

Coleman, J.E. 1997. 'Ancient Greek Ethnocentrism', in Coleman, J.E. and Walz, C.A. (eds) 1997, 175–220.

Coleman, J.E. and Walz, C.A. (eds) 1997. *Greeks and Barbarians. Essays on the Interactions Between Greeks and Non-Greeks in Antiquity and the Consequences for Eurocentrism*. Occasional Publications of the Department of Near Eastern Studies and the Program of Jewish Studies, Cornell University, No. 4. CDL Press, Bethesda, Maryland.

Colledge, M. 1987. 'Greek and Non-Greek Interaction in the Art and Architecture of the Hellenistic East', in Kuhrt, A. and Sherwin-White, S. (eds) 1987, 134–62.

ENEMIES OF ROME

Corbier, M. 1991. 'Family Behavior of the Roman Aristocracy, Second Century BC–Third Century AD', in Pomeroy, S.B. (ed.) 1991, 173–96.

Cottam, S., Dungworth, D., Scott, S. and Taylor, J. (eds) 1995. *TRAC 94 Proceedings of the Fourth Theoretical Roman Archaeology Conference*. Oxbow Books, Oxford.

Coulston, J.N.C. 1987. 'Roman Military Equipment on Third Century Tombstones', in Dawson, M. (ed.) 1987, 141–56.

Cunliffe, B. 1988a. *Greeks, Romans and Barbarians: Spheres of Interaction*. Guild Publishing, London.

Cunliffe, B. (ed.) 1988b. *The Temple of Sulis Minerva at Bath*. Volume 2: *The Finds from the Sacred Spring*. Oxford University Committee for Archaeology Monograph No. 16. Oxford.

Currie, S. 1996. 'The Empire of Adults: the Representation of Children on Trajan's Arch at Beneventum', in Elsner, J. (ed.) 1996, 153–81.

Curtis, C.D. 1908. 'Roman Monumental Arches'. *Supplementary Papers of the American School of Classical Studies in Rome II*, 26–83.

D'Ambra, E. 1993a. *Private Lives, Imperial Virtues. The Frieze of the Forum Transitorium in Rome*. Princeton University Press, Princeton.

D'Ambra, E. (ed.) 1993b. *Roman Art in Context*. Prentice Hall, Englewood Cliffs.

D'Ambra, E. 1998. *Art and Identity in the Roman World*. Weidenfeld & Nicolson, London.

Dannheimer, H. and Gebhard, R. (eds) 1993. *Das Keltische Jahrtausend*. Philipp von Zabern, Mainz.

Dauge, Y.A. 1981. 'Le Barbare: Recherches sur la Conception Romaine de la Barbarie et de la Civilisation', Coll. Latomus CLXXVI, Brussels.

Davies, P.J.E. 1997. 'The Politics of Perpetuation: Trajan's Column and the Art of Commemoration', *American Journal of Archaeology* 101, No. 1, 41–65.

Dawson, M. (ed.) 1987. *Roman Military Equipment. The Accoutrements of War*. BAR International Series No. 336, Oxford.

De Caro, S. 1997. 'I Barbari del Nord Visti da Roma', in *Riflessi di Roma: Impero Romano e Barbari del Baltico*, 25–9. L'Erma di Bretschneider, Rome.

Dench, E. 1995. *From Barbarians to New Men. Greek, Roman, and Modern Perceptions of Peoples of the Central Apennines*. Clarendon Press, Oxford.

Dirks, N. 1992. 'Introduction: Colonialism and Culture', in Dirks, N. (ed.) 1992, 1–25.

Dirks, N. (ed.) 1992. *Colonialism and Culture. Comparative Studies in Society and History*. University of Michigan Press, Ann Arbor.

Dobesch, G. 1991. 'Ancient Literary Sources', in Kruta, V. et al. (eds) 1991, 35–41.

Donaldson, L.E. 1992. *Decolonizing Feminisms. Race, Gender and Empire-Building*. University of North Carolina Press, Chapel Hill.

Dowling, M.B. 1994. 'The Clemency of the Times: Clementia on Public and Private Monuments', abstract, 95th Annual Meeting of the Archaeological Institute of America. *American Journal of Archaeology* 98, 335.

BIBLIOGRAPHY

Drexler, H. 1959. *Iustum Bellum*. Rheinisches Museum für Philologie 102, 97–140.

Ducati, P. 1910. 'Le Pietre Funerarie Felsinee', *Monumenti Antichi* XX, 362–729.

Dunbabin, K.M.D. 1978. *The Mosaics of Roman North Africa*. Oxford University Press, Oxford.

Dyer, R. 1993. *The Matter of Images. Essays on Representation*. Routledge, London.

Elsner, J. 1995. *Art and the Roman Viewer*. Cambridge University Press, Cambridge.

Elsner, J. (ed.) 1996. *Art and Text in Roman Culture*. Cambridge University Press, Cambridge.

Elsner, J. 1998. *Imperial Rome and Christian Triumph. The Art of the Roman Empire AD 100–450*. Oxford University Press, Oxford.

Erim, K.T. 1982. 'A New Relief Showing Claudius and Britannia from Aphrodisias', *Britannia* XIII, 277–81.

Erim, K.T. 1990. 'Recent Work at Aphrodisias 1986–1988', in Roueche, C. and Erim, K.T. (eds) 1990, 9–36.

Fantham, E., Foley, H.P., Pomeroy, S.B. and Shapiro, H.A. (eds) 1994. *Women in the Classical World: Image and Text*. Oxford University Press, Oxford.

Favro, D. 1994. 'Rome. The Street Triumphant: the Urban Impact of Roman Triumphal Parades', in Celik, Z. et al. (eds) 1994, 230–57.

Favro, D. 1996. *The Urban Image of Augustan Rome*. Cambridge University Press, Cambridge.

Fears, J.R. 1981. 'The Theology of Victory at Rome: Approaches and Problems', *Aufstieg und Niedergang der Römischen Welt* II 17, 827–948.

Ferris, I.M. 1995. 'Insignificant Others: Images of Barbarians on Military Art from Roman Britain', in Cottam, S. et al. (eds) 1995, 24–31.

Ferris, I.M. 1997. 'The Enemy Without, the Enemy Within. More Thoughts on Images of Barbarians in Greek and Roman Art', in Meadows, K. et al. (eds) 1997, 22–8.

Ferris, I.M. 1999. 'Invisible Architecture: Inside the Roman Memory Palace', in Leslie, A. (ed.) 1999, 191–9.

Ferris, I.M. 2001. 'The Body Politic. The Sexuality of Barbarians in Augustan Art', in Bevan, L. 2001 (ed.) *Sexuality, Society and the Archaeological Record*, 100–9. Cruithne Press, Glasgow.

Ferris, I.M. 2003. 'The Hanged Men Dance. Barbarians in Trajanic Art'. In Scott, S. and Webster, J. 2003. *Roman Imperialism and Provincial Art*, 53–68 Cambridge University Press, Cambridge.

Filmer-Sankey, W. 1996. 'The "Roman Emperor" in the Sutton Hoo Ship Burial', *Journal of the British Archaeological Association* CXLIX, 1–9.

Fischler, S. 1994. 'Social Stereotypes and Historical Analysis: the Case of the Imperial Women at Rome', in Archer, L. et al. (eds) 1994, 115–33.

Fishwick, D. 1989. 'The Sixty Gallic Tribes and the Altar of the Three Gauls', *Historia* 38, 111–12.

Formigé, J. 1949. *Le Trophée des Alpes*. Supplément à *Gallia* II.

ENEMIES OF ROME

Foss, C. 1990. *Roman Historical Coins*. Seaby, London.

Freeman, P. 1996. 'British Imperialism and the Roman Empire', in Webster, J. and Cooper, N.J. (eds) 1996, 19–34.

Freeman, P. 1997a. 'Mommsen through to Haverfield: the Origins of Romanization Studies in Late 19th Century Britain', in Mattingly, D. (ed.) 1997, 27–51.

Freeman, P. 1997b. '"Romanization" – "Imperialism": What Are We Talking About?' in Meadows, K. et al. (eds) 1997, 8–14.

Frothingham, A.L. 1915. 'The Roman Territorial Arch', *American Journal of Archaeology* XIX, 155–73.

Galinsky, K. 1996. *Augustan Culture. An Interpretive Introduction*. Princeton University Press, Princeton.

Garnsey, P.D.A. and Whittaker, C.R. (eds) 1978. *Imperialism in the Ancient World*. Cambridge University Press, Cambridge.

Gergel, R.A. 1986. *An Allegory of Imperial Victory on A Cuirassed Statue of Domitian*. Record of the Princeton Art Museum 45.1, 3–15.

Gergel, R.A. 1994. 'Costume as Geographical Indicator: Barbarians and Prisoners on Cuirassed Statue Breastplates', in Sebesta, J.L. and Bonfante, L. (eds) 1994, 191–212.

Gialanella, C. 1997. 'Echi del Barbaricum in Recenti Ritrovamenti a Pozzuoli', in *Riflessi di Roma. Impero Romano e Barbari del Baltico*, 89–90. L'Erma di Bretschneider, Milan.

Giardina, A. (ed.) 1993. *The Romans*. University of Chicago Press, Chicago.

Goldhill, S. and Osborne, R. (eds) 1994. *Art and Text in Ancient Greek Culture*. Cambridge University Press, Cambridge.

Gregory, A.P. 1994. '"Powerful Images": Responses to Portraits and the Political Uses of Images in Rome', *Journal of Roman Archaeology* 7, 80–99.

Gros, P. 1979. 'Pour une Chronologie des Arcs de Triomphe de Gaule Narbonnaise (à Propos de L'Arc de Glanum)', *Gallia* 37, 55–83.

Gruen, E.S. 1985. 'Augustus and the Ideology of War and Peace', in Winckes, R. (ed.) 1985, 51–72.

Gruen, E.S. 1990. 'The Imperial Policy of Augustus', in Raaflaub, K.A. and Toher, M. (eds) 1990, 395–416.

Gruen, E.S. 1992. *Culture and National Identity in Republican Rome*. Cornell University Press, Ithaca.

Hafner, G. 1969. *Art of Rome, Etruria, and Magna Graecia*. Harry N. Abrams Inc., New York.

Hall, E. 1989. *Inventing the Barbarian. Greek Self-Definition through Tragedy*. Clarendon Press, Oxford.

Hall, E. 1993. 'Asia Unmanned: Images of Victory in Classical Athens', in Rich, J. and Shipley, G. (eds) 1993, 108–33.

Hall, J. 1997. *Ethnic Identity in Greek Antiquity*. Cambridge University Press, Cambridge.

Hamberg, P.G. 1945. *Studies in Roman Imperial Art with Special Reference to the State Reliefs of the Second Century*. University of Uppsala, Uppsala.

BIBLIOGRAPHY

Hannestad, N. 1988. *Roman Art and Imperial Policy*. Aarhus University Press, Aarhus.

Hansen E.V. 1971a. 'A Bibliography of the Gallic Statues in the Art of Pergamon', in Hansen, E.V. (ed.) 1971b, 496–7.

Hansen, E.V. (ed.) 1971b. *The Attalids of Pergamon*. Cornell University Press, Ithaca.

Hartley, B. and Wacher, J. (eds) 1983. *Rome and her Northern Provinces*. Alan Sutton, Gloucester.

Hartog, F. 1992. *The Mirror of Herodotus. The Representation of the Other in the Writing of History*. University of California Press, Berkeley.

Hassall, M.W.C. 1977. 'Wingless Victories', in Munby, J. and Henig, M. (eds) 1977, 327–40.

Heather, P. 1999. 'The Barbarian in Late Antiquity: Image, Reality and Transformation', in Mills, R. (ed.) 1999, 234–58.

Hellenkemper, H., Horn, H.G., Koschik, H. and Trier, B. (eds) 1990. *Archäologie in Nordrhein–Westfalen. Geschichte im Herzen Europas*. RGZM, Mainz.

Henderson, J. 1994. 'Timeo Danaos: Amazons in Early Greek Art and Pottery', in Goldhill, S. and Osborne, R. (eds) 1994, 85–137.

Henig, M. 1977. 'Death and the Maiden: Funerary Symbolism in Daily Life', in Munby, J. and Henig, M. (eds) 1977, 347–66.

Henig, M. 1983a. 'The Luxury Arts: Decorative Metalwork, Engraved Gems and Jewellery', in Henig, M. (ed.) 1983b, 139–65.

Henig, M. (ed.) 1983b. *A Handbook of Roman Art. A Survey of the Visual Arts of the Roman World*. Phaidon, Oxford.

Henig, M. 1993. *Roman Sculpture from the Cotswold Region. Corpus Signorum Imperii Romani, Great Britain*, Volume 1: *Fascicule 7*. Oxford University Press, Oxford.

Henig, M. and Plantzos, D. (eds) 1999. *Classicism to Neo-Classicism. Essays Dedicated to Gertrud Seidman*. British Archaeological Reports International Series No. 793, Oxford.

Héron de Villefosse, A. 1902. *Le Trésor de Boscoreale*. Fondation Eugene Piot, Monuments et Mémoires 5. Paris.

Herrmann, G. 1980. 'The Sassanian Rock Reliefs at Bishapur, I. Bishapur III, Triumph Attributed to Shapur I', *Iranische Denkmaler* R2, Lfg. 9.

Hill, P.V. 1989. *The Monuments of Ancient Rome as Coin Types*. Seaby, London.

Hingley, R. 1993. 'Attitudes to Roman Imperialism', in Scott, E. (ed.) 1993, 23–7.

Hingley, R. 1994. 'Britannia, Origin Myths and the British Empire', in Cottam, S. et al. (eds) 1994, 11–23.

Hingley, R. 1996. 'The "Legacy" of Rome: the Rise, Decline, and Fall of the Theory of Romanization', in Webster, J. and Cooper, N.J. (eds) 1996, 35–48.

Holliday, P.J. 1982. *The Celtomachy in Etruscan Funerary Relief*. Abstracts, College Art Association of America 26. New York.

Holliday, P. (ed.) 1993. *Narrative and Event in Ancient Art*. Cambridge University Press, Cambridge.

Holloway, R. 1985. 'The *Spolia* on the Arch of Constantine', *Quaderni Ticinesi Numismatica e Antichita Classiche* Vol. 14, 261–9.

Holum, K.G. 1977. 'Pulcheria's Crusade of AD 421 and the Ideology of Imperial Victory', *Greek, Roman and Byzantine Studies* 18, 153–72.

Holum, K.G. 1982. 'Theodosian Empresses: Women and Imperial Dominion in Late Antiquity', University of California Press, Berkeley.

Hopkins, K. 1978. *Conquerors and Slaves. Sociological Studies in Roman History*, Vol. 1. Cambridge University Press, Cambridge.

Howard, S. 1983. 'The Dying Gaul, Aigina Warriors, and Pergamene Academism', *American Journal of Archaeology* 87, 483–7.

Huskinson, J., Beard, M. and Reynolds, J. (eds) 1988. *Image and Mystery in the Roman World. Papers Given in Memory of Jocelyn Toynbee*. Alan Sutton, Gloucester.

Hynes, S. 1976. *The Auden Generation: Literature and Politics in England in the 1930s*. Faber, London.

Jeppesen, K.K. 1994. 'The Identity of the Missing Togatus and Other Clues to the Interpretation of the Gemma Augustea', *Oxford Journal of Archaeology* 13 No. 3, 335–56.

Joplin, K. 1986. 'Ritual Work on Human Flesh: Livy's Lucretia and the Rape of the Body Politic', *Helios* 17.1, 51–70.

Jouffroy, H. 1986. *La Construction Publique en Italie et dans L'Afrique Romaine*. Études et Travaux Groupe de Recherche d'Histoire Romaine de l'Université de Sciences Humaines de Strasbourg. Strasbourg.

Juthner, J. 1923. *Hellenen und Barbaren*. Leipzig.

Kahil, L. and Auge, C. (eds) 1979. *Mythologie Gréco-Romaine, Mythologies Peripheriques: Études d'Iconographie*. Editions du Centre National de la Recherche Scientifique, Paris.

Kampen, N.B. 1981. 'Biographical Narration and Roman Funerary Art', *American Journal of Archaeology* 85, 47–58.

Kampen, N.B. 1991a. 'Between Public and Private: Women as Historical Subjects in Roman Art', in Pomeroy, S.B. (ed.) 1991, 218–48.

Kampen, N.B. 1991b. 'Reliefs of the Basilica Aemilia', *Klio (Beitrage zur Alten Geschichte)* 73, 448–58.

Kampen, N.B. 1994. 'Material Girl: Feminist Confrontations with Roman Art', *Arethusa* 27, No. 1, 111–49.

Kampen, N.B. 1996. 'Gender Theory in Roman Art', in Kleiner, D.E.E. and Matheson, S.B. (eds) 1996, 14–25.

Kampen, N.B. (ed.) 1996. *Sexuality in Ancient Art*. Cambridge University Press, Cambridge.

Kellum, B. 1986. 'Sculptural Programs and Propaganda in Augustan Rome: the Temple of Apollo on the Palatine', in Winckes, R. (ed.) 1986, 169–76.

Kellum, B. 1990. 'The City Adorned: Programmatic Display at the Aedes Concordiae Augustae', in Raaflaub, K.A. and Toher, M. (eds) 1990, 276–307.

BIBLIOGRAPHY

Kellum, B. 1996. 'The Phallus as Signifier: the Forum of Augustus and Rituals of Masculinity', in Kampen, N.B. (ed.) 1996, 170–83.

Kent, J.P.C. and Painter, K.S. 1977. *Wealth of the Roman World AD 300–700*. British Museum, London.

Keppie, L.J.F. 1975. 'The Distance Slabs From the Antonine Wall: Some Problems', *Scottish Archaeological Forum* 7, 57–65.

Keppie, L.J.F. 1979. *Roman Distance Slabs From the Antonine Wall. A Brief Guide*. Hunterian Museum, University of Glasgow, Glasgow.

Keppie, L.J.F. and Arnold, B.J. 1984. *Scotland*. Volume 1 *Fascicule 4, Corpus Signorum Imperii Romani. Great Britain*. Oxford University Press, Oxford.

Kleiner, D.E.E. 1978. 'The Great Friezes of the Ara Pacis Augustae. Greek Sources, Roman Derivatives, and Augustan Social Policy', *Mélanges de L'École Francaise de Rome Antiquité* 90, 753–85.

Kleiner, D.E.E. 1992. *Roman Sculpture*. Yale University Press, New Haven.

Kleiner, D.E.E. and Matheson, S.B. (eds) 1996. *I Claudia. Women in Ancient Rome*. University of Texas Press, Austin.

Kleiner, F.S. 1989. 'The Study of Roman Triumphal and Honorary Arches 50 Years After Kahler', *Journal of Roman Archaeology* 2, 195–206.

Kleiner, F.S. 1998. 'The Roman Arches of Gallia Narbonensis', *Journal of Roman Archaeology* 11, 610–12.

Koeppel, G. 1983. 'Two Reliefs from the Arch of Claudius in Rome', *Mitteilungen des Deutschen Archäologischen Instituts, Römische Abteilung* 90, 103–9.

Kruta, V., Frey, O.H., Raftery, B. and Szabo, M. (eds) 1991. *The Celts*. Thames & Hudson, London.

Kuhrt, A. and Sherwin-White, S. (eds) 1987. *Hellenism in the East: the Interaction of Greek and Non-Greek Civilisations from Syria to Central Asia after Alexander*. Duckworth, London.

Kuttner, A.L. 1995. *Dynasty and Empire in the Age of Augustus. The Case of the Boscoreale Cups*. University of California Press, Berkeley.

Lamboglia, N. 1983. *Il Trofeo di Augusto alla Turbia*. Istituto Internazionale di Studi Liguri, Bordighera.

La Rocca, E. 1994. 'Ferocia Barbarica', *Jahrbuch des Deutschen Archäologischen Instituts* 109, 1–40.

Laubscher, H.P. 1976. *Arcus Novus und Arcus Claudii: Zwei Triumphbogen an der Via Lata in Rom*. Vendenhoeck und Ruprecht. Göttingen.

Laurence, R. and Berry, J. (eds) 1998. *Cultural Identity in the Roman Empire*. Routledge, London.

Lefkowitz, M. 1993. 'Influential Women', in Cameron, A. and Kuhrt, A. (eds) 1993, 49–64.

Lepper, F. and Frere, S.S. 1988. *Trajan's Column*. Alan Sutton, Gloucester.

Leslie, A. (ed.) 1999. *Theoretical Roman Archaeology and Architecture. The Third Conference Proceedings*. Cruithne Press, Glasgow.

Levi, A.C. 1952. 'Barbarians on Roman Imperial Coins and Sculpture', *American Numismatic Society, Numismatic Notes and Monographs* No. 123.

Ling, R. 1991. *Roman Painting*. Cambridge University Press, Cambridge.

ENEMIES OF ROME

Lomas, K. 1998. 'Roman Imperialism and the City in Italy', in Laurence, R. and Berry, J. (eds) 1998, 64–78.

Long, T. 1986. *Barbarians in Greek Comedy*. Southern Illinois University Press, Carbondale.

Lovejoy, A.O. and Boas, G. 1935. *Primitivism and Related Ideas in Antiquity*. Johns Hopkins Press, Baltimore.

MacCormack, S.G. 1981. *Art and Ceremony in Late Antiquity*. University of California Press, Berkeley.

McCormick, M. 1986. *Eternal Victory. Triumphal Rulership in Late Antiquity*. University of California Press, Berkeley.

MacGregor, A. 1999. 'The Afterlife of Childeric's Ring', in Henig, M. and Plantzos, D. (eds) 1999, 149–62.

Mackendrick, P. 1975. *The Dacian Stones Speak*. University of North Carolina Press, Chapel Hill.

Mackintosh, M. 1974. 'Roman Influences on the Victory Reliefs of Shapur I of Persia', *California Studies in Classical Antiquity* 6, 181–203. University of California Press, Berkeley.

Mackintosh, M. 1986. 'The Sources of the Horseman and Fallen Enemy Motif on the Tombstones of the Western Empire', *Journal of the British Archaeological Association* CXXXIX, 1–21.

Mackintosh, M. 1995. 'The Divine Rider in the Art of the Western Roman Empire', *British Archaeological Reports*, International Series 607, Oxford.

Marsden, A.B. 1999. 'Imperial Portrait Gems, Medallions and Mounted Coins: Changes in Imperial *Donativa* in the 3rd Century AD', in Henig, M. and Plantzos, D. (eds) 1999, 89–103.

Marshall, E. 1998. 'Constructing the Self and the Other in Cyrenaica', in Laurence, R. and Berry, J. (eds) 1998, 49–63.

Marszal, J. 1994. 'The Death of Decebalus and the Motif of Barbarian Suicide', abstract of conference paper, *American Journal of Archaeology* 98, 335.

Mattingly, D. (ed.) 1997. 'Dialogues in Roman Imperialism. Power, Discourse, and Discrepant Experience in the Roman Empire', *Journal of Roman Archaeology*, Supplementary Series No. 23.

Meadows, K., Lemke, C. and Heron, J. (eds) 1997. *TRAC 96, Proceedings of the Sixth Theoretical Roman Archaeology Conference*. Oxbow, Oxford.

Mierse, W. 1990. 'Augustan Building Programs in the Western Provinces', in Raaflaub, K.A. and Toher, M. (eds) 1990, 308–33.

Miller, D.H. 1977. 'Ethnic Stereotypes and the Frontier: a Comparative Study of Roman and American Experience', in Miller, D.H. and Steffen, J.O. (eds) 1977, 109–37.

Miller, D.H. and Steffen, J.O. (eds) 1977. *The Frontier I: Comparative Studies*. University of Oklahoma Press, Oklahoma.

Mills, R. (ed.) 1999. *Constructing Identities in Late Antiquity*. Routledge, London.

Molyneaux, B.L. (ed.) 1997. *The Cultural Life of Images. Visual Representation in Archaeology*. Routledge, London.

BIBLIOGRAPHY

Momigliano, A. 1975. *Alien Wisdom. The Limits of Hellenization.* Cambridge University Press, Cambridge.

Montefiore, J. 1994. 'Socialist Realism and Female Bodies', *Paragraph* 17 (1), 70–80.

Montefiore, J. 1996. *Men and Women Writers of the 1930s. The Dangerous Flood of History.* Routledge, London.

Mosley, D.J. 1971. 'Greeks, Barbarians, Language and Contact', *Ancient Society* 2, 1–6.

Moxon, I.S., Smart, J.D. and Woodman, A.J. (eds) 1986. *Past Perspectives: Studies in Greek and Roman Historical Writing.* Cambridge University Press, Cambridge.

Moynihan, R. 1985. 'Geographical Mythology and Roman Imperial Ideology', in Winckes, R. (ed.) 1985, 149–62.

Munby, J. and Henig, M. (eds) 1977. *Roman Life and Art in Britain.* British Archaeological Reports, British Series 41, Oxford.

Museum of Fine Arts, Boston, 1976. *Romans and Barbarians.* Department of Classical Art.

Nelson, C. and Grossberg, L. (eds) 1988. *Marxism and the Interpretation of Culture.* University of Illinois Press, Urbana.

Nicolet, C. 1991. *Space, Geography and Politics in the Early Roman Empire.* University of Michigan Press, Ann Arbor.

Nielsen, M. 1975. 'The Lid Sculptures of Volterran Cinerary Urns', *Acta Instituti Romani Finlandiae* V.

Nochlin, L. 1989, 'Women, Art, and Power', in *Women, Art, and Power and Other Essays.* Thames & Hudson, London.

Nochlin, L. 1994. *The Body in Pieces. The Fragment as a Metaphor of Modernity.* Thames & Hudson, London.

Nochlin, L. 1999a. *Representing Women.* Thames & Hudson, London.

Nochlin, L. 1999b. 'The Myth of the Woman Warrior', in Nochlin, L. 1999a, 34–57.

Onians, J. 1979. *Art and Thought in the Hellenistic Age: the Greek World View 350–50 BC.* Thames & Hudson, London.

Onians, J. 1999. *Classical Art and the Cultures of Greece and Rome.* Yale University Press, New Haven.

Osborne, R. 1998. 'Men Without Clothes: Heroic Nakedness and Greek Art', in Wyke, M. (ed.) 1998, 80–104.

Overbeck, B.H. 1993. 'Die Kelten im Spiegel der Römischen Münzprägung', in Dannheimer, H. and Gebhard, R. (eds) 1993, 228–30.

Pacteau, F. 1994. *The Symptom of Beauty.* Reaktion Books, London.

Pallotino, M. 1946. *L'Arco degli Argentari.* Danesi Editore, Rome.

Payne, R. 1962. *The Roman Triumph.* Robert Hale, London.

Peirce, P. 1989. 'The Arch of Constantine: Propaganda and Ideology in Late Roman Art', *Art History* Vol. 12, No. 4, 387–418.

Petersen, E. *et al.* 1896. *Die Marcus-Säule auf Piazza Colonna in Rom.* Munich.

Petrikovits, H. von 1983. 'Sacramentum', in Hartley, B. and Wacher, J. (eds) 1983, 179–201.

ENEMIES OF ROME

Phillips, E.J. 1975. 'The Roman Distance Slab From Bridgeness', *Proceedings of the Society of Antiquaries of Scotland* CV, 176–82.

Phillips, E.J. 1977. *Corbridge. Hadrian's Wall East of the North Tyne. Corpus Signorum Imperii Romani, Great Britain.* Volume 1 Fascicule 1. Oxford University Press, Oxford.

Picard, G.C. 1957. *Les Trophées Romain. Contribution à l'Histoire de la Religion et de l'Art Triomphal de Rome.* Bibliothèque des Écoles Francaises D'Athènes et de Rome, Fascicule Cent-Quatre-Vingt Septième, Paris.

Picard, G.C. 1979. 'La Mythologie au Service de la Romanisation dans les Provinces Occidentales de l'Empire Romain', in Kahil, L. and Auge, C. (eds) 1979.

Pietela-Castren, L. 1987. *The Victory Monuments of the Roman Generals in the Era of the Punic Wars.* Helsinki.

Polito, E. 1999. *I Galati Vinti. Il Trionfo sui Barbari da Pergamo a Roma.* Electa, Milan.

Pollini, J. 1993. 'The Gemma Augustea: Ideology, Rhetorical Imagery and the Creation of a Dynastic Narrative', in Holliday, P. (ed.) 1993, 258–98.

Pollitt, J.J. 1986. *Art in the Hellenistic Age.* Cambridge University Press, Cambridge.

Pomeroy, S.B. 1975. *Goddesses, Whores, Wives, and Slaves. Women in Classical Antiquity.* Pimlico (British edn, 1994), London.

Pomeroy, S.B. (ed.) 1991. *Women's History and Ancient History.* University of North Carolina Press, Chapel Hill.

Pond Rothman, M.S. 1977. 'The Thematic Organisation of the Panel Reliefs on the Arch of Galerius', *American Journal of Archaeology* 81, 427–54.

Price, S.R.F. 1984. *Rituals and Power: the Roman Imperial Cult in Asia Minor.* Cambridge University Press, Cambridge.

Prieur, J. 1982. 'Les Arcs Monumentaux dans les Alpes Occidentales: Aoste, Suse, Aix-Les-Bains', *Aufstieg und Niedergang der Römischen Welt* Vol. 12.1, 442–75.

Raaflaub, K.A. and Toher, M. (eds) 1990. *Between Republic and Empire. Interpretations of Augustus and his Principate.* University of California Press, Berkeley.

Raditsa, L.F. 1980. 'Augustus' Legislation Concerning Marriage, Procreation, Love Affairs and Adultery', *Aufstieg und Niedergang der Römischen Welt* Vol. 2.13, 278–339.

Raftery, B. (ed.) 1995. *Sites and Sights of the Iron Age.* Oxbow Monograph 56. Oxbow Books, Oxford.

Raftery, J. (ed.) 1964. *The Celts. The Thomas Davis Lectures.* Mercier Press, Cork.

Ramage, E.S. 1997. 'Augustus' Propaganda in Gaul', *Klio (Beitrage zur Alten Geschichte)* 79, 117–60.

Rankin, D. 1987. *Celts and the Classical World.* Croom Helm, London.

Rawlings, L. 1998. 'Caesar's Portrayal of Gauls as Warriors', in Welch, K. and Powell, A. (eds) 1998, 171–92.

Reece, R. 1983. 'Late Antiquity', in Henig, M. (ed.) 1983, 234–48.

Reinach, A.J. 1911. *Les Galates dans L'Art Alexandrine.* Académie des Inscriptions et Belles-Lettres: Monuments et Mémoires 18, 37–15.

BIBLIOGRAPHY

Reinach, S. 1888. 'Le Gaulois dans l'Art Antique et le Sarcophage de la Vigne Ammendola', *Revue Archéologique* XII, 273–84.

Rich, J. and Shipley, G. (eds) 1993. *War and Society in the Greek World*. Routledge, London.

Richlin, A. 1983. *The Garden of Priapus: Sexuality and Aggression in Roman Humour*. Oxford University Press, Oxford.

Richmond, I.A. 1933. 'Commemorative Arches and City Gates in the Augustan Age', *Journal of Roman Studies* XXIII, 149–74.

Richmond, I.A. 1935. 'Trajan's Army on Trajan's Column', *Papers of the British School at Rome* 13, 1–40.

Richmond, I.A. 1967. 'Adamklissi', *Papers of the British School at Rome* 35, 29–39.

Richter, G.M.A. 1960. *A Handbook of Greek Art. A Survey of the Visual Arts of Ancient Greece*. 7th edn 1989. Phaidon, Oxford.

Rolland, H. 1969. *Le Mausolée de Glanum*. Supplément à *Gallia* XXI.

Rolland, H. 1977. *L'Arc de Glanum*. Supplément à *Gallia* XXXI.

Romm, J.S. 1992. *The Edges of the Earth in Ancient Thought*. Princeton University Press, Princeton.

Rose, C.B. 1990. '"Princes" and Barbarians on the Ara Pacis', *American Journal of Archaeology* 94, 453–67.

Rose, C.B. 1997. *Dynastic Commemoration and Imperial Portraiture in the Julio-Claudian Period*. Cambridge University Press, Cambridge.

Rossi, L. 1971. *Trajan's Column and the Dacian Wars*. Cornell University Press, Ithaca.

Rossi, L. 1972. 'A Historiographic Reassessment of the Metopes of the Tropaeum Traiani at Adamklissi', *Archaeological Journal* 129, 56–68.

Rossi, L. 1981. *Rotocalchi di Pietra: Segni et Disegni dei Tempi Sui Monumenti Trionfali dell'Impero Romano*. Milan.

Rotroff, S.I. 1997. 'The Greeks and the Other in the Age of Alexander', in Coleman, J.E. and Walz, C.A. (eds) 1997, 221–34.

Roueche, C. and Erim, K.T. (eds) 1990. 'Aphrodisias Papers. Recent Work on Architecture and Sculpture', *Journal of Roman Archaeology* Supplementary Series No. 1.

Ruggini, L.C. 1968. 'Pregiudizi Razziali, Ostilità Politica, Intollerenza Religiosa Nell'Impero Romano', *Athenaeum* 46, 139–52.

Saddington, D.B. 1961. 'Roman Attitudes to the "Externae Gentes" of the North', *Acta Classica* 4, 90–102.

Said, E.W. 1991. *Orientalism: Western Conceptions of the Orient*. Penguin, Harmondsworth.

Said, E.W. 1993. *Culture and Imperialism*. Chatto & Windus, London.

Scheid, J. and Huet, V. (eds), 2000. La Colonne Aurélienne. Autour de la Colonne Aurélienne. Geste et Image sur la Colonne de Marc Aurèle à Rome. Turnhout.

Schleiermacher, M. 1984. *Römische Reitergrabsteine: die Kaizerzeitlichen Reliefs des Triumphierenden Reiters*. Bouvier, Bonn.

Schmitt, H.H. 1958. *Hellenen, Römer und Barbaren. Eine Studie zu Polybios*.

ENEMIES OF ROME

Wissenschaftlo Beilage zum Jahresbericht d. Hum. Gymnasiums Aschaffenburg.

Schneider, R.M. 1986. *Bunte Barbaren: Orientalenstatuen aus Farbigem Marmor in der Römischen Repräsentationskunst*. Wernersche Verlaysgesellschaft Worms.

Scott, E. (ed.) 1993. *Theoretical Roman Archaeology: First Conference Proceedings*. Avebury, Hampshire.

Sebesta, J.L. 1998. 'Women's Costume and Feminine Civic Morality in Augustan Rome', in Wyke, M. (ed.) 1998, 105–17.

Sebesta, J.L. and Bonfante, L. (eds) 1994. *The World of Roman Costume*. University of Wisconsin Press, Madison.

Seikerk, R.P., and Breuninger, H. (eds), 1998. Kulturen der Gewalt. Ritualisierung und Symbolisierung von Gewalt in der Geschichte. Frankfurt.

Selzer, W. 1988. *Römische Steindenkmaler. Mainz in Römischer Zeit*. Katalog zur Sammlung in der Steinhalle, Landesmuseum Mainz. Verlag Philip von Zabern, Mainz.

Shapiro, H.A. 1983. 'Amazons, Thracians and Scythians', *Greek, Roman and Byzantine Studies* 24, 105–14.

Shaw, B.D. 1982a. 'Fear and Loathing: the Nomad Menace in Roman Africa', in Wells, C.M. (ed.) 1982, 29–50.

Shaw, B.D. 1982b. 'Eaters of Flesh, Drinkers of Milk: the Ancient Mediterranean Ideology of the Pastoral Nomad', *Ancient Society* 13, 5–31.

Sherwin-White, A.N. 1967. *Racial Prejudice in Imperial Rome. The Gray Memorial Lectures 1965–6*. Cambridge University Press, Cambridge.

Silberberg-Peirce, S. 1986. 'The Many Faces of the Pax Augusta: Images of War and Peace in Rome and Gallia Narbonensis', *Art History* 9 No. 3, 306–24.

Simon, E. 1968. *Ara Pacis Augustae*. New York Graphic Society, New York.

Smith, B. 1984. 'Captain Cook's Artists and the Portrayal of Pacific Peoples', *Art History* Vol. 7 No. 3, 295–312.

Smith, R.R.R. 1987. 'The Imperial Reliefs from the Sebasteion at Aphrodisias', *Journal of Roman Studies* 75, 88–138.

Smith, R.R.R. 1988. 'Simulacra Gentium: the Ethne from the Sebasteion at Aphrodisias', *Journal of Roman Studies* 78, 50–77.

Smith, R.R.R. 1990. 'Myth and Allegory in the Sebasteion', in Roueche, C. and Erim, K.T. (eds) 1990, 89–100.

Snitow, A. et al. 1983. *The Powers of Desire*. Monthly Review Press, New York.

Snowden, F.M. Jnr 1970. *Blacks in Antiquity: Ethiopians in the Greco-Roman Experience*. Harvard University Press, Cambridge, Mass.

Snowden, F.M. Jnr 1983. *Before Color Prejudice. The Ancient View of Blacks*. Harvard University Press, Cambridge, Mass.

Snowden, F.M. Jnr 1997. 'Greeks and Ethiopians', in Coleman, J.E. and Walz, C.A. (eds) 1997, 103–26.

Soprintendenza Archeologica di Roma 1998. *Museo Nazionale Romano, Palazzo Altemps*. Electa, Rome.

BIBLIOGRAPHY

Sparkes, B.A. 1997. 'Some Greek Images of Others', in Molyneaux B.L. (ed.) 1997, 130–58.

Speidel, M.P. 1970. 'The Captor of Decebalus. A New Inscription from Philippi', *Journal of Roman Studies* 60, 142–53.

Speidel, M.P. 1971. 'The Suicide of Decebalus on the Tropaeum of Adamklissi', *Revue Archéologique*, Fascicule 1, 74–8.

Spivak, G.C. 1988. 'Can the Subaltern Speak?' in Nelson, C. and Grossberg, L. (eds) 1988, 271–313.

Spivak, G.C. 1999. *A Critique of Postcolonial Reason: Toward a History of a Vanishing Present*. Harvard University Press, Cambridge, Mass.

Stallybrass, P. and White, A. 1986. *The Politics and Poetics of Transgression*. Cornell University Press, Ithaca.

Stella, C. 1987. *Guida del Museo Romano di Brescia*. Istituti Culturali del Comune di Brescia, Materiali e Studi per la Storia Locale 4, Brescia.

Stewart, A. 1997. *Art, Desire, and the Body in Ancient Greece*. Cambridge University Press, Cambridge.

Stonebridge, L. 1997. *The Destruction Element*. Macmillan, London.

Strong, D.E. 1961. *Roman Imperial Sculpture*. Alec Tiranti, London.

Strong, D.E. 1966. *Greek and Roman Silver Plate*. Methuen, London.

Strong, D.E. 1976. *Roman Art*. Penguin Books, Harmondsworth.

Thollard, P. 1987. 'Barbarie et Civilisation chez Strabon. Étude Critique des Livres III et IV de la Geographie', *Annales Litteraires de L'Université de Besançon* 365. Paris.

Thompson, L. 1989. *Romans and Blacks*. Routledge, London.

Tierney, J.J. 1960. 'The Celtic Ethnography of Posidonius', *Proceedings of the Royal Irish Academy* 60, 189–275.

Tierney, J.J. 1964. 'The Celts and the Classical Authors', in Raftery, J. (ed.) 1964, 23–33.

Tomaselli, S. and Porter, R. (eds) 1986. *Rape*. Basil Blackwell, Oxford.

Torelli, M. 1982. *Typology and Structure of Roman Historical Reliefs. Jerome Lectures 14*. University of Michigan Press, Ann Arbor.

Torelli, M. 1997. '"Ex his castra, ex his tribus replebuntur": The Marble Panegyric on the Arch of Trajan at Beneventum', in Buitron-Oliver, D. (ed.) 1997, 144–77.

Touati, A.M.L. 1987. 'The Great Trajanic Frieze. The Study of a Monument and of the Mechanisms of Message Transmission in Roman Art', *Skrifter Utgivna Av Svenska Institutet I Rom*, 4, XLV.

Toynbee, J.M.C. 1934. *The Hadrianic School: a Chapter in the History of Greek Art*. Cambridge University Press, Cambridge.

Toynbee, J.M.C. 1962. *Art in Roman Britain*. Phaidon, London.

Toynbee, J.M.C. 1964. *Art in Britain under the Romans*. Clarendon Press, Oxford.

Toynbee, J.M.C. and Painter, K.S. 1986. 'Silver Picture Plates of Late Antiquity: AD 300 to 700', *Archaeologia* CVIII, 16–65.

Tyrell, W.B. 1984. *Amazons: a Study in Athenian Myth Making*. Johns Hopkins University Press, Baltimore.

ENEMIES OF ROME

Vercoutter, J., Leclant, J., Snowden, F.M. Jnr and Desanges, J. 1976. *The Image of the Black in Western Art, I: From the Pharaohs to the Fall of the Roman Empire*. William Morrow, New York.

Vermeule, C.C. 1960. 'Hellenistic and Roman Cuirassed Statues', *Berytus* 13, 1–82.

Vermeule, C.C. 1968. *Roman Imperial Art in Greece and Asia Minor*. Harvard University Press, Cambridge, Mass.

Vermeule, C.C. 1980. *Hellenistic and Roman Cuirassed Statues*. Boston.

Versnel, H.S. 1970. *Triumphus. An Inquiry into the Origin, Development and Meaning of the Roman Triumph*. Brill, Leiden.

Veyne, P. 1993. 'Humanitas: Romans and Non-Romans', in Giardina, A. (ed.) 1993, 342–69.

Vulpe, R. 1963. 'Les Germains du Trophée de Trajan a Adamklissi', *Archéologie* 14.

Wace, A.J.B. 1907. 'Studies in Roman Historical Reliefs', *Papers of the British School at Rome 3*, 229–76.

Waelkens, M. 1985. 'From a Phrygian Quarry: the Provenance of the Statues of the Dacian Prisoners in Trajan's Forum in Rome', *American Journal of Archaeology* 89, 641–53.

Walbank, F.W. 1972. 'Nationality as a Factor in Roman History', *Harvard Studies in Classical Philology* 76, 145–68.

Walker, D.R. 1988. 'The Roman Coins', in Cunliffe, B. (ed.) 1988, 281–358.

Wallace-Hadrill, A. 1990. 'Roman Arches and Greek Honours. The Language of Power at Rome', *Proceedings of the Cambridge Philosophical Society* 216, 143–81.

Wallace-Hadrill, J.M. 1977. 'Raising on a Shield in Byzantine Iconography', *Revue des Études Byzantines* 33, 133–75.

Walter, H. 1986. 'La Porte Noire de Besançon. Contribution a l'Étude de l'Art Triomphal des Gaules', *Annales Litteraires de l'Université de Besançon* 321. Paris.

Walter, H. 1993. 'Les Barbares de L'Occident Romain. Corpus des Gaules et des Provinces de Germanie', *Annales Littéraires de l'Université de Besançon* 494. Paris.

Ward-Perkins, J. and Claridge, A. 1976. *Pompeii AD 79*. Exhibition catalogue, Royal Academy of Arts, Picadilly, London.

Warner, M. 1985. *Monuments and Maidens. The Allegory of the Female Form*. Weidenfeld & Nicolson, London.

Webster, G. 1993. 'Military Equestrian Tombstones', in Henig, M. 1993, 45–8.

Webster, J. 1995. 'The Just War: Graeco Roman Text as Colonial Discourse', in Cottam, S. et al. (eds) 1995, 1–10.

Webster, J. 1996. 'Ethnographic Barbarity: Colonial Discourse and "Celtic Warrior Societies"', in Webster, J. and Cooper, N. (eds) 1996, 111–24.

Webster, J. and Cooper, N. (eds) 1996. *Roman Imperialism: Post-Colonial Perspectives*. Leicester Archaeology Monographs No. 3, University of Leicester Press, Leicester.

BIBLIOGRAPHY

Welch, K. and Powell, A. (eds) 1998. *Julius Caesar as Artful Reporter: the War Commentaries as Political Instruments*. Duckworth with the Classical Press of Wales, London.

Wells, C.M. (ed.) 1982. *Roman Africa/L'Afrique Romaine*. The 1980 Vanier Lectures. Ottowa.

Wells, P.S. 1999. *The Barbarians Speak*. Princeton University Press, Princeton.

Whittaker, C.R. 1994. 'The Politics of Power; the Cities of Italy', in *L'Italie d'Auguste à Dioclétien. Actes du Colloque Internationale de l'École Française de Rome*. (CERAR 94), 127–43.

Whittaker, C.R. 1997. 'Imperialism and Culture: the Roman Initiative', in Mattingly, D. (ed) 1997, 143–63.

Wiedemann , T.E.J. 1986. 'Between Men and Beasts: Barbarians in Ammianus Marcellinus', in Moxon, I.S. et al. (eds) 1986, 189–201.

Wiedemann, T.E.J. (ed.) 1988. *Greek and Roman Slavery*. Routledge, London.

Winckes, R. (ed.) 1985. *The Age of Augustus*. Centre for Old World Archaeology, Brown University. Louvaine-La-Neuve.

Winter, I. 1996. 'Sex, Rhetoric, and the Public Monument. The Alluring Body of Naram-Sin of Agade', in Kampen, N.B. (ed.) 1996b, 11–26.

Woolf, G. 1998. *Becoming Roman. The Origins of Provincial Civilisation in Gaul*. Cambridge University Press, Cambridge.

Wyke, M. (ed.) 1998. *Gender and the Body in the Ancient Mediterranean*. Basil Blackwell, Oxford.

Young, R. 1995. *Colonial Desire*. Routledge, London.

Zadoks-Josephus Jitta, A.N. 1964. 'Imperial Messages in Agate', *Bulletin Antieke Beschaving: Annual Papers on Classical Archaeology*, 156–61.

Zahn, R. 1896. *Die Darstellung der Barbaren in der Vorhellenistichen Zeit*. Heidelberg.

Zanker, P. 1988a. *The Power of Images in the Age of Augustus*. University of Michigan Press, Ann Arbor.

Zanker, P. 1988b. *Bilderzwang: Augustan Political Symbolism in the Private Sphere*. In Huskinson, J., Beard, M. and Reynolds, J. (eds) 1988, 1–22.

Zanker, P. 1997. 'In Search of the Roman Viewer', in Buitron-Oliver, D. (ed.) 1997, 179–91.

Zanker, P. 1998. 'Die Barbaren, der kaiser und die Arena. Bilder der Gewalt in der Römischen Kunst', in Seiterle, R.P. and Breuninger, H. (eds) 1998, 53–86.

Zanker, P. 2000. 'Die Frauen und Kinder der Barbaren auf der Markussäule', in Scheid, J. and Huet, V. (eds) 2000, 163–74.

INDEX

Numbers in **bold** indicate plate numbers.

INDEX

INDEX

INDEX

INDEX

INDEX